To Dan —

— to help give you lots
of trouble-free driving.

Mom and Dad

Dec., '73

AUTO REPAIRS
You Can Make

Edited by Paul Weissler

Died in 2023

ARCO
New York

Published by ARCO PUBLISHING COMPANY, INC.
219 Park Avenue South, New York, N.Y. 10003

Copyright © Arco Publishing Company, Inc., 1971

All Rights Reserved

Parts of this book are © Science & Mechanics Publishing Co., 1971

Library of Congress Catalog Number 76-165211
ISBN 0-668-02508-5

Printed in the United States of America

Introduction

An estimated 25% of American car owners now perform their own tune-ups and minor repairs. This represents an increase of 15% from 1957, when there were far fewer cars on the road. One reason, of course, for this phenomenal increase is the fact that more and more car owners have come to realize that the average so-called mechanic often knows less than they do even though he charges exorbitant prices. Cars often have to be returned to the shop again and again for the same trouble; each time something else seems to be wrong. Finally the disgusted owner decides to locate and fix the trouble himself—and he usually does it with far greater success than the supposedly expert mechanic.

The main reason for this sorry state of professional service is the fact that there are not enough *trained* mechanics to go around. One expert estimates that at least 75% of the garage mechanics in the U.S. are insufficiently trained. The cost of having your car repaired is reaching astronomical heights, and gas pump jockeys are learning auto repair as they go along— at the customer's expense.

Obviously, then, it not only pays to do your own repairs because of the money you will save, but also because you will be sure that the repair will be done properly. To do this, you don't have to be a professional engineer. All you need is some common sense, patience, and basic knowledge of the workings of an automobile — something many so-called mechanics lack.

In this book we have attempted to show *how* you can make most of the common adjustments and repairs in a professional manner. Detailed how-to photos and drawings help explain the step-by-step instructions of the text, and, upon reading this book, it will be quite obvious that there are no secrets to keeping your car in proper tune and running shape. The contents cover most anything the average car owner will want to fix himself. No major tools are required for most of the repairs. The book is broken down into 10 major sections: Engine; Ignition; Fuel System; Pollution Control Devices; Cool-

3

ing System; Clutch and Transmission; Brakes; Tires and Steering; General Electrical Servicing; and Body.

This book does not pretend to be a complete manual for all repairs; if it were, it would have to cost ten times as much and you would need all types of special tools and equipment in order to make all the repairs shown. You certainly would not want to buy thousands of dollars worth of equipment. What you do want, though, and what this book will help you to achieve, is to make everyday repairs and adjustments — better and more efficiently than the average "professional" garage mechanic. You will discover that many of these repairs are not difficult, don't require special tools or knowledge, and can even be fun. They certainly will save you money and aggravation and will let you drive a car that is both better running and safer.

Contents

IV
POLLUTION CONTROL DEVICES

V
THE COOLING SYSTEM

VI
CLUTCH AND TRANSMISSION

VII
THE BRAKING SYSTEM

VIII
TIRES AND STEERING

IX

GENERAL ELECTRICAL SERVICING

X

BODY CARE

1

Taking Care of Your Engine

YOUR CAR'S DRIVING power starts with its engine, and just so long as cars continue to utilize internal combustion engines, engines will continue to receive the greater share of car maintenance. This is so because the engine, in addition to its own mechanical structure—block, head, oil pan, oil pump, crankshaft, pistons, rods, bearings, flywheel and timing gears—takes in the all-important ignition, carburetion, and cooling systems. And on today's smog-controlled cars, there is even more, such as Positive Crankcase Ventilation and special ignition timing controls.

If each of these individual units is kept up to standard, your engine will perform substantially as it did when new, even after thousands of miles of operation. But car owners usually become somewhat careless; when the thrill of new-car ownership has worn off, they tend to take their car and its engine for granted. Only when trouble shows up do they realize that a little attention at the right time would have forestalled trouble, saved them repair costs and—as a plus factor—made their car last much longer.

When you get your new car, every unit in it is brand-spanking new, and moving parts fit with just the right clearance. Then, in time, the engine parts gradually become worn so that clearances between rubbing metal enlarge, components in the ignition system become so worn that timing is late, spark plugs wear out and erosion of the plug electrodes widens the gaps so that plug performance falls off. Other parts loosen or disconnect. Dirt and other foreign matter impedes the operation of the fuel, lubrication and cooling systems, the power and zip of the engine falls off: in short, the engine ceases to purr. . . . Periodic attention could have prevented all of this.

Keep Your Engine Clean. It doesn't take a "mechanically minded" person to keep the outside of the engine clean. And keeping the outside of the engine clean is the first step towards getting the longest possible life from your engine.

Excess operating heat from your engine is dissipated by being passed to the atmosphere through the radiator core, the engine oil pan, and to some extent through other surfaces such as

9

block, cylinder head, and manifold. If you keep the outside of your engine clean, its operating temperature will have a better chance of remaining normal at all times. A dirt-caked oil pan, on the other hand, will not permit excess heat to escape and the bearings, crankshaft, pistons, rods and other parts will operate at higher than normal temperatures. The oil itself may overheat, oxidize, become black and lose much of its lubricating value.

Dirt and road film also can cause carburetor linkage to stick, mask an oil leak while it is still easy to cure, enter the brake master cylinder and contaminate brake fluid, and create electrical short circuits.

If you clean your engine just once a year, or twice a year in areas where winters are severe, you can greatly extend the life of many components.

You don't need an expensive steam-cleaning system to do the job correctly. For $2 to $3 you can buy an aerosol can of engine-cleaning solvent, and it will do an equally good job.

Just remove the air cleaner assembly and with clear cellophane household wrap, cover the generator end plate, top of the carburetor and the distributor body. (These must be cleaned separately with kerosene and a wire brush to keep dirt and water from entering these units.)

Spray the engine with the degreasing solvent, using a repeat spray on areas with caked-on film. If the cake of dirt is really thick, you may have to scrape it off. The solvent works best when the engine is warm.

Allow the solvent to work in for about fifteen minutes, then wash off with a garden hose.

A clean engine has the additional advantage, to a weekend mechanic, of being much easier to work on. Adjustment screws are easier to regulate when they are clean, and nuts and bolts can be tightened properly only when clean. (Dirt causes thread friction that gives a false sense of tightness.)

Keeping the engine clean means keeping *all* of it clean. In addition to brush-and-solvent cleaning of the generator, top of carburetor and distributor, also brush out well around the spark plugs, so that when they are taken out, no foreign matter will fall into the plug hole. Such dirt could lodge under a valve seat to prevent its seating, and it would take but a very short time for the valve and seat to burn, which would require an expensive and time-consuming repair.

Some Other Simple Steps. Over the miles, engine performance falls off gradually—but few engines ever have to have all adjustments and tune-up work done at one time. If your engine seems to be ailing, look first for one of the relatively simple sources of troubles listed in the table, "Simple Engine Troubleshooting."

With the possible exception of bringing the ignition distributor up to standard specifications, you can, with no special equipment, easily make all of the adjustments and repairs listed in the table.

You will be helped considerably in your efforts to keep the engine at its best by buying a set of socket and open end wrenches. If you cannot get these at a hardware store, you can at an automotive parts and equipment jobber. With a set of such wrenches you can go over all the various nuts in the en-

Engine cleaning can be done with an aerosol degreaser. Air cleaner should be removed and carburetor opening covered with plastic wrap. Distributor also should be plastic-wrapped.

After solvent has had a chance to work, spray it off with a garden hose.

This is the same engine as in the first illustration. The car is old, but the engine certainly doesn't show it.

gine, tightening those at such parts as intake and exhaust manifolds, carburetor joints, valve cover plates, timing gear cover, oil filter brackets, fuel lines, oil lines, oil pan—in fact, wherever the nuts are accessible. Be careful of the nuts on the cylinder head. These should be tightened with a torque wrench (a wrench which shows the exact amount of tension being placed on the stud upon which the nut is being tightened). See Chapter 5 in this book, "How Tight is Tight?" which discusses the torque wrench and how to use it.

Jacking Capability. If you presently have your car lubricated and the oil filter changed at a service station, you may wish to have underbody bolts and nuts, particularly oil pan bolts, tightened by the station attendant while the car is on the lift.

Jacking capability is needed for underbody work. Among the less expensive jacks available for weekend mechanics is this "trolley jack," which has three wheels for easy positioning and jacking.

Once car is raised, safety stands should be placed under lower A-frames. You don't need expensive ones. 5000-pound capacity stands illustrated cost only $8 for the pair.

But if you have a late-model "lubricated for life chassis" you should consider changing the oil and filter yourself. You can normally buy the oil and filter at discount houses and auto supply stores for less than the list price the service station charges.

Most cars have spin-on filters which require only an inexpensive wrench to replace. The oil pan drain plug requires only a simple box or open-end wrench. The elimination of the chassis lubrication means that you do not need to use an air-pressurized grease gun or struggle with a small hand grease gun.

You will, however, need good jacking capability to do this work. But you will need this for many routine underbody jobs, including underbody nut and bolt tightening, which you will then be able to do yourself. See the chapter, "How to Change Your Car's Filters," which discusses jacking and the oil filter.

Using a Vacuum Gauge. A vacuum gauge is a handy and inexpensive (under $7) instrument that can tell you much about engine condition. When an engine is performing properly, the downward stroke of the pistons creates a healthy vacuum in the intake manifold. Engine malfunction often shows up as changes in intake manifold vacuum, which you can measure with the vacuum gauge.

The vacuum gauge is easily connected to either the base of the carburetor or to the intake manifold itself. (The intake manifold is the tubular unit that sits below the carburetor. It carries the fuel mixture into the cylinder head.) See the chapter, "Pinpointing Ailments with a Vacuum Gauge."

Testing Compression. Good operation of your engine depends to a great extent upon having uniform compression in all the cylinders. A compression gauge tests for this. Before removing spark plugs from all cylinders to make such a test, the engine should be operated long enough to bring it to its normal operating temperature. Next, loosen all plugs two turns to crack internal carbon, then start and "gun" engine to blow out this carbon. Then remove the spark plugs, open the carburetor throttle valve wide and block the accelerator pedal if necessary to hold it in this position. Also make sure that the carburetor choke valve is wide open. Place the compression gauge in the plug hole of the first cylinder (hold it firmly in place), and with ignition off have someone crank the engine. Watch the pointer of the compression gauge and count the number of revolutions necessary to bring the hand to its highest indication. Acutally, you do not count the engine revolutions, but rather the *whrr whrr* of the starting motor. Jot down the reading and do the same with the remaining cylinders.

If you have the correct grade and amount of oil in the engine and if pistons, rings, cylinders, valves and gaskets are in good condition, the highest readings on all cylinders should be within 25 percent of the lowest readings. If there is a greater variation, there is an engine mechanical problem, and normal tuning will have very limited effect. Example: if the highest compression reading is 160 psi, the lowest should be 120.

The important thing to watch for in this test is the action of the com-

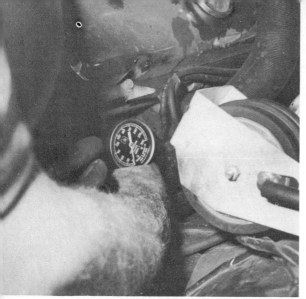

Top: When making compression test, make sure all plugs are out, engine is warm and throttle is blocked open. Watch action of compression gauge needle for indication of condition of valves. Above: Fuel pump capacity test is made by cranking engine with fuel line end disconnected from carburetor and aimed into can. Pump should deliver pint in 30 seconds on V-8, 45 seconds on a six.

pression gauge pointer. For example, if the pointer does not climb steadily, but remains at rest during the cranking process, indications are that the valve of the cylinder on test is holding open. Or, if on the first turn of the starting motor the hand goes to 35, for example, then remains at 35 on the next turn but climbs higher on succeeding strokes, it is likely that the cylinder has a sticky valve. Such a valve condition will show up on the first few revolutions during the test.

Note: on many V-8 engines, it will be impossible to hold the compression gauge in the spark plug hole as required, and still be able to read it as the pointer rises. If you have a V-8 and this is the case, you will need a compression gauge with a hose. One end of the hose has a threaded fitting for the spark plug hole. The other end has the gauge, which can be held away from the plug hole and read easily.

Head gasket leakage is generally indicated by low compression readings on adjacent cylinders. If the readings you have jotted down show definite lack of uniformity between cylinders, you can often restore normal conditions by using a special gum solvent or similar preparation sold by service stations for this purpose. Valves and piston rings freed in this way may again seat firmly to restore compression; but if the valves are burnt, the obvious remedy is replacement of the old valves with new. See the chapter, "Tackling Valve and Ring Jobs."

The cooling system dissipates the excess heat from the engine. It must always be kept in the best of condition. At one time it was necessary to drain the system twice a year, once in the spring, again in the fall.

But today's cooling systems are designed differently. They require only once-a-year draining, and year-round use of anti-freeze. See Section V, "Engine Cooling Systems," for details.

The fuel pump draws gasoline from the tank and forces it up into the carburetor, usally through a gasoline filter. It is a simple unit that normally functions for up to 50,000 miles and more without giving trouble.

The pump has two valves, both spring-loaded but in different directions, and a diaphragm that is connected to an arm. The engine camshaft has a lobe that moves the arm to flex the diaphragm.

As the diaphragm flexes downward, it creates a suction that pulls open one of the two valves, called the inlet. The suction also draws in fuel from the gas tank.

As the camshaft turns, it relieves the pressure against the arm, and a spring pushes the diaphragm up. The spring pressure against the diaphragm forces the fuel against the other valve —the outlet—opening it and pushing the fuel out of the pump and up the tubing to the carburetor.

Eventually, however, the diaphragm may be come punctured by dirt in the gasoline, or porous, and insufficient fuel will be pumped to the carburetor. And over a period of time, the diaphragm arm may become excessively worn.

Fuel pumps can be tested with a pressure gauge that reads to about nine psi. All vacuum gauges sold for engine troubleshooting also have a pres-

Fuel pump pressure test is made with fuel line end disconnected from carb and vacuum-pressure gauge attached. Check manufacturer's specifications, which will tell you what pump output should be.

sure gauge built in, so you need not purchase an additional test instrument.

The pressure gauge is normally connected onto the end of the fuel line at the carburetor. The engine is cranked, or even started (and operated for a moment on the fuel in the carburetor, while the pump output pressure is read on the gauge).

The correct pressure varies according to make of car. In general, a six-cylinder pump is satisfactory if it develops 2.5 to four psi. A V-8 pump normally develops three to as high as eight psi. Inadequate pressure causes fuel starvation; too much pressure causes carburetor flooding.

In addition to a pressure check, a volume check should also be made. This is done by cranking the engine and holding a can to catch the flow

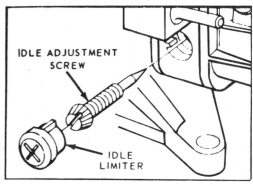

IDLE ADJUSTMENT SCREW

IDLE LIMITER

Left: Adjustment of carburetor idle mixture on late model cars is restricted by plastic idle limiter. However, you should be able to get an acceptable idle within its range. Right: Drawing shows that limiter is nothing more than a plastic cap over the conventional idle mixture adjustment screw.

from the fuel line, and is most conveniently performed immediately after the pressure check. A six-cylinder pump should deliver a pint into the can in 45 seconds at most. A V-8 pump should deliver a pint in 30 seconds.

If fuel pump delivery is not up to specifications, the problem may be caused by a clogged gasoline filter. On many cars, the fuel pump is a sealed assembly and must be replaced if defective; on others, it can be rebuilt. See the chapter, "Your Fuel Pump," for details.

The Carburetor. Modern carburetors can be complicated units, particularly if they have two or four barrels. You can, however, do some car-

buretor service work yourself even with little experience. (If you have more experience, you can do the work described in the chapters, "Put New Life in Your Carb," and "How to Rebuild a Four-Barrel Carburetor".)

Light carburetor service is limited to the following:

1. *Adjusting the carburetor.* You will need a tachometer for this. The tachometer, which is an engine speed indicator, is normally sold as a combination unit with a dwellmeter, which is needed for checking ignition point adjustment.

Inexpensive tach-dwellmeters for weekend mechanics are sold by discount and auto accessory stores for about $15 to $20.

Connect the tachometer as specified by the instrument manufacturer (normally to the thin-wire "CB" or minus sign terminal on the coil, and to an electrical ground, such as a cylinder head bolt).

With the engine fully warmed up, you should adjust the idle mixture screw. This screw is near the base of the carburetor. Turn it clockwise until the engine starts to falter, then counterclockwise one turn.

Note: on late-model cars with emission controls, the idle mixture screw may have a plastic cap that limits how much it can be turned. Somewhere within this range of adjustment, the engine should idle smoothly. Otherwise, the plastic cap may require removal and the carburetor adjustment by a professional shop with an exhaust analyzer.

Once the mixture is set, you can adjust the idle speed. This is controlled by a screw against the throttle linkage, which you can identify by its return spring (or by stepping on the accelerator pedal and seeing what moves).

Turning the screw clockwise increases idle speed; turning it counterclockwise decreases it. On most automatic transmission cars, idle speed is set with the emergency brake applied and the transmission shift lever in "drive" position.

A satisfactory idle speed is normally about 500 rmp for a V-8, 600 rpm for a six-cylinder, although on a somewhat older engine, you may have to increase the speed 150 rpm to obtain a smooth idle.

There is a limit to how high to set the idle speed on automatic-transmission-equipped cars. Most automatics will creep if the idle is too high, an inconvenience most motorists will not accept.

2. Checking the accelerator pump. Most carburetors have an accelerator pump, which squirts extra fuel into the air horn when you floor the accelerator suddenly. The extra fuel prevents fuel starvation under hard acceleration, which could cause "flat spots." If your engine hesitates on hard acceleration, remove the air cleaner with the engine off, and have someone pump the gas pedal while you peer into the carburetor air horn. With the pedal being pumped, there should be squirts of fuel into the air horn.

If there are none, the carburetor requires disassembly and replacement of the accelerator pump. If the squirts are very weak, perhaps the problem is that the pump arm is not connected to the correct hole of the external linkage. For maximum pump stroke, the pump linkage (which you can identify by watching what moves on top of the carburetor) should be connected to the top hole if there are more than one. To change the rod adjustment, take off the retaining clip, move the rod to the top hole and refit the clip.

The pump must have its longest stroke in winter, its shortest stroke in summer.

3. On some older Holley-brand carburetors, you also can check the fuel level in the carburetor bowl. If you see a plug threaded into the side of the bowl, remove it with the engine running; fuel should just dribble out. If no fuel comes out, or if the fuel really pours out, the fuel level is too high and

the top of the carburetor must come off (see the chapter "Put New Life in Your Carb").

Thermostatic Controls. Modern engines use either of two means (and occasionally both) to warm up the incoming air mixture for better fuel vaporization (and better combustion) when the engine is cold.

The most popular system over the years is the manifold heat control valve, also called a "heat riser." For service information on this, see the chapter, "The Heat Riser."

On late model cars, a "thermostatic air cleaner" is used. This is nothing more than a valve in the air cleaner snorkel and a duct over the exhaust manifold. A thermostatic control ducts air warmed by the exhaust manifold into the engine during cold operation. As the engine warms up, the valve pivots to close off the exhaust manifold duct and open the snorkel to intake air flow. Information on servicing this system is in Section IV, "Pollution Control Devices."

Valve Adjustment. The valves in your engine may be adjustable, even if the valve lifters are the "hydraulic" type. In addition, all valves with mechanical lifters are adjustable.

Most foreign cars, most six-cylinders and most Ford and Chevrolet V-8s have adjustable valves, whether hydraulic or mechanical. Valve adjustments are well within the ability of the weekend mechanic. See the chapters, "Valves: Tapping for Service" and "Taking the Tap Out of Tappets" for how-to information.

Valves should be adjusted at least once a year. Wear in the valve train creates the need, and periodic adjustment makes certain the valves open and close at exactly the right times for good engine performance.

The Ignition System. Periodic checking and replacement of the spark plugs will not only prolong engine life, but will help you to get maximum fuel mileage. Spark plugs when correctly chosen for the engine operate for a long period, but eventually lead in gas, oil and combustion heat cause gradual deterioration. The insulators literally wear out and oxidation takes place, often causing the spark to jump across the insulator up inside the plug rather than across the intended gap. The electrodes, too, become eaten away so that the gap becomes wider than the normal setting called for.

In adjusting electrode gap, always bend the outer, never the center, electrode. Gaps vary from .022 to .040 inch, the average being about .035 inch. Spark plug makers and service stations have specifications listing all makes of cars and the correct gap setting for each model. When the plugs are installed, tighten them only enough to compress the gasket. When buying new plugs, be sure they are of the heat range specified for your engine. Plugs are classified hot or cold according to the exposed interior length of the insulator. A hot plug does not have a "hotter spark." Hot plugs burn off fouling deposits in low-speed driving. Cold plugs prevent insulator blistering from the heat generated in high-speed driving. See chapter, "Sparkplug Troubleshooting," for details on servicing and inspecting plugs.

So far as the ignition distributor it-

Normally, ignition points can be replaced and adjusted without removing distributor. End view of Ford distributor shows the problem of installation. Note hexagonal hole in center and gear that must be engaged.

self is concerned, it should not be removed from the car unless absolutely necessary, as for replacement. Ford distributors, for example, have a gear and a hexagonal slot on the shaft, and engaging both properly can be a very difficult job.

Most routine checks of the distributor can be made on the car, as can replacement of the ignition points and condenser. See chapter 14, "Engine Tuning for Power," for more information; it does contain distributor removal information.

Muffler and Tail Pipe. A badly corroded muffler, broken or disarranged baffle plates, together with a kinked pipe, may produce enough back pressure to offset all of your other good work.

TABLE A—SIMPLE ENGINE TROUBLESHOOTING

If This Is Happening—	Look for This Trouble—	And Fix It Like This—
Low gas mileage.	Dirty air cleaner.	Remove and clean unit with kerosene, gasoline or a cleaning fluid.
Starter works too slow; lights almost go out when starting; engine does not start; lights brighten when engine speeds up.	Battery at low charge.	Have battery charged and tested for condition of cells.
Sluggish starting motor; engine starts hard, lights dim with engine not running.	Loose, corroded, frayed or broken battery cable or ground strap.	Tighten terminals or replace old cable and ground strap with new ones.
Water dripping when car is at rest.	Leaking water hose connection, defective water pump or radiator cap.	Tighten hose clamps or replace hose with new one. Have professional shop check pump and cap.
Engine overheats; water in cooling system boils.	Loose or broken fan belt or defective radiator cap.	Adjust tension of belt or install a new belt. Have professional shop check cap.
Engine starts hard or fails to start; poor gasoline mileage; fuel drips from carburetor.	Choke sticking partly closed.	Remove air cleaner and free up choke valve or linkage with kerosene or aerosol solvent.
Erratic engine operation; engine starts hard.	Loose cable in primary ignition circuit.	Tighten cable connections on switches, coil and distributor.
Slow acceleration when "stepping on gas."	Wrong seasonal setting of carburetor.	Make correct setting of seasonal adjustment for cold, hot or normal temperature.
Misfiring; rough operation; poor gasoline mileage; hard starting.	Worn out or wrong type of spark plugs.	Replace plugs with a new set of correct type and heat range.
Flooding carburetor.	Dirt or chip stuck under carburetor float valve.	Remove carburetor float bowl cover, remove float and float valve. Watch for foreign matter on valve or its seat.
Rough engine operation; misfiring; hard starting.	Pitted or wrongly spaced distributor contact points.	Install new points if old are badly worn.
Low gasoline mileage; engine lacks power and pick-up.	Heat control valve sticking.	Squirt aerosol solvent on shaft and tap lightly with hammer.

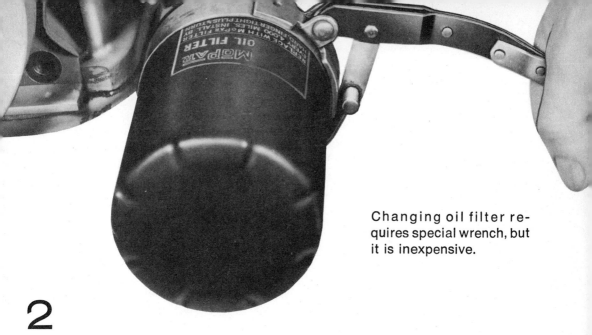

Changing oil filter re-quires special wrench, but it is inexpensive.

2

How to Change Your Car's Filters

SERVICING YOUR CAR'S filters is an excellent beginner's job for anyone interested in becoming a weekend mechanic.

Filter service is simple—no complicated disassembly required.

It also is the most frequently-needed service on a car. Oil filters normally are replaced three or four times a year, air filters once a year and gasoline filters once a year.

Name brand filters you can trust are available at discount prices (40 percent off list) in auto supply stores and the auto departments of discount houses.

The leading brands are: Purolator, AC, Fram and Wix. Stick to a name brand when buying filters. A poorly-made filter is no bargain at any price.

Oil Filter Replacement. For this job you need a filter wrench (an inexpensive tool, about a dollar in discount houses) and jacking capability.

Jacking capability is necessary to raise the front of the car several inches off the ground so you can get in underneath.

Although the oil filter may be accessible from the top of the engine compartment, the filter is replaced as part of an oil change. The engine oil drain plug is underneath and you've got to get underneath to remove it.

The car's bumper jack will raise the car, but it is hardly safe enough. The

Left: Replacing most air filters is simple. Take off the cover, lift it out and put in a new element. Right: To service oil bath air cleaner, remove cover, which contains wire mesh. Clean wire mesh in solvent and allow to air dry.

car should be supported on safety stands, which are available for as little as $7 to $9 a pair.

If the car's bumper jack is so inadequate that it will not raise the car high enough to slip the safety stands under the front suspension's lower control arms, then you need a better jack (there is no bumper jack worth talking about anyway, so you really should have something better).

For under $10, you can buy a scissors jack. This can be slipped under the front crossmember and will raise the frame (and carry the suspension with it) for enough to get the safety stands in position.

For about $30 you can get a trolley jack, which is similar to the scissors jack but has a tri-cycle stand, making it very easy to position and safer to use.

You will also need a drain pan (which you can make out of a flattish container of at least one-gallon capacity; or you can use an inexpensive plastic wash basin). The drain pan

must be large enough to hold the oil you will drain from the engine and most engines have a five-quart capacity. However, only four quarts at most will come out when you pull the drain plug.

With the car up on safety stands, remove the drain plug and allow the engine oil to drain out. For best results, the oil should be hot (it takes a fifteen to twenty mile drive to heat up the oil).

After the oil has finished pouring out of the drain hole, the oil filter can be removed. The wrench, as illustrated, wraps around the filter body and you just apply counterclockwise pressure.

Before installing the new filter, lubricate the filter's rubber gasket with clean engine oil.

Hand tighten the filter—do not use the wrench.

Cartridge Filters. Some foreign cars have replaceable cartridge filters (American cars dropped this design many years ago in favor of the easy-to-install and replace spin-on unit).

With the replaceable cartridge type, you must clean the container to remove sludge. Use a general purpose automobile solvent (such as the type used to clean carburetors).

The through-bolt that holds the container has one or more sealing O-rings on it, and these should be checked for a tight fit, and replaced at least every fourth oil change.

The filter container seals against a rubber gasket, which should be replaced every time the element is changed.

Air Filter Replacement. On most cars, there is nothing simpler than replacing an air filter element. A wing nut holds the filter cover; just remove it, pull out the old element and install the new. Some cars have spring clips to hold the cover, but that doesn't really make things any more difficult.

On some cars, however, the filter is cleaned, not replaced. Most Volkswagens have oil bath, wire mesh air cleaners, and many GM products have polyurethane foam filters.

Servicing Oil Bath. Remove the entire air filter assembly. Undo the wing nut that holds the wire mesh and remove it.

Inside you will see the oil reservoir. Dump out the old oil, clean the reservoir with solvent and refill to the level mark with clean engine oil. Dunk the wire mesh assembly in solvent, agitate, remove and allow to air dry.

Refit the reservoir assembly, then bolt the wire mesh assembly to it.

Servicing Polyurethane Foam. Gently remove the foam from its metal cage, soak in solvent and gently squeeze dry (do not wring). Allow to

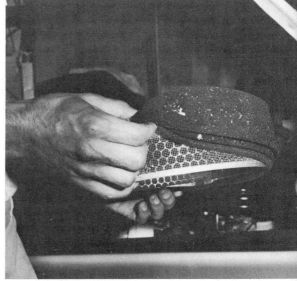

Top: Fill oil bath reservoir to mark with clean engine oil. Above: Polyurethane foam filter is removed from cage for service. Dunk it in carburetor solvent, agitate and gently squeeze dry. Allow to air dry.

air dry and dunk in clean engine oil. Gently squeeze out the excess oil and refit to the cage.

Replacing Gasoline Filter. There are three popular gasoline filters used in recent years: one is an element type on the fuel pump; a second is in the carburetor fuel inlet boss, and the third (and most popular) is in the fuel line between pump and carburetor.

23

Left: Oil polyurethane foam with clean engine oil. Right: Squeeze out excess oil (gently) from polyurethane foam element and refit to cage. Below: Pump-type gas filter is replaced by removing cover, taking out old element and installing new one.

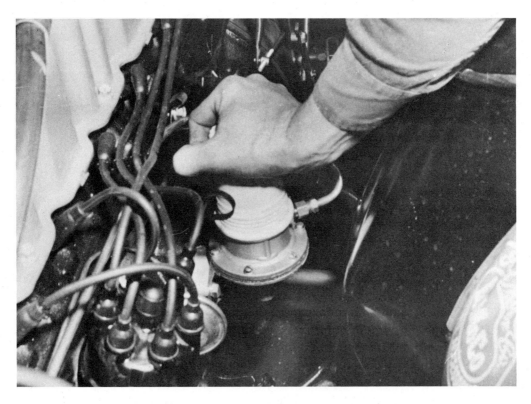

The fuel pump type is replaced by simply unscrewing the cover, lifting out the element, installing a new one and refitting the cover.

The type in the carburetor fuel inlet boss requires undoing the fuel line fitting. Pull the fuel line out of the carburetor inlet boss and inside you'll find the tiny element, made of sintered bronze or pleated paper. You will also find a filter positioning spring.

This type of filter is best discarded completely. If it is sintered bronze, it has poor filtering ability and will pass dirt particles 10 times larger than a good paper filter. If it is paper, it's so small it will clog in only a few thousand miles and the constant replacement is a nuisance.

The discarding of the carburetor boss filter doesn't mean you have to leave your fuel system unprotected. You can install an in-the-line gasoline filter, which will last a year because it is so much larger. Many cars are factory equipped with this type, but it does cost more than the smaller one, and Detroit has its penny-pinchers.

In-line Gasoline Filter. This type of filter is available in kit form, for installation on cars with no fuel filtration or with the inadequate carburetor boss type.

The kit differs from the replacement filter only in the inclusion of two short hoses. The boxes for both contain four spring clamps.

To replace the filter on a car so equipped, remove the clamps. The original equipment clamps are a pry-off type that you discard. Pull the hoses from the filter necks, and discard the filter.

This is sintered bronze filter in carburetor boss, accessible after removing fuel line (on some cars, filter is accessible after removing plug in carb side).

Installing in-line gasoline filter begins with disconnection of fuel line at carburetor.

Then cut out six-inch section of fuel line with tube cutter. Type used in illustration is combination tube cutter and hose clamp pliers.

Fit short hoses and secure with spring clamps furnished with kit.

The finished job. Run engine and check for leaks.

Fit a spring clamp onto each hose. This can be done by spreading the tangs of the clamps with a pair of ordinary pliers, but it isn't easy. By filing a notch in the center of the top edge of each jaw, you will be able to hold the tangs for easy spreading. Or you can purchase a pair of hose clamp pliers, which are designed for the purpose. Such pliers are available in combination forms with tubing cutters, and if you are planning to install a kit, they are a worthwhile purchase.

Then install the filter, making sure that the arrow on the side of the filter container points toward the carburetor.

With the hoses firmly in place spread the tangs of the clamps and move the clamps to positions on the hoses over the filter necks.

Installing the Kit. The kit takes about 15 minutes to install and requires a tubing cutter, such as the type that is built into some hose clamp pliers.

Find a six-inch section of fuel line between pump and carburetor that is reasonably straight and accessible, and with the tubing cutter, chop it out. You may find it easier to brace the fuel line by disconnecting it at the carb and holding it.

Fit a short hose on to the necks of the filter and secure with a spring clamp.

Position the entire assembly in the gap in the fuel line and secure with the remaining clamps. (Slip the clamps onto the line before you put the hose on; that's the easy way.)

After you have changed oil and a few filters, you will begin to feel more comfortable about working on a car, and can tackle other jobs.

Vacuum gauge can pinpoint many engine ailments.

3

Pinpointing Ailments with a Vacuum Gauge

NATURE MAY ABHOR a vacuum, but the economy-minded motorist is all for it. He knows that high engine vacuum readings indicate superior driving efficiency, excellent engine performance, and more miles to the gallon. And he measures the vacuum of his car's engine with a vacuum gauge.

Showing you how to squeeze more mileage from a tankful of gas is not a vacuum gauge's only virtue, either. It's also a top-notch troubleshooter—quick to diagnose over 30 engine ailments—

all the way from sticking valves, bad carburetor adjustment, worn timing chain, leaky head gasket and clogged muffler, to rings in poor condition, loose valve guides and faulty cylinders.

You can obtain one of these "engine doctors" for anywhere from $5 to $12 from auto accessory stores. It is installed by connecting it to the intake manifold. On cars equipped with a vacuum-operated windshield wiper, you remove the windshield wiper hose and attach the vacuum gauge hose. If the car has a vacuum-booster pump, take off the booster line at the manifold and plug the opening.

Unfortunately, very few cars have vacuum-operated windshield wipers. Electric wipers have been standard on virtually all cars for many years (some current American Motors cars are a low-sales exception).

On some cars with electric wipers, there is a plug in the intake manifold. Remove it and thread in the fitting normally supplied with the vacuum gauge. If the fitting is not the correct size, you can obtain another from most auto parts houses.

If there is no plug, you can obtain a T-shaped fitting from an auto parts house and install it in the hose to the power brake unit. Do not install the vacuum gauge T-fitting in the line to the distributor vacuum advance, although this would seem to be a logical place. On many cars, the location of the vacuum advance port is such that you will not get a true vacuum reading at engine idle.

Reading a Vacuum Gauge. Many automobile engines in good condition show a steady vacuum reading somewhere between 17 and 22 as most gauges are calibrated.

Note: on some high-performance engines, the vacuum gauge reading may flicker slightly.

This reading will drop 1 point for each 1,000 feet that the car is above sea level. Technically, these points on the gauge are referred to as "inches of mercury." Originally, vacuum gauges were U-shaped glass tubes with mercury at the bottom of the U. The greater the vacuum, the higher the column of mercury. Measured in inches, the standard for vacuum reading became *inches of mercury.*

Let's look at some typical readings. The first is a *steady* reading showing 20 inches. But compare this with the next. Here the needle is slowly swing-

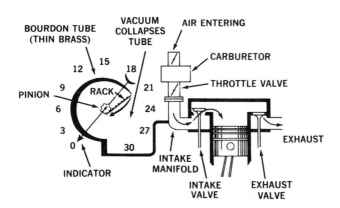

Drawing shows how vacuum gauge works. Tip of Bourdon tube moves toward center as vacuum increases, moving rack, pinion and gauge hand. Opening throttle lowers vacuum reading; closing throttle increases it. Variation in piston speed causes gauge to pulsate. Air leaking into intake manifold, or compression pressure escaping into it, lowers gauge reading.

Finding a connection point for a vacuum gauge may be difficult. On this car, a multiple vacuum hose connector is the choice.

ing back and forth on either side of 18. Something is making the engine speed up and slow down. This something is usually faulty carburetion, though the action may also be due to air leaks between the base of the carburetor and the manifold, or between the manifold and the engine block.

If such oscillation of the hand is noted, tighten the bolts that hold the carburetor to the manifold and those that hold the manifold to the block. Then turn the low-speed mixture, adjusting screws of the carburetor *in* (clockwise), possibly ¼ turn, until the vacuum gauge suddenly reduces its reading two or more divisions of the scale. Then turn the mixture screws *out* (counterclockwise) until the gauge reading reaches the highest obtainable value.

If the hand still continues to swing,

then the carburetor may have a high float level, or the air cleaner may be clogged, or the fuel pump may have high pressure. Any of these conditions could give a rich mixture that would result in the oscillating gauge reading. If cleaning the air cleaner does not cure the trouble, try bending the carburetor float level down 1/16 inch and repeating the test. If no improvement is noted and the carburetor has gone 30,000 to 40,000 miles, try a new or rebuilt carburetor.

Note that the vacuum gauge hand in the third reading is steady, but at the *low* end of the acceptable range. This *could* happen on a new engine due to stiffness which necessitates extra throttle opening. Or it could happen on an engine that has not warmed up and is using heavy oil.

The reading in that illustration

merely means that the throttle is opened wider—thus admitting more outside air—in order to keep the pistons moving. There are a number of possible causes for this wider throttle opening. It may be because of a new engine, or because valve and ignition timing are late as the result of worn timing gears or timing chain. Or, late ignition alone could cause this low gauge reading. Since the ignition is not efficient and full power is not delivered to the pis-

ton, the throttle must be opened farther to keep the engine running. And, as we know, opening the throttle lowers the vacuum reading.

Greatest value of the gauge results when you check your engine vacuum from time to time. Then if you find the vacuum reading *reducing,* you are on the trail of lost efficiency.

Finally, a totally dead cylinder, blown head gasket, burned distributor contact points, or a leaking intake

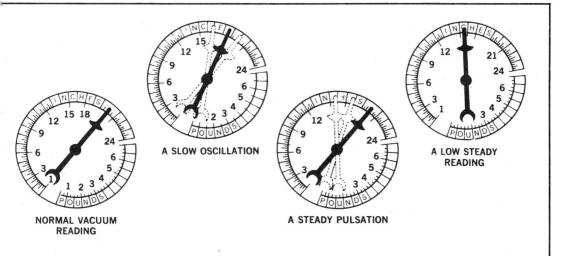

A SLOW OSCILLATION

A LOW STEADY READING

NORMAL VACUUM READING

A STEADY PULSATION

Some vacuum gauge indications. Chapter explains what they mean.

valve could cause the considerable pulsation at a steady rate indicated in the final reading.

Understandably, these vacuum gauge indications become even more valuable when followed by compression tests. When we have a condition such as that indicated by the vacuum gauge in the final reading, a compression reading would show whether or not the trouble was due to faulty valves.

Experienced users of the vacuum gauge do more than just watch the reading at low idle, however. If the reading is a little low, the operator will open and close the throttle suddenly. If the gauge drops to zero and then shoots up between 20 and 22 when this is done, the chances are that the engine needs new rings. A compression test should follow in order to check whether this is the case or not.

If the reading is quite low—between

10 and 15—loosen the clamp on the ignition distributor. Turn the distributor *against* the ignition cam rotation while watching the gauge. Turning the distributor housing against distribution shaft rotation advances the spark. If this brings the vacuum reading up one or two or more points, it is a sure indication that the car has been running with a retarded spark. Since wear of the fiber block on the moving arm in the distributor retards the spark, check the condition of the distributor contact points and either adjust them or put in new ones.

Bleeding Air. On old cars, you will often find air bleeding into the intake manifold through a worn carburetor throttle shaft. Air may also get in if the carburetor gasket is broken, or if the carburetor is loose on the manifold. A quick check for these conditions is made by some mechanics by placing a small quantity of gasoline in an oil can and, with the engine idling—and being careful of the fire hazard involved—applying a drop of gasoline at each end of the carburetor throttle shaft. If this causes the vacuum gauge reading to vary at all, it means that the gasoline is being drawn into the engine.

Make the same kind of test at the base of the carburetor to see if air is being sucked in at the gaskets. The same check can also be made by dripping gasoline at the exposed edge of each manifold-to-engine gasket.

If any of these other tests show an air leak as indicated by the gauge reading varying from one to five points, tighten the part or replace the gasket.

Spark-plug gaps are often set up to .005 in. wider than specifications call for to give smooth idling and quick starting. Smooth idling from *any* cause gives a steady vacuum gauge reading. Spark plug gaps are also often set .003 to .005 inch closer than specifications call for in order to gain greater top speed. Some individuals may overdo these variations from specifications. If the vacuum gauge oscillates over a range of one or two points, it may be because spark plugs are set too close. If you get such a swing on your car, check the spark plug gaps and set them properly to specifications.

When cars overheat or fail to reach expected road speed, you may have a restricted exhaust system from carbon in the exhaust pipe or muffler, or a bent or clogged tail pipe. To test this, run the engine at about 2,000 rpm. This would be about what would give the car 40-50 mph on the road. If the vacuum gauge reading reduces gradually from a normal value of between 17 and 22 to almost zero, and then begins to climb slowly, you may be sure that the exhaust system is offering excessive resistance and should be checked.

Power Balance Test. If, because of low or irregular vacuum gauge readings you suspect that a cylinder is faulty, how can you tell which one it is? The answer is that you make a *power balance* test, by shorting out certain groups of spark plugs and noting the effect on the gauge reading.

For an efficient power balance test, regular automotive trouble shooters often use as many as six ground wires attached to a common ground clamp. To avoid electrical shock, attach the common ground clip from the ground-

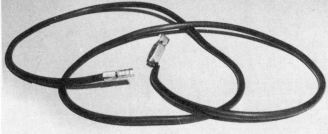

Above: Squirting a little gas at base of carburetor, if it increases vacuum reading, indicates leaking carburetor gasket. Right: Homemade grounding wire for power balance testing.

ing wires to the engine first. Then attach the wires to the spark plugs.

In order to attach these wires (which are made from ordinary spark plug wire) to the spark plugs, you will need special adapters, which are available from auto parts houses.

The adapters provide a clip-on point for the grounding wires, which normally are fitted with alligator clips. Without these adapters, the plug wire terminal would cover the plug terminal and there would be no way to attach the grounding wires.

The idea of the balance test is to short out all but a pair of companion cylinders. These are the cylinders whose pistons are in the same position at all times, but on different strokes.

When one piston is going down on the intake stroke, the companion is going down on power stroke. When one is coming up on compression stroke, the other is coming up on exhaust.

To determine the companion cylinders, you must know the firing order of the cylinders and how they are numbered.

The firing order for all in-line six-cylinder engines is the same: 1-5-3-6-2-4, and the cylinders are numbered

1-2-3-4-5-6, starting from the front. V-8s vary all over the lot, and we suggest you ask the counterman where you buy your auto parts.

To pair off the companions, take the firing order and divide it in half. Place the second half under the first half, and the companions are the cylinders directly above and below.

Examples: six-cylinder in-line 1-5-3
6-2-4
companions are 1 and 6, 5 and 2, 3 and 4.

V-8 with firing order 1-8-4-3-6-5-7-2
1-8-4-3
6-5-7-2

With the grounding wires, short out all cylinders but one companion pair and run the engine on the pair with a tachometer and vacuum gauge connected, and the engine warmed up.

Note engine speed and vacuum gauge reading.

Do the same for the other companion pairs.

If, on this power balance test, the vacuum gauge shows a variation greater than one inch between *pairs* of cylinders being tested, these cylinders are off balance, (If you used a tachometer, the speed variation should be no greater than 40 rpm between pairs of cylinders being tested). To isolate *one* weak cylinder, short out half of the cylinders in an in-line engine, or an entire bank in a V engine. The bank that gives the lower vacuum gauge reading *includes* the weak cylinder.

These, then, are some of the more important of the many applications of the vacuum gauge. It can save you money; it can give you the satisfaction of having a smooth-running efficient car. Unfortunately, it can't remedy the faults it finds. But it can and does simplify that job tremendously.

Replacing carburetor begins with removal of complete air cleaner assembly. On late-model car, this involves several hose disconnections and perhaps loosening or removing a bracket or two.

4

Replacing Engine Parts

WHEN YOUR CAR needs a new generator, starter, fuel pump, carburetor, transmission, or engine, you can replace it with an exchange unit, doing the removal and installation yourself to save a big part of the repair bill. Buying rebuilts is convenient when you don't have the time, tools and/or know-how to rebuild your own.

In addition, many parts houses give discounts from list price to weekend mechanics, though professionals do, of course, receive larger ones.

The exchange unit is a rebuilt. At one time, rebuilts were very risky purchases. But today, there are excellent assembly-line and semi-custom rebuilders all over the country, and their products are reliable.

There also are poor rebuilts. Take a carburetor for example. A "cheapie" rebuilder will merely clean out the old carburetor, replace the gaskets and perhaps the needle valve and seat assembly. A quality rebuilder will replace power valves, jets, accelerator pump and choke too.

With a fuel pump, the cheapie rebuilder will just replace the pump diaphragm. The quality rebuilder will change the diaphragm spring, and also check valves and pump arm, if worn.

Top: Most late-model cars have an electric solenoid to regulate the precise position of the throttle. Solenoid holds throttle open slightly for idling and when engine is shut off, allows it to close completely so engine does not run on. Disconnect solenoid wire. Above: If new carburetor doesnt come with throttle solenoid, remove old one for transfer.

How can you be assured of a quality rebuilt? The answer is to buy from the auto parts houses that the professionals patronize, and not from the stores that also sell toys and garden hoses.

Carburetor Replacement. One of the most frequent troublemakers is the carburetor. Remove the air cleaner and disconnect the throttle, choke linkage and the fuel line from the fuel pump. Two to four studs hold the carburetor body to the flange. Buy an exchange carburetor to fit your car from your rebuilt parts dealer. The carburetor represents a real savings. A new 4-barrel carburetor costs around $75 to $110, while the price of a rebuilt is perhaps half that, including the trade-in of your old carburetor.

The new carburetor, depending on the rebuilder, will often require transfer of some pieces of linkage from the old carburetor to the new. So before you hand in your old carburetor, place it side by side with the new and determine what parts must be transferred.

Installing a rebuilt carburetor is the reverse of pulling the old one, although it is good practice to install a new gasket between the carburetor and the intake manifold.

To get a precise adjustment, you can use a vacuum gauge, installed as described in the chapter, "Pinpointing Ailments with a Vacuum Gauge."

Turn out the mixture screw or the two screws, in the case of a two or four barrel carb, until the engine idles smoothly without rolling or galloping. The indicator on the vacuum gauge should remain stationary, but if it oscillates in a slow floating motion, keep adjusting the idle-speed screw along with the idle-mixture screws until the gauge shows the highest vacuum without vibration. Then adjust the idle-speed screw alone for the best idle speed before the engine warms up

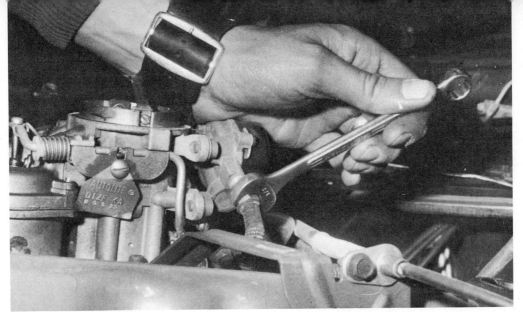

Disconnect automatic choke heat tube on carbs with incarburetor coil. On carbs with well choke, disconnect link from coil to choke plate.

thoroughly. On cars with automatic transmissions, it may be necessary to readjust the idle speed somewhat lower if the car tends to creep too much at a stoplight.

The procedure for distributor testing and removal is in the chapter, "Engine Tuning for Power."

If the engine will not start after installation of the rebuilt distributor (and it was running, even poorly, before), chances are you have installed the distributor incorrectly and ignition timing is far off.

Many distributors will go in only one way, but many more will go in any number of ways, but the timing will be wrong and the car won't start.

The best procedure is to prevent an error by carefully marking the distributor body and the engine adjacent, and noting the position of the rotor, as also explained in "Engine Tuning for Power."

If you have made an error (or are assisting a friend who has), here is a procedure to get the engine timed close enough to get it started, after which you can use a power timing light to set timing accurately.

With the distributor removed, crank the engine in very short bursts until the timing mark on the crankshaft pulley or damper is lined up with the timing indicator on the front of the engine.

At this point, the ignition system should be ready to fire either No. 1 cylinder or its companion, No. 6 (you will have to know how the cylinders are numbered, and the ignition firing order).

Put the distributor partly back in, lining up the body as close as you can remember to its original position. The location of the vacuum hose or tube to the distributor vacuum advance may assist your memory.

Disconnect fuel line from carburetor.

Left: Disconnect throttle linkage. The arrangement from one carburetor to another varies, so you will just have to see what is used. On this particular carb, pushing off a spring clip does the job. Below: Disconnect any vacuum hoses to the carburetor.

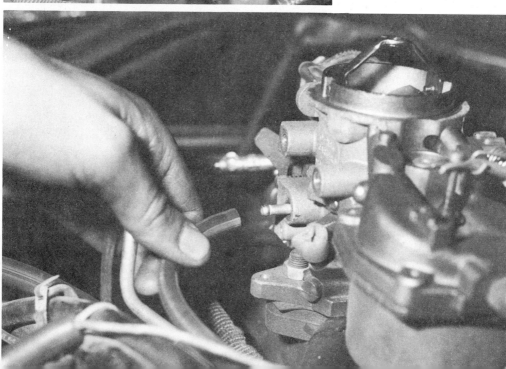

Swing the distributor cap back into position but do not fasten it down. Just note the location of the No. 1 and No. 6 spark plug wires and aim the tip of the rotor for either of them. With the rotor so aimed, slip the distributor back in all the way. (This may take time on such as Ford products, where the distributor shaft must engage both a gear and a hex fitting.)

Refit the distributor cap and try to start the engine. If the engine seems to be trying to start, move the distributor body in short arcs, and if the engine starts, you now are ready for precise timing with the power timing light.

If it shows no sign of starting, take out the distributor and re-install, aiming the tip of the rotor for the other cylinder. Refit the distributor cap and again try to start the engine, also moving the distributor body in short arcs if the engine seems to be trying to start.

If the term "trying to start" is unfamiliar, here is what it means: the engine will fire then die immediately. This is an indication that ignition timing is close, but not close enough.

Special Technique. Here is a technique that you can use to determine which cylinder (No. 1 or No. 6) is ready to fire when the timing marks are lined up. It eliminates the 50-50 odds you face otherwise.

Remove the No. 1 cylinder spark plug and watch the timing mark on the crankshaft pulley or damper. When it is several inches from the timing indicator on the engine, insert a compression gauge into the No. 1 spark plug hole and continue cranking until the marks are very close. Remove the compression gauge and see if there is a reading on it. (It won't be a normal one, but it should be something if No. 1 piston is coming up on compression.)

If there is no reading, No. 1 piston is coming up on exhaust and No. 6 is coming up on compression. The rotor tip should be pointed toward No. 6.

Generator and Voltage Regulator. The generator (whether an older DC type or the newer alternator) can be confidently replaced with a rebuilt, at a saving that could exceed 60 percent over a new unit.

The voltage regulator is integral with the alternator on many new cars, but it is a separate unit on most others, and has always been a separate unit with DC generators.

Never install a rebuilt conventional voltage regulator. There are many reasons a voltage regulator can fail, and the rebuilding jobs we have seen on them are limited to replacement of the vibrating contacts.

Fully-electronic regulators have no moving parts and seldom fail. Rebuilt units of these are not readily available, although they should soon be, and may be worth considering.

It is important that you definitely determine that the trouble is in the generator before you replace it. Broken connections, a faulty regulator and a slipping fan belt are far more likely problems.

See Section IX, "General Electrical Servicing," for troubleshooting information.

Replacing a generator is a very straightforward job, but there is one precaution: always disconnect the battery ground cable before you start.

Left: Undo the nuts or bolts that hold the carburetor to its base, and remove. Right: The carb is ready for removal. Just lift it up and out. Installation is a reversal of the removal procedure.

Two or three bolts and nuts will hold the generator, and there are two or three electrical connections. If the terminals are not sufficiently different, make a sketch showing where each wire goes before you remove anything.

Fuel Pump. When a fuel pump fails, replacing it with a rebuilt is a simple job. See the chapter, "Fixing Your Fuel Pump," for troubleshooting information.

The typical fuel pump is a mechanical unit, driven by the engine. The only exceptions are some foreign cars and the Chevrolet Vega, which have electric pumps.

The mechanical pump is held by two bolts or studs and nuts. To replace the pump, just undo the two fuel line connections (one inlet line from the gas tank, the other an outlet line to the carburetor).

Then remove the two bolts or nuts and pull the pump straight out. On cars with a flexible hose or hoses, it may be easier to take out the bolts or nuts first and lift the pump to a position where the hose connection is easier to get at.

Warning: on Chevrolet engines, the fuel pump arm is moved by a cylinder that is in contact with the camshaft. This design can make it difficult to install a replacement pump. There are special tools available to hold the cylinder up and in its bore, so that the replacement pump can be fitted. If you don't have this tool, you can do the job with a piece of stiff wire and patience.

Virtually all Ford products have sealed pumps, so they cannot be rebuilt except at a factory. Even if your pump is rebuildable, the low price of a factory rebuilt (generally under $10) makes it the best choice for a time-saving repair.

On Chevrolet Vega, the only American car with an electric pump, the pump is in the gas tank, which is held

Replacement of a regulator is simple. Regulator is held by two or four screws. Hold replacement regulator next to defective unit and transfer one wire at a time.

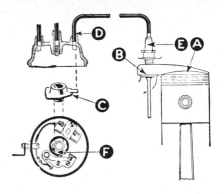

If you make a mistake while replacing a distributor, drawing shows how to set up ignition timing close enough to get engine started, at which point timing light can be connected. Piston (A) of No. 1 cylinder is at top dead center of cylinder on compression stroke. Rotor (C) points to No. 1 spark plug wire in distributor cap (D). Lobe on cam (F) is about to open breaker points. E is the No. 1 spark plug, which is about to fire.

by two straps. To get at this pump, undo the strap nuts at the rear of the tank, lower the tank and remove the pump from its bracket.

Engine. When the engine in your car is so badly worn that it needs a complete overhaul, such as reboring, new pistons and rings, engine bearings, crankshaft regrinding, valve job, ring gear on the flywheel, etc., a rebuilt or used engine is the best answer.

You can save at least $400 by buying a rebuilt instead of a new engine, even if you could get a new engine. The rebuilding art is so highly developed in the engine field that few car makers even supply complete new engines. In many cases, all they supply are short blocks, which are engine blocks with crankshaft, connecting rods, pistons and rings. To get a complete engine, you have to buy all the accessories and cylinder heads.

Even if the car maker lists a complete engine, it will not be easy to get.

The few that are made are for warranty use.

So your choice is either a factory rebuilt, a semi-custom rebuilt or a used engine from a wrecking yard.

If you can obtain a late-model used engine from a wrecking yard, this is the most economical choice. There is very little risk if you buy from a reputable wrecking yard, for it surely will have run the engine before it was pulled from the chassis, and therefore will not sell it if it burns oil or has piston slaps or bearing knocks. It also will advise you of the mileage on the engine.

The rebuilt engine offers a bit more security, for it comes with a firm guarantee. In the rebuilt area, there are two choices:

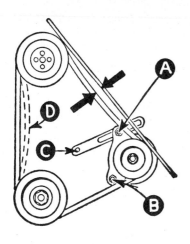

Above: Replacement of a generator is difficult only if the generator is inacces-sible. Normally it is held by two or three bolts and is removed by taking out bolts A and B, pushing generator in along pivot C, and removing belt D. There are two or three electrical connections on the generator and if they look the same, tag them so you can refit them correctly. Below Left: Replacing fuel pump is normally not difficult if the pump bolts are accessible, and they usually are with ordinary tools. First step is to disconnect the fuel lines. In the case of this pump, only one line has to be disconnected, as other is a hose which can be swung up with the pump and removed from the top of the engine compart-ment more easily. Below Right: Socket wrench makes short work of the two fuel pump bolts.

Pump now can be lifted up and hose connection taken off. This particular pump is from a Chevrolet, and a special tool is very helpful in refitting the pump so that the pump arm will properly be under an actuating cylinder.

1. the factory rebuilt. This is an engine that went down an assembly line much like the one that put it together.

2. the semi-custom rebuilt. This is an engine that was rebuilt in a smaller shop with a lot more human inspections. It is 10 to 20 percent more than a factory rebuilt.

If you have an older car, or one that just wasn't a big seller, the factory rebuilt engine may not be readily available. The semi-custom rebuilding job will be done on your engine, and your car may be out of action less than a week.

Engine Removal. There are no complete sets of hard-and-fast rules that will cover engine removal on all cars. Some general information, however, may help you:

1. You will need a chain or cable hoist, and this can be rented for a day for about two dollars.

2. You will need something from which to hang the hoist. A heavy beam across the top of your garage or a sturdy basketball backboard normally are acceptable.

3. When you make disconnections of either tubing or wiring, tag everything so you'll know where it goes when the replacement engine is ready for installation.

4. The engine on all front-engine-rear-drive cars comes out from the top of the engine compartment, so the hood may have to be removed. Inasmuch as hood re-installation and alignment is a time-consuming procedure, you may be able to reduce it by scrib-

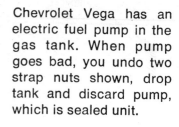

Chevrolet Vega has an electric fuel pump in the gas tank. When pump goes bad, you undo two strap nuts shown, drop tank and discard pump, which is sealed unit.

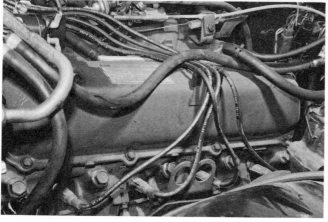

Many engines have lifting hooks, which makes the job of removing them a bit easier. There are two on this V-8, one on each side between second and third spark plugs.

ing around the bolts or nuts in elongated adjustment holes with a sharp instrument.

5. Do not try to do this job without a complete set of wrenches. You will need a complete socket set (preferably both 1/2-inch and 3/8-inch drive), in addition to open-end and box wrenches.

6. If the car is a manual transmission, you will have to align the clutch. Inexpensive but satisfactory wooden alignment tools are available for $2 or less; don't waste your money on the expensive professional-type alignment tools.

7. Although engine removal is often a one-man job, installation is never so. Have a husky friend lined up for the day you install the replacement engine. Better still, have two husky friends.

8. Keep related parts and nuts and bolts together, using envelopes appropriately marked or muffin tins. It is very easy to become impatient when pulling an engine, and just pile up nuts and bolts. But when the job of installation comes later, one misplaced nut or bolt could hold you up for an hour or more.

9. Rebuilt engines are supplied stripped of accessories, but including all innards. It's best to equip the rebuilt block with rebuilt carburetor, distributor, fuel pump, generator and other parts subject to wear.

10. If you can, obtain a factory shop manual. It won't make the job that much easier, but it may keep you from breaking something.

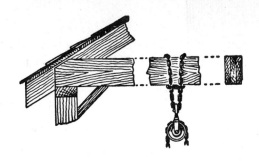

Chain sling over built-up beam across caps of garage walls supports chain hoist to lift out engine.

11. If the engine seems to be stuck, either coming out or going in, look for a reason instead of applying heavy force. And be very careful not to pinch tubing or lines.

12. On virtually every engine pull, you will have to do the following:

a. drain engine oil and cooling system; disconnect hoses.

b. disconnect ignition system at the coil's "SW" or plus terminal.

c. disconnect the fuel system from the tank. Because of clearance problems, you may also have to pull the fuel pump and carburetor.

d. disconnect the exhaust pipe from the exhaust manifold, and if clearance is limited, remove the exhaust manifold.

e. disconnect the electrical ground strap from the chassis to the engine. On late-model cars, a split ground strap is sometimes used, with one part going from battery to chassis, the other part from battery to engine. If your car doesn't have this, look for a separate strap from engine to chassis. It may be buried underneath, and would, if left connected, keep the engine from coming out.

f. disconnect the engine mounts. Most cars have two (there is a third support at the transmission).

13. If the engine compartment looks a bit crowded, remove any accessories that are reasonably easy to get at, such as alternator, oil filter, possibly the starter.

14. The last item on this list should actually be the first on yours: always disconnect the battery cables before you start working. In fact, removing the battery and both cables will not only give you more room, but in part is necessary for engine removal (the cable to the starter has to come out).

With the engine out, clean the compartment of all grease and mud with a putty knife and rags soaked in solvent. Examine the rubber engine mounts and replace them if they are flattened, broken or uneven. It is inexpensive insurance to replace the mounts, as they will have become worn by the time the engine needs replacing.

Once you install your practically new engine, use a new fan belt, ignition wiring, battery cables and hose connections to complete the installation. Install new spark plugs of proper heat range and gapped for your engine. (Check with your service station to determine the correct gap for your engine. Most older cars use a .025 inch plug gap; all recent cars use a gap of .035, and most plugs manufactured today are sold with the wider gap.)

Installing replacement parts is not limited to engine parts. Replacement *transmissions, universal joints, muffler* and *exhaust pipes, brakes, front suspension* parts and *shock absorbers* are available. Some are rebuilt, some new.

The torque wrench can be used to tighten anything you can get it on, including spark plugs.

5

How Tight is Tight?

EVER-INCREASING USE of lighter and softer metal components in automobiles, power mowers, outboard motors, and many household appliances means that homeowners who do their own repairs can no longer rely on hand-tightening nuts and bolts just enough to do the holding job, yet not so tight as to cause damage and premature failure.

Gone are the days when it was permissible to tighten nuts until they squawked or snugged up. To get the proper clamping and holding force from any fastener demands that just the right amount of tension be placed on the fastener to stretch it to the predetermined amount of elasticity.

Too much tightening force can stretch the fastener past the point from which it can snap back into original shape after being stretched, making it unfit for further use. It will also cause the metal component to warp or twist.

On the other hand, too little tension reduces the fastener's ability as a clamping device. Consequently, that part of the assembly will either loosen, fracture, or fail prematurely. General torque tightening specifications are in the table included in this chapter.

Function of the Torque Wrench is to measure the amount of tightening force applied to the fastener. Today's close-tolerance assemblies require pure precision to establish the correct tightening tension.

All torque wrenches are designed on the principle of the lever. Torque is based on the fundamental law of the lever, which states that force times distance equals the torque about a given point. Force refers to the amount of pull applied to the wrench handle by the operator. Distance is the length of the wrench measured between the centerline of the force being applied to the handle and the centerline of the drive square. To arrive at torque, multiply force times distance.

Most commonly used torque wrenches are the pound-inch and the pound-foot. The occasion often arises when it may become necessary to convert lb./in. into lb./ft., or vice versa. To convert a lb./ft. reading on the scale of the wrench to lb./in., multiply the scale reading by 12. To convert lb./in. to lb./ft., merely divide the reading on the lb./ft. scale by 12.

Increase Capacity of the torque wrench by using an extension or adapter to gain access to hidden fasteners and nearly double the calibrations on the torque scale.

A fitting equal to the lever length of the wrench will multiply the torque by two; thus a 100 lb./ft. wrench can be used to tighten bolts up to 200 lb./ft.

There are a number of such fittings available for torque wrenches; in fact, most any socket adapter or extension will fit a torque wrench.

Although these fittings enable you to get maximum utility from the wrench, they also increase the length of the wrench and have the overall effect of increasing the length of the lever so the torque scale will not give an accurate torque reading.

By using the illustrated formula, you can see that a 10-in. torque wrench with a 4-inch adapter or extension will over-torque by 4 lb./ft. even though the scale reads 10 lb./ft.

Using the Torque Wrench is no more difficult than a regular ratchet or pull handle. There is no hard and fast rule as to whether you should push or pull. The only requirement is that you do not twist or bind the handle.

The pivoted handle, or floating handle as it is sometimes called, is so designed that it conveniently fits the operator's hand and concentrates the pulling force at a fixed point on the torque wrench.

When using the wrench, the force should be applied to a specific point rather than spreading it out over the entire area of the handle.

Important Points to keep in mind when tightening down threaded fasteners are thread resistance, fastener seizure, and tightening procedure.

General Torque Tightening Specifications.

Bolt Size	Cast Iron	Aluminum	Brass
1/4-20	80 lb./in.	60 lb./in.	61 lb./in.
1/4-28	100 lb./in.	84 lb./in.	77 lb./in.
5/16-18	11-12 lb./ft.	8-10 lb./ft.	8-9 lb./ft.
5/16-24	13-14 lb./ft.	10-11 lb./ft.	9-10 lb./ft.
3/8-16	21-23 lb./ft.	17-19 lb./ft.	14-16 lb./ft.
3/8-24	23-25 lb./ft.	19-21 lb./ft.	15-17 lb./ft.
7/16-14	33-35 lb./ft.	27-29 lb./ft.	24-26 lb./ft.
7/16-20	35-37 lb./ft.	30-31 lb./ft.	25-27 lb./ft.
1/2-13	46-48 lb./ft.	37-41 lb./ft.	33-35 lb./ft.
1/2-20	48-50 lb./ft.	42-44 lb./ft.	35-37 lb./ft.
9/16-12	60-62 lb./ft.	57-58 lb./ft.	44-46 lb./ft.
9/16-18	67-69 lb./ft	63-64 lb./ft.	49-51 lb./ft.
5/8-11	104-106 lb./ft.	93-96 lb./ft.	73-75 lb./ft.
5/8-18	116-118 lb./ft.	101-104 lb./ft.	93-95 lb./ft.
3/4-10	144-146 lb./ft.	128-131 lb./ft.	102-104 lb./ft.
3/4-16	140-142 lb./ft.	132-134 lb./ft.	100-102 lb./ft.
7/8-9	218-220 lb./ft.	191-194 lb./ft.	157-159 lb./ft.
7/8-14	217-219 lb./ft.	196-198 lb./ft.	156-158 lb./ft.
1-8	323-325 lb./ft.	293-298 lb./ft.	232-234 lb./ft.
1-14	292-294 lb./ft.	264-266 lb./ft.	210-212 lb./ft.

* These specifications can be followed when specific factory specifications are not available. The many variables of fasteners and materials make the above table useful as a guide only. On especially critical applications, individual manufacturer's specifications must be followed.

Thread resistance is caused by damaged or rusted threads. The rule of thumb to follow when tightening fasteners on such threads is to add the thread resistance to the torque specification for the final torque reading. For instance, if the specification calls for 20 lb./ft. torque for a certain nut, and if it takes 3 lb./ft. to overcome the thread resistance, tighten the nut to a torque of 23 lb./ft.

To determine just what is the amount of thread resistance, note the torque required to pull the nut through its last full turn before exerting any tightening torque. Never check thread resistance anywhere except during the last full turn of the nut.

All manufacturers' specified torque readings are for clean and lightly oiled threads. You can't use rusted bolts or nuts and expect to get reliable settings, even if you compensate for thread resistance.

FORMULA FOR CALCULATING EXTRA TORQUE FOR ACCESSORIES

$$TA = \frac{TW \times (L + A)}{L}$$

TA = Torque exerted at end of the adapter or extension
TW = Torque wrench scale reading
L = Lever length of wrench
A = Length of the adapter extension

The torque wrench should always be used to tighten cylinder head bolts or nuts, connecting rod and bearing caps, clutch pressure plate bolts, wheel bearing nuts and any aluminum parts, including intake manifolds.

The tightening of cylinder head bolts or nuts is a standard part of a major tuneup. Cylinder head gaskets take a "compression set" and to prevent compression losses, they must be periodically retightened.

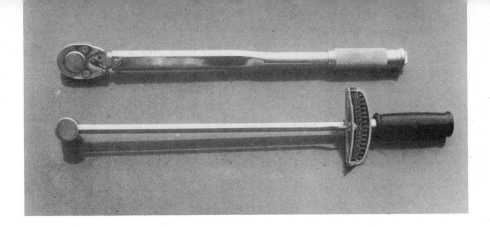

Top: These are the two most commonly used types of torque wrenches. The top wrench is a professional tool, with a ratchet feature and a torque-setting feature in the handle. When pre-set torque is reached, the wrench clicks. Lower unit is inexpensive weekend mechanic's type. Professional version is $35 to $45. Weekend mechanic's version is $10 to $15. Right: Cylinder head gasket should always be torqued with torque wrench, following manufacturer's recommended sequence. Most torquing sequences start at the center and work toward outside, and the one illustrated is typical.

Right: Intake manifold is made of aluminum, and therefore tightening with torque wrench is desirable. You can almost always get the wrench in, and as you notice, this torquing sequence, like the cylinder head, starts at the center and works toward the outside.

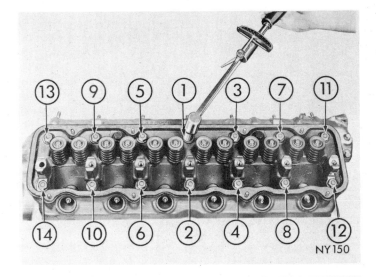

All car manufacturers specify a sequence for tightening cylinder head bolts or nuts, and the sequence should be used whenever available.

If unavailable, you should tighten the bolts or nuts from the center out, as illustrated, on cast-iron engines. Aluminum engines are another matter; always obtain the manufacturer's sequence.

Tightening to specifications should always be done in stages. If the specified torque is 50 ft./lbs. or under, tighten all nuts or bolts in three roughly equal stages, such as 15, 30 and 50.

If the specified torque is more, tighten all nuts or bolts in four roughly equal stages. Example: if final torque is 85 ft./lbs., tighten first to 20, then to 40, then to 60, then to 85.

In addition to those situations where the use of the torque wrench is mandatory, use it wherever it can fit in. Uniform tightening of all nuts or bolts on a particular assembly can only help its long-term performance.

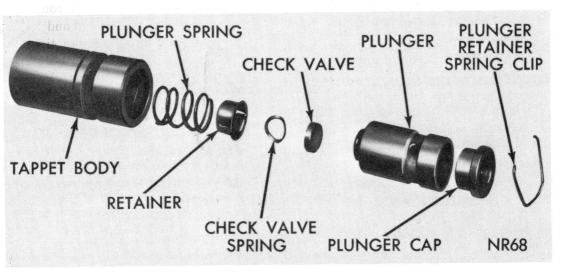

PLUNGER SPRING

CHECK VALVE

PLUNGER

PLUNGER
RETAINER
SPRING CLIP

TAPPET BODY

RETAINER

CHECK VALVE
SPRING

PLUNGER CAP

NR68

Hydraulic valve lifter disassembled.

6

Taking the Tap Out of Tappets

MANY MOTORISTS WITH some of the finest and latest cars are plagued by a tapping sound under the hood. This noise may be light or heavy; it may continue for only a few seconds when the car is first started, or it may not clear up for many miles. And, in some cases, the noise may not stop at all.

The sound is probably caused by the hydraulic tappets. These tappets were designed to assure quiet engine operation with maximum power but, when they fail, the result is noisy operation and loss of power.

The lifter rides on the camshaft and carries a push rod which operates the rocker arm, which in turn opens and closes the valve. Strictly speaking, the rocker arm does not *close* the valve. This job quite obviously is done by the valve spring as the cam allows the valve lifter to descend and the push rod and rocker arms are allowed to "retreat."

There is always the possibility in any engine that carbon is causing valve sticking, with resultant noise and loss of engine performance. And, while we are concerned at the moment with the quiet and efficient performance of valve lifters, we cannot ignore valve conditions. It is a good idea on any engine checkup operation to use one of the commercial valve oils in order to be sure of smooth valve performance. One-pint containers, holding enough for an average engine, may be purchased at automotive supply stores. The instructions on the container usually recommend on overhead valve jobs that the oil be squirted directly onto the valve stems while the engine is running, and frequently also suggest that some oil be introduced through the air intake of the carburetor (air-cleaner removed) while the engine is running.

There is basically no difference in the job of the hydraulic valve lifter in a straight engine (whether six or eight cylinder) and the job performed in a V-8. The thing to get clearly in mind is that an engine warms up at varying rates and consequently is subject to varying degrees of expansion when going into service. This varying expansion upsets valve clearances in any engine utilizing solid valve lifters. Picture what happens when the engine first starts up. Combustion at extremely high temperature is present in each cylinder and on each piston so the engine begins to warm up through the cylinder block. The first heating up takes place near the top of the block. As the heat progresses down the cylinder walls and up into the cylinder head, expansion actually lifts the whole valve rocker assembly, since this is mounted on the head. To the extent of a few thousandths of an inch, this increases clearances in the valve train.

With hydraulic valve lifters, the clearance is taken up and valve action remains unchanged. With solid lifters, the lifter has to travel a little farther to take up the clearance that has developed before it can open the valve. This influences valve timing slightly and has an adverse effect on engine power. True, the difference is small; no driver would notice this. But engineers who are trying to corral the very last horse in their favorite engine consider these fine points. Naturally, this valve action goes on at one-half engine speed.

To clear up that point, let's review the engine operation. This begins with the intake stroke in which the intake valve is opened and the piston is going down into the cylinder bore. This fills the cylinder with a combustible mixture. Somewhere near the bottom the intake valve closes. The exhaust valve is already closed. So the piston goes up to top dead center, compressing the charge. Near top dead center the spark occurs and, with both valves still closed, the piston goes down on the power stroke. Near the bottom of the stroke, the exhaust valve opens and remains open while the piston goes up on the exhaust stroke.

So we see that there is a complete cycle of valve movements at every other revolution of the engine. This fact can help in identifying tapping sounds. For example, if a tapping sound is present in the engine at what appears to be about engine speed, then the piston pins, rings, or connecting rods are more likely to be to blame than the valves. But, if the sound occurs at what appears to be about *half* engine speed, there is good reason to believe

How Hydraulic Valve Lifters Work

WITH engine valve closed there is no pressure on the push rod (1 in Fig. A), so the plunger spring (2) pushes up the plunger (3). Oil from the engine's lubrication system enters at (4), passes through the lifter valve (5) into space (6) below the plunger into the lifter body (7).

When the cam has turned to open a valve as in Fig. B, lifter valve (5) closes making the body (7) and plunger (3) a solid hydraulic ram. Thus the hydraulic lifter acts like a solid unit forcing up the push rod and opening the engine valve.

So we see that automatic *takeup of clearance* in the valve train is handled by the relatively light plunger spring (2 in Fig. A) moving up the plunger as any play develops. The oil then holds the plunger up.

Continuous pressure on the plunger, however, will force the plunger down due to *slight intentional leakage* between the plunger and the body. This continuous pressure is present on one or two valves when a car is left standing, for example overnight. This is why hydraulic lifters may be noisy for just a second or two when the engine is first started after having been idle for a period. Understanding that a *light* plunger spring takes up noise-producing clearance explains why even a little gum within the lifter body or foreign matter between the plunger and the body will cause noise. The plunger spring simply isn't strong enough to take up the clearance that develops in the system as the engine expands and contracts with changes in temperature.

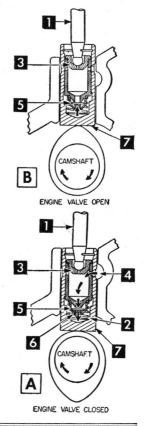

ENGINE VALVE OPEN

ENGINE VALVE CLOSED

that the fault lies in the valve action somewhere.

To check for valve lifter noise you can either listen or feel, or use both methods as a double check. The first step in either case is to remove the rocker cover. Be careful of the gasket: it can often be used again. With the rocker cover (of a straight six or eight) or the covers of a V-8 removed, start the engine and let it idle (about 400-500 rpm). To listen to the sound of individual valves and their lifters, hold one end of a length of garden hose firmly to your ear and hold the other end close to one valve at a time. Some noise will be picked up from each valve. But if you come to one that sounds like a lonesome woodpecker on a drainpipe, you have located your trouble.

To *feel* the valve action, place one or two fingers on the top of one valve spring retainer at a time, while the engine runs slowly. If the valve lifter is not performing as it should, there will be a distinct stinging or snapping effect on your finger. In other words the hammering that you hear will be the hammering that you feel. Now let's see what causes this annoying and power-destroying action.

If you experience a hard rapping noise contrasted with a moderate rapping noise, it is likely that the plunger is sticking in the bore of the lifter body. This means that the return spring within the valve lifter is unable to push the plunger into the working position to take up play or looseness (see sketch). This trouble is generally due to gum or varnish deposits from the oil used or to carbon formation.

There is also the possibility that the metal itself has galled. This galling, or picking up of metal, is commonly the result of the presence in the engine oil of abrasive dirt that was not filtered out. The best preventive is the use of heavy-duty or high-detergent oil and the frequent replacement of the oil filter—at least every 4,000 miles on a car using hydraulic valve lifters.

A moderate rapping noise heard during the garden hose check indicates considerable wear within the valve lifter or in the rest of the valve train, such as the valve stem tip and the rocker. All Chevrolets and most Fords have a moderate range of adjustment provided in the rocker arm retaining nut, to compensate for valve train wear.

To adjust, simply warm up the engine and run it at slow idle. (Turn back the idle speed screw until the engine will just lope along without stalling.) This will minimize oil squirting through the pushrods (which are hollow), all over the engine and you.

If the oil squirting is unbearable, you can use large paper clips over the ends of the rockers, with one end of the paper clip stuck into the hole in the rocker, through which it is lubricated by the pushrod.

With a socket wrench, back off the rocker nut until the lifter begins to chatter (counterclockwise). Then turn the nut clockwise until the chatter is just eliminated, and then one full turn more to position the lifter plunger properly.

Note: sometimes excessively fast lifter leakdown can be confused with wear in the valve train. To check, insert the thickest feeler gauge that will fit, between rocker and valve stem tip.

If the problem is wear in the valve train, the lifter will not make any more noise so long as the feeler is in place. If the problem is excessive leakdown (a bad check valve or worn plunger), the noise will return in seconds.

If you find it hard to determine which valve is the noisiest and yet the whole system is annoyingly loud, check up on the quantity and quality of the oil in the engine. Frequent short runs in cold weather, excessive use of the choke, or cold running will contribute to crankcase dilution. And this dilution of the crankcase oil will allow a rate of leakdown that will let the lifters become noisy. The first step in this case is to drain the oil while the oil is thoroughly hot and put in oil of the correct grade as specified by the engine manufacturer for the particular time of year.

If the valve lifter noise is the type that comes and goes, it may be caused by a very small piece of dirt which prevents the check-valve in the lifter from sealing tight. There is, of course, the possibility that the valve itself may have a small defect on it. And as the valve shifts around, this defect may occasionally interfere with action and cause the valve lifter to be noisy. At other times the defect does not interfere and the valve lifter is quiet.

Before undertaking expensive mechanical work, try a commercial gum-dissolving solvent or special oil that will clean up any varnish or gum deposit in the hydraulic valve lifters. The methods of using the hydraulic valve lifter oil vary all the way from a normal oil change to a highly specialized lubrication system servicing.

For example, one additive maker specifies that the engine should be drained, the oil filter cartridge removed and the engine then refilled with a quart of SAE low oil plus 4 quarts of kerosene in which his additive has been installed. Then, due to the cleansing effect of this mixture, the engine must be run at what would give 15 to 20 mph for two hours, *outside* of the shop or garage. Then it is drained, the oil filter replaced, and the regular oil for the particular engine put in. Usually this clears up the entire valve lifter problem. Where the valve lifter noise has continued so long that mechanical damage has occurred or where the noise was due originally to wear or damage to the parts, then, of course, the use of a special solvent will accomplish nothing. So this brings us up to the job of removing, cleaning, inspecting, reassembling and installing the lifters.

First, you will have to remove the one rocker cover on an in-line engine or two covers on a V-8. On an in-line engine, the side plate over the push rods will also have to be removed. In a V-type engine the intake manifold will have to be taken off. Then, whatever the engine design, the valve rocker arm assembly must either be loosened sufficiently to release the push rods or removed entirely if that becomes necessary in order to get the push rods out.

Now use the starter to turn the engine over at least two revolutions. This will push all of the hydraulic valve lifters up as high as they go in normal operation. If they fall down again, it merely indicates that they are fairly free in their guides. Sometimes carbon or gum in the valve lifter guide *above* the normal travel of the lifter will interfere with lifter removal, requiring a strong hook in order to get the lifter up. (Note: a special tool is available for "impossibly stuck" lifters.) The lifters have one or two holes near the top to facilitate removal. To make a hook for one with two holes, straighten out a 20-inch length of heavy wire coat hanger and bend over exactly in the middle. Then bend the two free ends out with a ⅛-inch base for each "L" shape. Spread the wire sufficiently so that it will tend to spring out in the top of the valve lifter and grip the holes.

Place each valve lifter in the cup of a muffin tin. Use one muffin tin to represent the left block, another for the right block, and number the individual compartments from front to back so that each lifter can be returned to its original engine position. Soak

To prevent oil squirt as you adjust hydraulic lifters, use large paper clips around rocker, with tip inserted in hole in end of rocker as shown.

With engine idling, back off rocker nut until valve just starts to clatter, then turn clockwise to just eliminate clatter and a specified amount more (usually one turn, but check car maker's specs.

If you have a question about lifter wear, crank engine until valves for a cylinder are closed (piston up on compression stroke). Push on back of rocker to force oil out of lifter. Check valve clearance with feeler gauge and compare with manufacturer's specifications.

each lifter in a commercial gum and varnish solvent such as Gumout; then, for complete cleaning, disassemble each lifter and return parts to the solvent. Keep the parts of each lifter together in the properly numbered compartment of the muffin tin. Plungers and lifter bodies are a selective fit when manufactured, and as they wear together it becomes increasingly important that the same parts continue to work together.

Disassemble lifter by pressing the plunger down with one of the push rods from the engine and lift out the lock-ring. If, with the wire out, hydraulic lifter assembly cannot be shaken apart due to gum on the plunger or inner core of the body, let it soak for a half-hour. Then strike the assembly softly against a piece of soft wood, holding it in the right hand with the opening facing down. The inertia of the plunger will carry it out of the bore. Occasionally brush the parts soaking in the solvent with a one inch varnish brush to speed up the cleaning action. Then lift out the assemblies one by one and shake them dry. Compressed air may be used, but do not wipe parts with a cloth as the lint can cause trouble. Inspect each part for damage such as scratching or galling. Then try the plunger in the lifter body. It should move in and out freely of its own weight but should not have any noticeable looseness or side play.

Now replace all parts in the order in which they were removed. Be sure that the locking spring has not been collapsed. Spring it outward about ⅛ inch before installing so that it will snap firmly into the groove in the lifter body. When the lifter is assembled, you may be able to hear the check valve rattle when the assembly is shaken. Reassembly is easiest when done with all parts upside down. That is, place the push rod seat on the bench and put the plunger in position on top of the seat. Then put the check valve with its retainer on top of the plunger and the plunger spring on top of the valve-retainer. Pour about a spoonful of SAE low engine oil over this plunger assembly, then slide the valve lifter body down over it. Holding the assembly in place in the body with the tip of one finger, turn the lifter right side up. Then, using a push rod to force the plunger down into the body, put the spring lock ring into position in the body groove.

Now submerge the lifter in a clean container of SAE 10 engine oil. Pump the plunger up and down so that the lifter becomes filled with oil, then press down firmly on the plunger. If the plunger can be pushed down into the lifter body, it indicates excessive leakage between the lifter and the body or through the valve. Discard such lifters and substitute new ones purchased from your car dealer or automotive supply house. Test these as previously described before installing.

Now you can reassemble the engine. Remember, there is a limit to the take-up of a hydraulic lifter. For this reason on engines that provide no mechanical adjustment in the rocker arms each lifter should be collapsed after it is installed by applying continuous pressure on the push rod. When the lifter is collapsed by having forced out all the oil there should be .030 to .070 inch of clearance between the rocker arm and the valve stem. In checking this, crank the engine until the piston of the cylinder in which the valves are being checked is at top dead center of the compression stroke. On many engines it is possible to see the camshaft. On these it is only necessary to have the valve lifter on the "heel" of the cam—the lifter's lowest position—when checking the clearance. Obviously there can be no clearance when the cam is turned so as to open the valve. And it is very important that the cam is not in some mid-position which eliminates *some* of the clearance though the valve has not yet opened.

Another easy way to check for dead center position of the piston is to use the distributor rotor. The rotor points to the distributor cap terminal of the piston that is at top dead center of the compression stroke. Should the clearance when checked prove to be less than .030 inch—which is most unlikely—it will be necessary to grind the end of the valve stem to give the required clearance. If the clearance is greater than .070 inch, replacement of the worn parts will be necessary. This could involve rebushing the rocker arm, renewing the rocker arm shaft or installing a new valve. Note: most engines with hydraulic lifters have in-dependently mounted rockers—no rocker shafts. No one can tell which will be required until the job is inspected. Occasionally where no adjustment is provided, mechanics have improvised by shimming up or filing off the brackets that support the rocker arm shaft. A .004 inch shim between the base of the rocker arm support bracket and the cylinder head will increase valve clearance about .008 inch.

Since checking the hydraulic lifters in the block required compressing them and thus discharging all oil, they will be a little noisy until the engine oil has worked into them again. With the lifters in place, the pushrods replaced and the rocker arm assemblies tightened down, start up the engine and let it idle. With the rocker arm covers still off, take a recheck of operations by listening at each valve for unusual noise, then feeling each valve spring as the engine idles. There should be no stinging shock on your fingertip. If you have followed the foregoing procedure step-by-step you have saved at least $50, and you have the plus-satisfaction that comes from realizing that hydraulic tappets don't have to be noisy—that they can, in fact, give you a bonus of silence and power when properly used and serviced.

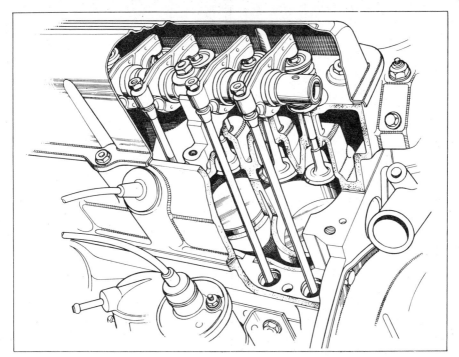

This is an overhead-valve engine with mechanical lifters that can be adjusted with the engine running. Note the self-locking nuts on the pushrod side of the rocker arms.

7

Valves: Tapping for Service

"SOLID" MECHANICAL VALVE lifters will be with us as long as there are small engines that can't afford a power loss and owners of big V-8s that won't tolerate one.

Hydraulic self-adjusting lifters are nice, but don't provide as precise valve timing as the solids. The solids, on the other hand, do not compensate for minor valve train wear, and need adjustment at about 6,000-mile intervals, or the accuracy of the solid setup is lost.

With few exceptions (overhead cam engines), overhead valve trains all are adjustable at the rocker arm. (Ford once made a six-cylinder with self-adjusting solid lifters, but there are not many of that design.)

The rockers are adjustable in either of two ways: a self-locking hex-head screw, or a slotted screw and hex-head locknut.

Clearance between rocker arm and valve stem tip should be checked with a good feeler gauge. (Weekend mechanics will find the go-no go type gauge easiest to use.)

If, because of wear, intake valve clearance is excessive, valves will open late and close early. An insufficient amount of fuel mixture will get into the cylinders and they will develop less power.

If exhaust valve clearance is excessive, exhaust gases won't be adequately purged. This will limit (and contaminate) the fuel mixture that can get in, and again, less power results.

Too little clearance also creates problems. The valves open early and close late in this case, spending less time on their seats. The valves are cooled by transfer of heat to the seats, so if the clearance is inadequate, the valves will burn. Also, the incorrect timing of the valves will often cause rough idle and poor performance.

Always begin the job by tightening the cylinder head to specifications with a torque wrench. Tightening the head is a standard part of a major tuneup, and if it is done after the valve adjustment, the adjustment will be changed.

This is because the tightening of the head nuts or bolts compresses the head gasket, reducing the height of the engine.

Most American cars with solid lifters have the self-locking hex-head screw. Old timers may remember the slotted screw and hex-head locknut of American cars of years ago, and they will find this arrangement on most foreign cars.

Valve clearance on cars with the self-locking hex-head screw is set with the engine fully warm and running at slow idle. The self-locking screw is easy to adjust. However, after an engine has a fair amount of mileage on it, the screw loses some of its self-locking ability and the valves require adjustment more often—perhaps twice a year.

Just slip the appropriate size feeler gauge (check manufacturer's specifications) between rocker and valve stem. If it won't fit in, turn the screw counterclockwise a bit until the gauge will fit. Then turn the screw clockwise until the feeler gauge can be moved in and out with moderate drag.

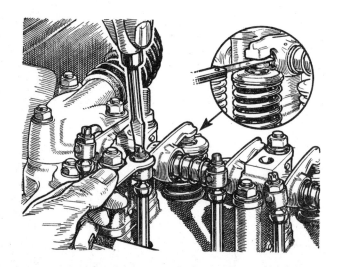

Overhead-valve clearance on many foreign engines is adjustable by slotted screw with locknut and measured between the valve stem and the rocker tip with a feeler gauge. It will be difficult to adjust if the rocker tip at the point in contact with valve stem is worn.

Don't confuse inability to withdraw the feeler momentarily with tightness. The engine is running and when the valve is open, the feeler is locked between rocker and valve stem. The moderate drag is for the instant that the valve is closed.

This means that the feeler should not alternate between plug wire for the cylinder with the piston on TDC compression.

The valves of that cylinder are in position for adjustment—fully closed.

Try to insert the specified size feeler gauge between the valve stem and rocker. If it fits in and can be withdrawn only with moderate drag, it is in proper adjustment—leave it alone.

If there is insufficient or too much clearance for the gauge, slacken the locknut. Turn the adjusting screw counterclockwise to increase clearance, clockwise to reduce it.

When there is just enough clearance between rocker and valve stem to produce moderate drag on the feeler gauge, tighten the locknut while holding the screw with a screwdriver.

After tightening the locknut, re-check clearance. If it has changed, you will have to redo the adjustment.

When you have some experience, you will be able to set the clearance right the first time. One technique that often works is to set the clearance for light drag, hold slight counterclockwise pressure with the screwdriver on the adjusting screw, and allow the tightening of the lock to pull the adjusting screw clockwise just enough to reduce clearance to moderate drag on the feeler gauge.

To set up the other valves for adjustment, connect a test lamp between the breaker points terminal of the coil and ground. Turn on the ignition and the test lamp will light.

Crank the engine in very short bursts with a remote starter switch. When the points close, the test lamp will go out, locked and slipping around. It either should be locked or be capable of being pulled out with moderate drag.

NOTE: The specified clearance for intake valves usually is different from the clearance for exhaust valves, so you should note the valve arrange-

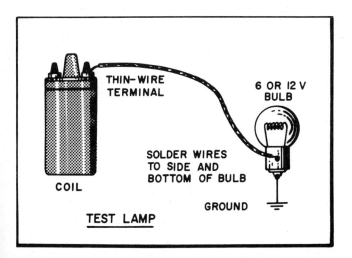

THIN-WIRE TERMINAL

6 OR 12 V BULB

SOLDER WIRES TO SIDE AND BOTTOM OF BULB

COIL

GROUND

TEST LAMP

Illustration shows how to make a test lamp. Lamp is connected to negative terminal (may be marked "CB" or with minus sign) of coil, and to ground.

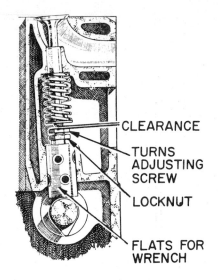

CLEARANCE

TURNS
ADJUSTING
SCREW

LOCKNUT

FLATS FOR
WRENCH

Side-valve adjustments are made after removing the tappet cover on the side of the engine under the exhaust manifold. Measure between the valve stem and topnut. Job is time-consuming; fortunately, side-valve engines are a rarity today.

ment. The typical layout of intake and exhaust valves for a V-8 is E-I-I-E-E-I-I-E (each bank).

If the engine has the slotted screw and locknut, the valves should be adjusted with the engine off. Check to see if the clearance specifications are for engine hot or engine cold—the difference is important. Metal expands when hot and changes the clearances in the valve train.

Most imported cars have in-line engines so the valve arrangement is easy to see. The most popular import, however, is Volkswagen, and the valve arrangement on its pancake engine is not easy to see. It is E-I-I-E on each side.

To adjust valves with the engine off, you must make the adjustment with the piston at top dead center ("TDC") on the compression stroke, for this is the time the intake and exhaust valves are closed and there is maximum clearance in the valve train. The manufacturer's clearance specifications are designed for this situation.

To determine when a piston is at TDC on compression, line up the timing marks. Either No. 1 cylinder or its companion in the firing order will be at TDC on compression (actually a few degrees before or after, but the marks will get you close enough).

To find out which piston is on compression, lift the distributor cap and see to which plug wire insert the rotor points. Follow the spark plug wire from the distributor cap insert; it will go to the spark for the ignition current will flow through the points instead of the lamp.

When the distributor cam just cracks open the points, the test lamp will go on again, indicating that the ignition system is ready to fire another spark plug (in a cylinder that is on TDC compression).

Stop cranking the instant the test lamp goes on. The valves for the next cylinder in the firing order are ready for adjustment. If the firing order is 1-4-3-2 (for example Volkswagen), and you adjusted No. 1, you next would adjust valves for No. 4 (then No. 3, then No. 2 cylinders). If the first set of valves adjusted was on No. 3 (the companion cylinder to No. 1 in a 1-4-3-2 firing order), you next would adjust No. 2 (then No. 1, then No. 4).

All manufacturers number their cylinders differently, so you should be familiar with the numbering system. (Most mechanic's specifications manuals give this information.) If you are not, you will have to see which plug wire the rotor points to, and follow it to the cylinder.

NOTE: on most cars, the adjustable screw is on the pushrod side of the rocker. On Volkswagen, however, it is on the valve stem side. This difference does not affect the adjustment procedure.

Many cars are equipped with overhead crankshaft engines. The imports in many cases have shim adjustments, which should be left to an import car mechanic. However, American cars have some form of adjusting screw, and because the camshaft is exposed, you can tell when a valve is closed, making the job quite easy.

The Pinto adjustment is illustrated. The other popular overhead-cam engine, in the Chevrolet Vega, has an Allen wrench hole in the side of the tappet for adjustment. Because of internal construction of the adjusting mechanism, the adjusting screw must be given a complete turn, which changes clearance by about .003-inch, or the adjustment won't hold.

Although this might make precise adjustment impossible, there is no problem. Chevrolet specifies an .002-inch range (.014 to .016-inch on intake valves; .029 to .031-inch on exhaust valves), engine cold.

The screw inside will lock in position when a complete turn is made. At that time, check clearance between tappet and valve stem.

Top: This overhead-cam Pinto engine has mechanical lifters. Loosen locknut with lower wrench and turn adjusting screw with upper wrench. Exposed camshaft makes it easy to see when valve is closed.

Above: Feeler gauge is inserted between cab lobs and rocker on Pinto engine while adjusting screw is turned with wrench. When specified feeler can be withdrawn with moderate drag, tighten locknut. Adjustment is complete.

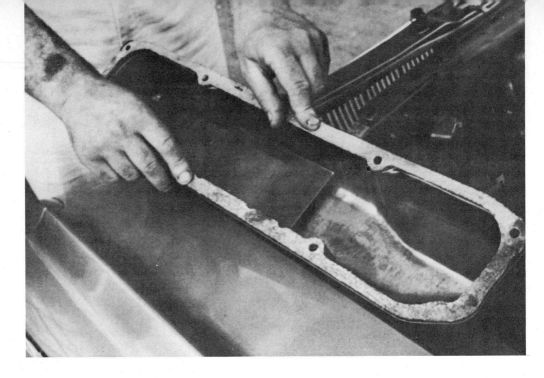

8

Don't Blow Your Gasket — Fix It

LOTS OF GASKETS, particularly engine cylinder head gaskets, "blow." Maybe it has happened to you, and maybe you thought the fault lay in the quality or construction of the gasket. Actually, gaskets usually blow because of incorrect application. It's the way you do or do not prepare the surfaces to be gasketed together that counts, and counts heavily. The gasoline mileage you get, the engine's cooling efficiency, compression, lubrication, silencing of the exhaust, tightness of the rear axle housing and a lot of per-formance factors depend on the ability of gaskets to seal well; to maintain pressure; and to keep out dirt and water. The oil, water or even fuel that drips on your garage floor overnight may indicate leaky gaskets. And the leakage may be worse when the car is running because parts get hot, metal expands and the gasket-packed joints widen, creating greater leakage. If you want to track down guilty gaskets, first inspect the car's engine carefully. If you see rusty and gooey-looking seep-age around the cylinder block and head joint, your engine needs a new head gasket. The same evidence around the crankcase and oil pan joints, the water inlet elbow flange and head, the fuel pump connection to crankcase, the front end chain housing cover, and the water pump flange and manifolds —is a sign that gasket trouble has arrived.

It's always a good rule to install a new gasket every time a joint is opened. The old gasket might "look good" but it has done its job even if it hasn't "blown," so toss it out and use a new one. There's always the temptation to use the old cylinder head gasket, for example, especially if it comes off clean, stays flat and has that nice shiny copper color. But you can't re-seal the joint adequately with the old gasket. In the first place, the joining surfaces between the cylinder block and head, while "milled" to substantially smooth surfaces, are never completely smooth. Under a microscope, you see a lot of hills and valleys. When the head is bolted down tightly, the copper of the gasket (usually made of asbestos between two thin layers of copper or steel) squeezes into the tiny imperfections of the metal and with the asbestos filler makes a tight seal against compression and coolant losses. Obviously, this compression of the gasket flattens and conforms it to irregularities of the block and head, so that if the head is later removed, it is practically impossible to replace the gasket (which has lost much of its compressibility) and get a perfect seal against all the little irregularities again.

Also, the old gasket may be bent in removing it so that the asbestos filler

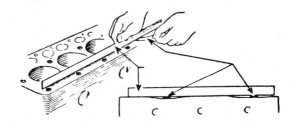

Checking block with a straight edge and a feeler gauge. Same procedure can be used for cylinder head gasket surface.

breaks when the gasket is straightened for reuse—and the gasket is liable to burn through at this weak spot and lose its effective seal.

You can find out whether you have a broken and leaky head gasket by checking these points. If the coolant boils at normal atmospheric temperatures and your radiator takes a lot of water, it could indicate a broken gasket. When you make a cylinder compression test and find two adjacent cylinders reading much lower than the others, the gasket may have blown at the spot between the two cylinders. Sometimes you can see bubbles in the top of the radiator, which can be from a blown gasket. There is available an inexpensive air hose adapter that threads into the spark plug hole. You can use it to find out whether the head gasket is faulty and allowing leakage into the coolant. To use it, fill the radiator to the top with coolant, run the car until it reaches normal operating temperature, then remove the spark plugs and test each cylinder as follows: Take off the distributor cap so you can watch the rotor. Turn

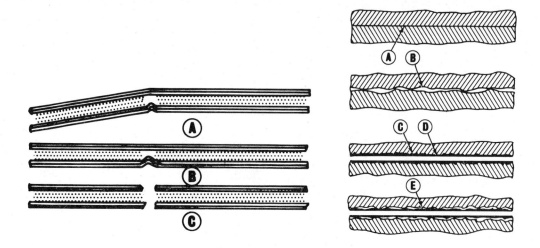

Left: Instead of an unobtainable perfect joint (A) between the machined surfaces of a cylinder head and engine block, there are a series of microscopic hills and valleys (B). Note how the metal of the gasket (C) fills the irregularities of the block and head, making a tight joint. (D) is the asbestos filler. After a head gasket has been compressed, it is almost impossible to again seal the irregular surfaces (E).

Right: If a cylinder head gasket of the copper asbestos type is bent, the asbestos filler may break at A. If the gasket is then straightened (B), it may look O.K., but later burn through and "blow" at the break in the asbestos (C).

the engine slowly (with fan belt or by jacking up one rear wheel with the transmission in gear), until the rotor is lined up with one of the cap electrodes if the cap were in place. The valves of that cylinder will then be closed. Screw the tester into the spark plug hole of that cylinder and from a hand pump or air supply, apply air to the tester valve. If there is gasket leakage you can see or hear the bubbles at the radiator neck with the filler cap off to allow you to look in.

To replace this gasket, you will have to strip the engine of such parts as the air cleaner, carburetor, spark plugs and wiring harness, perhaps the oil filter bracket, the hose connection at the water inlet elbow and other parts depending on the make and type of engine. Then you take out the head bolts or loosen the nuts on the block studs so you can lift off the head. But before you loosen the nuts and bolts, let the engine cool to the surrounding temperature of the atmosphere or room.

Next, clean the block and cylinder head of all carbon deposits by scraping, wire brushing, and with a metal parts cleaner. You can use an ordinary hand tire pump to blow out any foreign matter on the piston heads, bolt holes and water passages. Also, blow out the passages inside the cylinder head to prevent any carbon particles from dropping on the new gasket (such particles can form pockets in the gasket and cause leakage). With the block and head surfaces clean, check the surfaces with a straight edge for indications of distortion or warping.

Since the cylinder head gets hotter than the block, warpage is more likely to occur in the head. If you run into such a condition, better have an automotive machine shop true the surface of the head on a surface grinder. This removal of metal, however, should be held to a minimum as it increases compression ratio—perhaps more than is good for the engine. On old engines, especially, if the cylinder has been re-machined more than once, it's wise to replace the head with a new one.

Make a careful inspection of the cylinder head studs in the block (or the bolt holes, if the head is held down with bolts). If you find there is a buildup of metal around the studs or bolt holes, you can use a chamfering tool to trim enough off so the studs

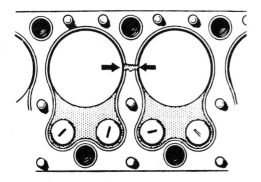

Occasionally a cylinder head gasket breaks at a point between two adjacent cylinders, shown by the heavy arrows.

or bolts can be firmly tightened with clearance for the gasket. But make sure you don't remove too much metal with the chamfering tool, particularly where a stud is located very close to two cylinders (removing too much metal in such places may cause gasket to blow). Some mechanics prefer to dress the block with a large file, which also removes the rough spots.

Now check the new gasket for correct fit on the cylinder block. Some gaskets are marked "Top," "Front" or "Up." Check for these markings before installing and follow the directions they indicate. All of the water holes and bolt holes should tally with those in the block. On some engines like the older 6-cylinder Ford, be sure that the gasket is positioned with the cut-off corner at the left front corner of the cylinder block; otherwise water will leak externally at the left rear corner of the engine between the cylinder head and block. Never enlarge any of the water passage holes in the gasket, as the rear cylinders might overheat. Watch out for a bent gasket. The method of applying the gasket depends on the type of gasket material. The steel and the asbestos head gaskets usually have a sealing coat put on them by the gasket manufacturer. This clear coating ordinarily does not require any additional gasket cements. But if this type of gasket does not have a coating you can use a non-hardening gasket compound such as Permatex "Form-A-Gasket." This material is a liquid applied with a brush and changes in a few seconds to a paste. It produces a non-drying elastic, adhesive, heat-resisting seal. You can also use it with copper asbestos gaskets. If you wonder

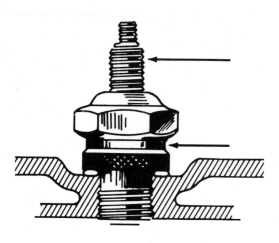

A handy tester to check for a blown gasket can be made by brazing a tire valve into a spark plug shell. You also can isolate a blown head gasket of the two-adjacent-cylinders type by compression testing. If you prefer the air pressure test, but have no brazing equipment, you can buy the equivalent of the plug shell and tire valve tool at auto supply stores.

why both steel and copper asbestos gaskets are used, each has certain advantages. For example, where high octane fuel is used and detonation is likely, steel resists breakdown better than copper. But this advantage is offset to some extent by the superior heat conductivity of copper. Copper also makes a better seal with less likelihood of compression leakage that might cause burning of the gasket back of the edge of the cylinder opening. Steel has a natural tendency to corrode where exposed to the coolant at water

holes or where the gasket itself is exposed to the coolant. Some steel gaskets are made with copper grommets at the water holes. Remember, however, that gaskets with copper ferrules must never be used with aluminum heads.

Some cars use an embossed type of steel cylinder head gasket. This is said to provide an even and uninterrupted flow of heat between the cylinder head and engine block. The design and formation of the embossing makes the flow of metal under compression even, producing a good seal.

If you don't want to blow your new gasket, better check for clearance of the new gasket around the cylinder bores. The engine may have been rebored and fitted with oversize pistons, In this case the edge of the metal around the gasket might be very close to or even slightly overlap the cylinder bore openings. Thus, on the upstroke, the pistons might strike the head of the gasket, causing early gasket failure or blowout. The minimum clearance from the edge of the gasket to the edge of the cylinder bore opening should be 1/32 inch. This permits correct gasket compression and prevents direct flame contact burn-out. If you find you cannot get this clearance, check the tops of the pistons for a number such as +.010 which indicates an oversize piston, and buy a gasket to match it.

Make a final check to make sure that the gasket is correctly centered. If the head is held by studs, this is easy. But if long cap screws or bolts are used, buy a couple of longer bolts, cut off the heads and screw these into a couple of holes at the end of the block. These will serve as pilots and after the head has been dropped and a half dozen or so of the head bolts inserted finger-tight, remove the pilot bolts with pliers.

You are now ready to tighten the head, which must be done with a torque wrench, to factory specifications. See the chapter, "How Tight Is Tight?" for details.

After you have replaced the accessories you previously removed, run the engine for 15 or 20 minutes at a fast idle and then go over the head bolts on the cast-iron head again, once more tightening them about a quarter turn. On aluminum heads, the engine must first be cooled to room temperature before tightening the bolts down. You should tighten again after about 300 or 400 miles of operation, using the same recommended sequence.

When you install intake and exhaust manifold gaskets, alignment is important. If the gasket does not line up with the port holes, the reduced port opening area cuts down on engine power and, in the case of the exhaust, might cause engine overheating. On manifold gaskets, the gaskets are positioned by the bolts holding the manifold on the head. On overhead-valve V-8 engines, tighten the bolts holding the intake manifold. If they are loose, air is pulled into the manifold, making a lean mixture, and also ruining the gasket.

Intake manifold gaskets are additionally important on some V-8 engines, where they seal off the valve

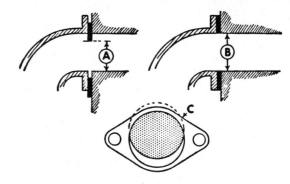

Intake and exhaust manifolds must have their gaskets in alignment; otherwise the port openings are reduced. Note the small opening (A) compared to what it should be (B). The effect of misalignment on port opening is shown at (C).

tappet chamber. A poor gasket seal in such a situation could cause the engine to leak oil.

Other Gaskets. Although the cylinder head and intake manifold gaskets involve a great deal of work and care, there are other gaskets that are more prone to failure. These include the rocker cover, oil pan, fuel pump, thermostat housing, timing chain cover, rear axle cover, and transmission pan.

There's nothing complicated about gasket replacement, but unless you do it correctly, you can find yourself with an expensive comeback. Clearly, a gasket is supposed to seal, and if it leaks, something is wrong.

To insure a leak-free seal, regardless of what gasket is being replaced, takes just a bit of care and know-how.

Start by making sure that if the bolts that hold the cover or part are of different length, you know exactly

69

Note that some of bolt holes in this transmission oil pan have gasket residue. It must be cleaned out (along with gasket surface and the pan itself) before fitting a new gasket.

Minor irregularities in a pan or rocker cover can be straightened with a hammer and the pan or cover on a flat surface, such as a block of wood.

where they go, so you can refit them properly. A simple technique is to push them through a piece of cardboard in the pattern that they go on the engine or transmission.

When you remove the cover, pan or part, scrape all gasket particles from both gasket surfaces, using a scraper. A screwdriver often will do the job, but it is a blunt instrument and you may gouge a gasket surface using it.

This is particularly true of an aluminum part, such as a thermostat housing. Aluminum is quite soft and it does not take much to damage it.

On sheet metal parts with a narrow groove in the gasket surface, however, a thin screwdriver is about the only practical way to clean the groove, particularly if the gasket is cork or if a coating of sealant was applied.

Cleaning out gasket material from

bolt holes is very important. Pieces of gasket material can prevent the bolt from seating properly. Remove large pieces with an awl and blow out small pieces with compressed air.

At this time, inspect the bolt holes. If any go through to water jacket or oil passage, the bolts will have to be coated with thread sealer when you re-assemble.

Once the gasket surfaces are absolutely clean, you can fit the new gasket.

There are four common choices in gasket material for sealing fluids under low pressure: cork, composition cork, neoprene and treated paper.

Treated paper has little resiliency and does a relatively poor job of compensating for any warpage in parts. It should not be used except in emergencies when nothing else is available.

Cork has been a popular gasket material for many years. It does a fine job of compensating for irregularities in sealing surfaces, but it is somewhat brittle and it shrinks when stored in a dry place for some time.

Composition cork is a combination of cork and other fibers. It is less brittle than cork, less prone to shrinkage, and is almost as resilient.

Neoprene is the best material. It is the easiest to handle, does the best job of sealing, doesn't shrink and doesn't break. If you can get a particular gasket in neoprene, this should be your choice.

Unfortunately, you don't always have a choice. Some gaskets for certain cars are only available in cork, or composition, or perhaps just treated paper.

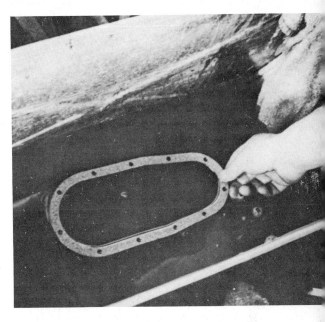

If a cork gasket has shrunk, it can be soaked in warm water.

If a cork or composition cork gasket has shrunk, don't try to force it in place, or it will probably break. Soak it in warm water for fifteen minutes and it will stretch to properly cover the gasket surface.

If the old gasket was leaking badly, don't just install a new one. See if the gasket flange is distorted by lining up a straight edge against it.

A mildly-distorted flange can be straightened with a hammer, as illustrated, by holding the flange against a flat wooden surface. Don't try to straighten one that is badly cocked; replace the part.

Many pans and covers have retaining features for the gasket, such as cutouts for gasket tabs. With such designs, a sealant frequently is unnecessary.

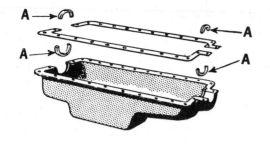 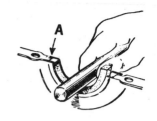

Engine oil pans usually have two cork gaskets. When they are replaced, the crankshaft oil seal packings (A) should also be replaced, as illustrated. The oil seal packings should be rolled in place, also as illustrated.

If a sealant is necessary to hold the gasket in place, or to provide additional sealing for a hard-to-seal surface, only apply the sealant to the cover or pan, not to the engine or transmission. That pan might have to come off again some day, and if the someone who has to do the job is you, you won't want to scrape sealant and gasket off two surfaces.

Gasket shellac is a glue that will keep a gasket from shifting position during installation in a tight spot. It is not as good a sealant as the flexible setting type and should be avoided. It certainly is difficult to scrape off completely.

Never overtighten a gasket. Excessive tightening is the major cause of distortion of a cover or pan. If a leak won't stop with a new gasket, coating of sealant, and tightening to specifications—something is wrong, probably a warped pan or cover.

Don't leave out the bolt washers. Many pans and covers rely on the washers, which often are specially shaped, to distribute the bolt tension evenly and contribute to a good seal.

Making Your Own Gaskets. You can buy sheet cork and treated paper and make your own gaskets. This procedure is recommended for emergency use only. Gaskets are cheap, and although with care you could make one that is almost as good, you also might not.

Caution on Oil Pan Gaskets. On many cars, replacing the oil pan gasket is anything but easy. To avoid removing the pan, which requires jacking the engine well up off its mounts for clearance on many cars, you will be working in tight quarters with the oil pan hanging down just a few inches. Be sure you take the time to scrape off the old gasket completely, clean the side packing grooves and check the mating surfaces in the engine for any burrs, which can be smoothed with an oil stone if not deep.

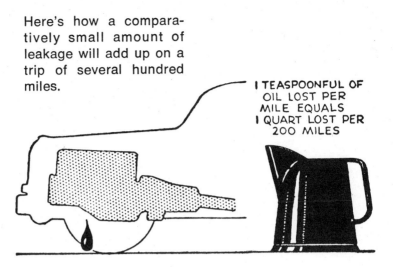

Here's how a comparatively small amount of leakage will add up on a trip of several hundred miles.

I TEASPOONFUL OF OIL LOST PER MILE EQUALS I QUART LOST PER 200 MILES

9

Stopping Engine Oil Loss

YOU'VE HEARD THE summer month vacationist say the trip was fine but that he "used a lot of oil," but, did he? Perhaps instead of *using* he was *losing* oil; there is a difference. You've seen those familiar dark streaks stretching endlessly along both sides of concrete highways—they are mute evidence of precious engine oil relentlessly dropped from motor vehicles.

How much can plain everyday oil leakage amount to? If your engine has an external leak which lets a teaspoonful of oil drip from the engine every mile, you'll lose nearly a quart of oil every 200 miles of travel. Of course, every normal engine uses oil when operating because some oil naturally is consumed in the combustion process. If this were not so you wouldn't have

to "add a quart" now and then to bring the crankcase oil level to normal. And, like excessive fuel consumption that goes along with sustained high speed driving, oil consumption, too, goes up with high speeds.

But there is such a thing as excessive oil consumption at normal driving speeds. Sometimes the cause may be hard to diagnose, but like a headache, excessive engine oil consumption tells you something is wrong somewhere.

If your engine has a lot of miles on it and the oil burning has been gradually becoming worse, the only cure is to go inside the engine.

Interestingly enough, worn rings are not the most common cause of high-mileage oil consumption. The ring

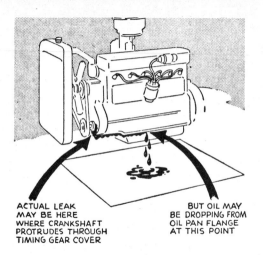

ACTUAL LEAK
MAY BE HERE
WHERE CRANKSHAFT
PROTRUDES THROUGH
TIMING GEAR COVER

BUT OIL MAY
BE DROPPING FROM
OIL PAN FLANGE
AT THIS POINT

If you suspect your engine of leaking oil externally, spread clean paper under the engine and allow it to run awhile. Then watch where the oil is dripping to localize leakage source.

manufacturers have done an excellent job of making rings that last, and their oil control rings are singularly good.

A more likely cause of high mileage oil burning is worn valve guides or damaged valve stem seals. The seals can be replaced with special tools without even pulling the cylinder head. Valve guide replacement requires pulling the head, but even that is not an extremely difficult job. See the chapter, "Tackling Valve and Ring Jobs," for more information.

If you suspect your engine may be leaking oil, start your investigation by taking a look at your garage floor or wherever you normally park the car. The familiar "gooey" spot on the floor under the engine is a dead give-away of dripping oil. A good test is to spread some clean newspapers on the floor under the engine. Then run the engine at a speed substantially above idling. Allow the engine to run long enough to bring it up to idling temperature and for 5 or 10 minutes thereafter. If oil drips on the paper, get under the car and check where it is coming from. Remember that though the oil drops straight downwards with the car at rest, the source of leakage actually may be farther away with the oil creeping along inside the engine until it finds a convenient spot from which to drip. Also remember that the car's forward motion often makes excess oil show up where a leak is actually not occurring. If you suspect external oil leakage, look for "oil washed" areas on the engine; such areas are evidence of leakage *ahead* of the washed areas. While excessive oil consumption also may take place inside the engine, let's first troubleshoot and correct the external leaks.

Very often just tightening a joint, installing a new gasket or tightening the oil pan drain plug stops external leaks.

Oil loss can also be caused by too much pressure in the engine crankcase.

On older cars (1962 and earlier), crankcase pressure and turbulence (caused by wear of the piston rings, which allowed exhaust and unburned gases to leak into the crankcase), would break the oil up into droplets, and these droplets would blow out the crankcase ventilating tube.

Since the introduction of positive crankcase ventilation, the oil droplets-laden gases now are pulled out of the crankcase and dumped into the intake manifold, where they go into the com-

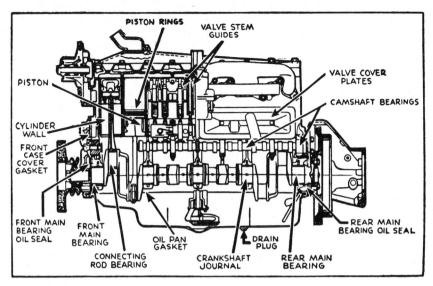

This illustration shows the engine parts involved in both internal and external oil leaks. Loose joints on such parts as the oil pan and front end timing gear cover do not allow gaskets to seal tightly. Internally, such worn parts as cylinders, rings and bearings, cause excessive oil consumption.

bustion chamber for burning. In high-speed driving, the engine will suddenly start to burn oil.

The positive crankcase ventilation system also can cause oil leaks. If the PCV valve is partly or fully clogged, the gases cannot escape. Crankcase pressure builds up and when it is very high, it can create leaks through any weak spots in the oil pan and other engine gaskets, including fuel pump, rocker cover, tappet cover, intake manifold (on some cars), and timing chain.

An increasingly common cause of oil burning on GM and Ford products creates an unusual mystery. The smoke is pouring out the tailpipe, but the engine dipstick doesn't seem to be showing any oil loss. In this case, check the transmission oil level, you will find it down. How can transmission oil burn in the engine? Very simple, on auto-matic transmissions with vacuum modulators.

The vacuum modulator is a transmission device that is connected by a hose to the engine's intake manifold. It contains a diaphragm that helps regulate transmission shifting according to changes in engine manifold vacuum. If the modulator diaphragm cracks or becomes porous, the intake manifold vacuum draws transmission oil up through the hose into the engine. See Chapter 27, "Servicing Automatic Transmissions," for information on replacing modulators.

The switch to electric windshield wipers eliminated the combination fuel-vacuum booster pump that was used on most cars with vacuum windshield wipers. And this booster pump was responsible for many cases of sudden high oil consumption. The pump was operated by intake mani-

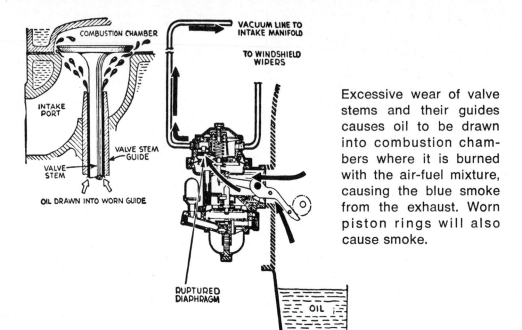

COMBUSTION CHAMBER

VACUUM LINE TO
INTAKE MANIFOLD

TO WINDSHIELD
WIPERS

INTAKE
PORT

VALVE STEM
GUIDE

VALVE
STEM

OIL DRAWN INTO WORN GUIDE

RUPTURED
DIAPHRAGM

OIL

Excessive wear of valve stems and their guides causes oil to be drawn into combustion chambers where it is burned with the air-fuel mixture, causing the blue smoke from the exhaust. Worn piston rings will also cause smoke.

fold vacuum, and if its diaphragm leaked, the vacuum would draw oil from the engine block, into which the pump was bolted, up into the manifold. Only a few American Motors cars use vacuum wipers today, but you may have an older car that also has them, and you should not forget this possibility.

Checking for Leakage

To check vacuum pump diaphragm leakage (indicated by sluggish windshield wiper action when the engine is accelerated) have the wiper in operation and disconnect the vacuum pipe at the manifold. Then hold a piece of clean paper near the open end of the pipe. If you get an oily discharge, it shows that oil is passing through the vacuum pump requiring replacement of the diaphragm.

Other reasons why your engine may be using or losing too much oil are:

piston rings with too little "end" or "gap" clearance; rings installed upside down in grooves; wrong type rings for the engine; distorted cylinders caused by unequal tightening of cylinder head stud nuts; connecting rods bent or twisted; late valve timing; too much oil pump pressure (can be corrected on some engines by regulating oil pressure relief valve where such a valve is fitted); dirty oil; clogged oil passages; air-fuel mixture too lean (engine may overheat causing rings to stick or break); dirty cooling system, causing local hot spots, distortion and overheating of the engine. In some cases the remedies are obvious; in others, it means a tear-down and rebuild job which should be done by a well-equipped shop.

The more mileage on the engine, the more likely it is to use more and more oil. And it usually will take more

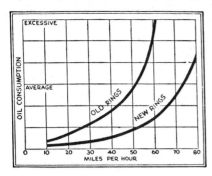

Above: Curves showing how oil consumption goes up with high road speeds. Consumption is greater with old or worn piston rings. Right: Because modern engines breathe so deeply, the intake valve guide, when worn, is a major cause of oil consumption. Improved seals, such as the spring-loaded teflon type illustrated, can be installed to prevent oil loss from this problem.

than just a "ring job" to bring back normal conditions with normal oil consumption. Wear is usually distributed over the entire engine so that when cylinders have to be reconditioned it's safe to say the valves, bearings, timing chain or gear, camshaft and crankshaft need reconditioning or replacement. The popularity in recent years of "rebuilt" or "exchange" engines testifies to the fact that fixing only part of the job certainly won't overcome high oil consumption in a worn engine. Oil consumption also goes up with high road speeds; as is true with gasoline, moderate speeds will save you money by using less oil.

Although rings have dropped to near the bottom of the list as a cause of engine oil burning, they still must not be ignored. Rings have a tough job to do in any engine. They must act as a guide for the piston, must con-

form to the cylinder walls, and seal against compression and combustion pressures, besides keeping the correct amount of oil on the cylinder walls. They have to constantly battle other hardships like oil dilution, cold weather starting, gum and foreign matter, all of which induce wear or cause sticking and breakage. Worn, broken, or sticking rings (rings that stick in the grooves of the pistons, due to gum, carbon, etc.), when removed and replaced with a new set of rings, often bring oil consumption back to normal.

But here is a point to watch. Blue smoke blowing from the exhaust pipe doesn't always mean the rings are to blame. Perhaps the rings are in fairly good shape but not able to handle the excessive oil "throw-off" from the bearings. Remember that bearings, too, have a lot to do with high oil consumption. Engines are fitted with piston rings known as "oil rings" which are there to control the amount of oil for the cylinder walls. The oil rings scrape excess oil back to the crankcase, but when excessive bearing clearance allows too much oil to be thrown on the cylinder walls, the oil rings just can't handle the great volume of oil.

Therefore, when your engine uses a lot of oil and the trouble is traced to "rings," you are in for a job of (a) replacing the old rings with new, or (b) reconditioning the cylinders, fitting new pistons, pins, rings, main and connecting rod bearings. Along with this a "valve job" will be done because when an engine is "down" for major work on cylinders, pistons and bearings, the valves are sure to need replacement or reconditioning.

Many times, the effect of worn rings will be exaggerated. Worn compression rings and low compression readings do not mean that oil consumption must be high, or that the rings are the major cause of the problem.

Often, repairing a few minor leaks, replacing valve stem seals with new, improved seals, and servicing the positive crankcase ventilation system will restore oil mileage to an acceptable level.

Oil Additives. Engine oil additives have become very popular in recent years as a performance improver. These very thick lubricants actually increase the oil's ability to resist thinning out as the engine warms up. As such, they can be helpful in reducing oil burning by preventing the oil from becoming thin enough to slip past worn rings and through worn valve guides. In conjunction with other measures, they can help keep oil mileage at reasonable levels without the expense of an overhaul, which on an older car may not be economically justifiable.

10

Tackling Valve and Ring Jobs

THIS CHAPTER IS limited to overhead valve engines, which represent the overwhelming majority of engines in cars on the American road. There are a few foreign and domestic cars with overhead camshaft engines. Such engines require special handling and/or tools to maintain or restore the relationship between the crankshaft and the camshaft. Clearly, when the cylinder head on an overhead camshaft engine is removed, the camshaft comes with it. Because of the special complexities, we do not recommend you attempt the work in this chapter on overhead camshaft engines unless you have a factory shop manual and considerable experience.

If your engine pressure readings indicate trouble, you probably have a valve or piston ring job in the planning stages.

The first step is to isolate the problem. Squirt oil into a cylinder and take a compression reading. The oil will temporarily seal off the piston-to-bore clearance, so if compression readings rise to near normal, the problem is in the valves.

If the readings do not rise significantly, the compression loss is because of worn rings.

In either case, you must remove the cylinder head (the procedure is the one you must follow to replace a cylinder head gasket).

Oil squirted into spark plug hole temporarily seals worn rings. Compression gauge reading will rise sharply when you retest.

The Valves. Before removing the cylinder head, or heads, drain the water, remove the water hose if it is an in-line engine, and remove any other accessories fastened to the head or valve covers.

Next, remove the intake manifold. You'll have to disconnect the fuel line and the carburetor throttle linkage and take off a few hoses.

Normally the exhaust manifold can either be disconnected at the exhaust pipe and pulled with the cylinder head, or disconnected at the cylinder head and pulled away from it, permitting you to lift the head out.

Next, remove the pushrods, and if you wish, also the rocker arm assemblies. If the engine has ball-socket rocker arms, they are simply loosened and turned aside where necessary to reach the head bolts. A heavy T-handle and socket on an extension are used

to loosen the head bolts. After all bolts are removed, the head should lift off easily. If it sticks, bump it with a mallet, but do not pry between the head and block with a screwdriver. Lay the head, or heads, aside and clean the piston tops by turning the engine to bring them to the top of the block. Scrape off the carbon and clean off any gasket cement you notice on the block.

Take the complete head assembly or assemblies into a jobber's. He disassembles the head, cleans it, faces the valves, and seats and reassembles the head. Cost for V-8s is $12.50 to $15 per head, for 6s the price is $17 to $20 per head. A jobber can do the valve job so much quicker than you that his price is well worth it. A big C-shaped spring compressor quickly pops out the valve keepers and the valves are removed, the head or heads are degreased and checked to see that they are true on the gasket face, and, if it is necessary, the face of the head is milled to true it up; cost is $7.50 to $10 per head. (If you are a hot-rodder who wants higher compression, up to about .100 inch can be milled away for an additional $3 to $5 per head.)

Stems, Seals and Springs. If you determined that the valve guides were allowing a lot of oil to be wasted, the jobber can now modify the upper ends of the valve guides to permit the installation of premium oil seals, such as Perfect Circle seals, to prevent oil leakage past the stem of the valve.

While the heads are in the jobber's shop, the valve springs can be tested to see if they have the correct pressure, and that there is no great variation between the pressures in the set.

Top: Cylinder head is pulled with pushrods removed and rocker shaft left in place. Above: Scrape off carbon from tops of pistons, and gasket residue from block and cylinder head (as shown), using gasket scraper.

The jobber slips each spring into a tester that permits it to be compressed a definite amount, to a certain length. A table furnished by the manufacturer gives the specifications that the valve springs from any particular engine should meet. Correct springs are available from the jobber to replace any springs that do not meet specifications.

The valve guides are reamed with a tool chucked in a drill motor and pilots are inserted in the guides over which is fitted the tool that refaces the valve seats. The pilots come in sets, varying from oversize to undersize in steps of one thousandth of an inch. The valves themselves are refaced on a machine that rotates them against a rotating stone, while a liquid coolant is

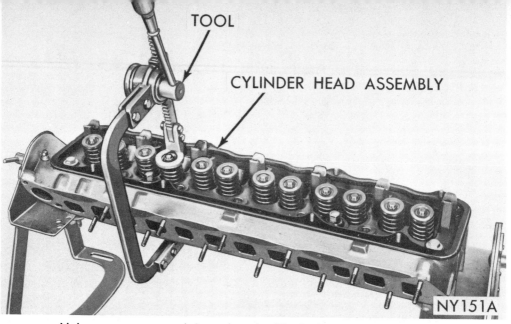

TOOL

CYLINDER HEAD ASSEMBLY

NY151A

Valves are removed from head with C-shaped compressor.

pumped over the valve. Many conscientious jobbers handlap the valves with grinding compound, assuring that final fit.

The jobber will reassemble your overhead-valve head, so all you have to do is reinstall it.

Tightening down the cylinder head does require a torque wrench. See the chapter, "How Tight Is Tight?" for details.

Adjustment. After all the valves have been installed, loosen the tappets so each valve is loose and the lifter can be moved slightly up and down when the valve is seated. Using a feeler gauge, set all the exhaust valves .002 inch wider than the hot specifications (if a hot setting is specified) and .001 inch wider for the intake valves. After the head and accessories are reinstalled, start the engine and warm it. Presetting when cold will result in only a few of the tappets requiring a resetting when hot.

The above information is for a solid lifter engine. If your engine has hydraulic tappets, tappet clearance usually is zero spacing. To be sure of this, as well as other specifications in your engine, always use the service manual for your model automobile.

See Chapters 6 and 7, "Taking the Tap Out of Tappets," and "Valves: Tapping For Service," for more details.

The Ring Job. Before plunging into the job, remove the accessory system parts that will interfere with the job. Then, the head, or heads in the case of a V-8, must come off, the oil pan must be removed, connecting rod caps taken off and the pistons slipped out from the top of the cylinder block. In all probability you'll have to remove the "ridge" which occurs at the top of the cylinder bore. The ridge is caused by the wearing action of the upper edge of the top piston ring and is fairly sharp. In many cases you cannot slip the piston out because the ring catches on the ridge and there is danger of breaking the piston or ring lands.

The lands also may be sprung so that you will have trouble installing new rings. Here is where you should get help from a shop man who has a ridge reamer. This tool reams or cuts away the ridge left by the old rings. The job should be done while the pistons are still in the bores, and you probably can rent a reamer from an automotive job shop, but if you have a shop man come to your garage to do the job for you, he probably can also "mike" the cylinders for taper and out-of-round wear and run a hone in the cylinder bores to break the glaze to make a better seat for the new rings.

Start by draining the cooling system, and the engine oil from the crankcase. Then, using a socket wrench with a T-handle, remove the cylinder-head stud nuts or bolts, and lift the head.

Note the tops of the pistons. There may be an arrow or mark, such as the "dimple" on the piston denoting which way the pistons are installed. If there is no mark, make one with a sharp center punch so you can reinstall them correctly. If you see any strange marks on the heads of the pistons, a valve has been hitting the piston head. This could have been caused by a broken valve spring, or one that is weak, or by someone having the cylinder heads milled to raise the compression ratio, and overdoing it. In some cases there would be a clatter that could be heard when the engine was running.

Connecting Rods. To remove the oil pan, jack up the car and put a couple of supports under the front end

Top: Valves are refaced on special machine as shown. Liquid coolant may be poured over valve during this operation.

Valve seats are refaced with special grinding stones to precise angles.

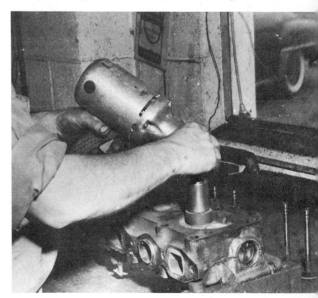

to give yourself more room to work. Be sure the supports are sturdy.

When the oil pan is off, you will find some of the connecting rods in a position where you can remove the cotters or other "locks" on the nuts. Remove the caps of these rods and mark them (if they are not already marked) so that you will know from which rod the cap was removed and in what position it was on the rod. On an in-line engine, the rods usually have marks on the rod and cap on the camshaft side of the engine. If you can, have a helper handy to turn the engine crankshaft slowly with the fan belt so the other rods can be brought into position for removal.

Gather up the connecting-rod caps and place them in proper sequence on a bench or board. Then rub the tips of your fingers up and down the cylinder bores at the top to determine if you are confronted with a ridge removal job. (Odds are that you will be.)

If you feel a ridge, get the shop man and tell him to bring along a dial gauge, inside micrometer and cylinder hone. After he removes the ridge at the top of the bores, the pistons and rod assemblies can be pushed out of the block. Then the shop man can check each cylinder for taper and out-of-round condition. Many piston ring manufacturers say that where cylinders are not to be rebored, the glaze at least should be removed to let the new rings seat. The shop man will use a spring-loaded hone for this. He may also tell you what rings to use depending on what his cylinder measurements show.

Variety of Rings. The ring makers have done a good job in producing various kinds of rings to meet cylinders with considerable wear. For example, if the taper or out-of-round wear is around .002 to .003 inch, practically any of the standard rings will do a good job. However, if it ranges between .004 and .008 inch you can get piston rings supported with expanders that will do the work. In any event, you will have the shop man's measurements and any automotive supply or jobber will recommend the specific rings you should use.

To remove the old rings from the pistons, mechanics use a special tool called a ring spreader, but in its absence you can do it by cutting four strips of thin sheet metal about ⅜ x 3 inches. Slide these strips under the rings and work them around the piston until equally spaced. The rings will then be expanded so they can be pulled off the piston over the strips. Most mechanics simply pull the ring ends apart and break the rings. If you try this, use gloves, since the ring ends can puncture fingers.

The job of cleaning the pistons and their grooves is very important; the measurements for the new rings depend upon it. Also clean out the cylinder bores which have previously been conditioned with the hone.

Inspect the piston for cracks, broken lands or excessive wear of the ring grooves. Here again it will pay you to let the jobber size up the piston-ring groove. He may advise regrooving, a process that also increases the width. Fillers are now obtainable which you slip into the groove over the piston

Above: Valve spring tension is checked on special rig with torque wrench. Manufacturers supply spring tension specifications. Right: Valve guides must be measured for wear. This split ball gauge is often used. Gauge adjusts for width until it is a tight fit in guide, then its diameter is measured. If guide is worn, it must be replaced. If guide is good, it can be cleaned with a reamer.

ring to take up the extra space, resulting from regrooving.

Finally, while the jobber has the pistons, have him resize the piston skirt. There are various processes used for this, one of which is Nurlizing, which actually makes worn pistons practically as good as new at only a fraction of the cost of replacing them.

The process gives a closer fit without scuffing or scoring, prevents piston slap which you might otherwise get even with new rings, and assures adequate piston lubrication.

Fitting the Rings. Now comes the actual fitting of the rings to the pistons and cylinder bores. A common practice is to locate two compression rings and

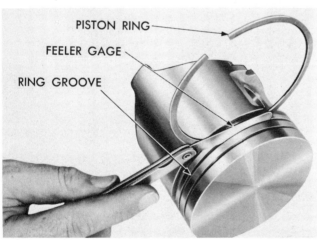

PISTON RING

FEELER GAGE

RING GROOVE

Above: Piston (without rings) also must have adequate clearance in its bore. This is checked by pushing piston with appropriate feeler gauge into bore (piston upside down) as shown.

Left: Piston ring clearance in groove must meet specifications. Clearance is measured with feeler gauge as shown.

two oil rings above the pin. The rings must be fitted into the cylinders so that the rings pass the smallest part of the bore with enough end or gap clearance to prevent binding, but no more than enough.

Place the top compression ring of cylinder No. 1 into the cylinder and push it downward with the top of the piston to the unworn portion of the bore. By pushing it with the piston, it will be square in the bore. If your pistons are not flat, but angle or "pent-roof" type, have your jobber loan you a flathead piston of the approximate size to make this test. With a feeler gauge, check the gap for end clearance of the ring according to the ring manufacturers' instructions that come with the rings.

If the specified feeler gauge will not pass through the gap, remove the ring and file it by pushing it back and forth across a flat, smooth-cut file held in a vise. Do this carefully so that the gap is not distorted, but is square top, bottom, sides, front and back. Check the other rings for piston No. 1 in the same way. Now take the top ring of No. 1 piston and roll it around the groove to see that it is free. To make sure that the clearance between the ring and its groove is correct, refer to the instructions packed with the rings or look in your shop service manual for the specifications, and check with a feeler gauge. Then proceed with the other rings for the rest of the pistons.

To slip the new rings into their respective grooves, a tool called a piston-ring applier or expander is used. If you don't want to rent one, you can use the strips of metal which you previously used to slide off the old rings — only this time reverse the procedure.

Replacing Pistons. You are now ready to reinstall the piston and rod assemblies in their respective cylinders. Be sure to install them in the same bore and position from which they were removed. Check the mark on top of the pistons. On a three-ring piston, arrange the rings so the gaps are 120° apart; on a four ring piston, 90° apart. Arrange them so that no ring gaps come directly in line with the pin.

Then, grasping the connecting rod of the piston, dunk the piston and rings in heavy oil and spread a film of oil around the bore of the cylinder. Then lower the piston-and-rod assembly into the cylinder, having compressed the rings into the grooves with a ring compressor. This compressor is inexpensive, but like the other tools used, you don't have to buy it; it can be rented or borrowed for the job. With the crankshaft turned so the journal for the cylinder is all the way down, push the piston-and-rod assembly down so the upper rod bearing contacts the journal. Have a helper under the car to guide the lower end of the connecting rod. The rod bolts may project and if they strike against the smooth surface of the journal, a gouge or nick could result that would chew up the bearing insert.

At this point you consider doing some work on the connecting rod bearings. It could very well be that some of the oil consumption was due to worn bearings, in which case the oil throw-off was too much for the old rings to handle. You may give the new rings a much better chance by installing new bearing inserts in the connecting rods. See Chapter 11, "Engine Bearings," for details.

It is important, after tightening the connecting-rod caps, to secure the nuts with cotters or other "locks." Some connecting-rod nuts are "self-locking," having plastic inserts, or they are designed with an inside taper that automatically locks them in place. Especially for this latter type setup, a torque wrench should be used, each nut being tightened according to the manufacturers specifications. Clean the oil pan thoroughly and reinstall it, using new gaskets and oil seals on the pan ends. Reinstall the cylinder heads and other parts using new gaskets, and refill the cooling system and oil pan to the required level.

After you have the job buttoned up, start the engine and run it at fast idle (1500 to 1800 rpm) for about 15-20 minutes or until the engine coolant is warm.

Drive the car easily for 50 to 100 miles, then seat the rings by taking the car out on a highway and doing about a dozen full-throttle accelerations from 35 to 55 mph (cruise at 35, full throttle to 55, drop back to 35 and cruise for a mile, then full throttle to 55, etc.).

Laborious break-in procedures over a thousand or more miles are out of date. Use a good quality multi-grade oil (an additive is unnecessary).

11

Engine Bearings

IT'S COMMON FOR weekend mechanics to think of engine bearings as little as possible, and then merely as the super-smooth supports for the engine's moving parts. The reasoning is that bearings are nothing for the weekend mechanic to worry about because they should last a long time, and if they don't, there is nothing he can do about it. But good maintenance practices will prolong bearing life, and if replacement is necessary for the most heavily loaded bearings—those on the crankshaft—the job often can be done by a weekend mechanic without exotic tools. Even if you have the work done by a professional, you should know what is involved and what types of crankshaft bearings are available for installation.

Let's review crankshaft properties:

Load-carrying ability: the downward pressure on the piston of the exploding gasoline mixture is transmitted by the connecting rod to the crankshaft. This pressure creates a load which must be carried by the bearings within the connecting rod and the crankshaft support caps (called the main bearing caps). The more powerful the engine, the greater the pressure developed by the exploding gasoline mixture, and the greater load.

High fatigue strength: the ability of the bearing to withstand the cumulative effect of a repeatedly applied force. In other words, the bearing can take a lot of pounding without getting "tired." (In the case of a bearing, when it gets "tired," it cracks.) The higher the fatigue strength, the longer the bearing will last under a certain load.

Slipperiness: when the engine is being cranked, and under other severe conditions, there is no oil film to provide lubrication. So the bearing surfaces must have a natural slipperiness, to avoid scoring the journals (the mirror-smooth round surfaces of the crankshaft, around which the bearings are fitted.)

Corrosion resistance: as a result of combustion, corrosive agents are form-

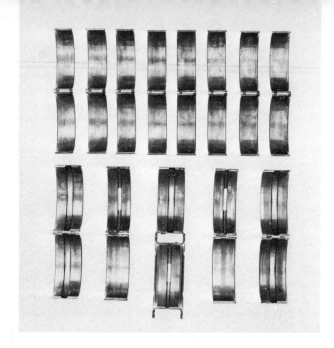

These are the engine's main and connecting rod bearings. The eight sets of connecting rod bearings and five sets of main bearings are for typical V-8.

ed in the oil pan. The engine oil contains additives that neutralize these corrosive agents, but if the additives are used up, the bearing itself must be resistant to corrosion.

Ability to withstand high temperatures: crankcase temperatures can exceed 200 degrees, which can affect the strength of a bearing material.

Conformability: manufacturing tolerances prevent the bearing surface from being exactly parallel with the journal surface it supports. The ability of a bearing material to "creep" or "flow" to be reasonably parallel is called conformability.

Heat transfer: both the oil and the bearings must transfer heat from the cylinders. The bearing must do its part of the job.

No one metal can do everything, so bearings are made of layers of different metals. The usual procedure is to use a steel backing for maximum overall strength and a top layer of babbitt, an alloy of tin and lead. Babbitt has superb natural slipperiness and conformability, making it an ideal bearing material in these respects. It also has good embeddability, which means it can "absorb" dirt particles so they can't score journals. (With today's oil filters, embeddability isn't overly significant, but it's helpful in cases where the oil filter isn't changed at proper intervals.)

Unfortunately, babbitt has relatively low fatigue strength and load-carrying ability. So a layer of babbitt on a steel back would work only in light-duty applications. In such cases, either a lead-base or tin-base babbitt is used. The lead base has a slightly higher load-carrying ability.

Today's powerful engines use bearings with a layer of a secondary bearing material between a thin babbitt outer layer and the steel backing. This design serves two purposes: The thin babbitt layer (.0005 to .0015 inch)

A bearing shell is a multi-layer part. Outer layer is soft babbitt; backing is steel. One or two layers inbetween vary according to manufacturer and load-carrying needs.

actually has a higher fatigue strength than a thick layer; that is, it is less prone to cracking. However, once the babbitt layer wears through, there has to be a reasonably suitable bearing surface. The usual choices for the second bearing layer are sintered (powdered) copper-lead, aluminum alloy, cadmium nickel and cast copper-lead. It is the second layer that essentially determines the bearing's load-carrying ability.

Cadmium nickel has better fatigue strength and load-carrying ability than babbitt, but isn't as slippery, doesn't conform as well, and has far less embeddability. It is sometimes plated with indium for greater corrosion resistance.

Aluminum alloy: a very satisfactory bearing material for medium to fairly heavy-duty use.

Sintered copper-lead: not as slippery as babbitt, but good fatigue strength and load-carrying ability; fine for medium-duty use.

Cast copper-lead: the super-heavy-duty material. It has the highest fatigue strength and load-carrying ability. A nickel barrier of 30 to 50 millionths of an inch separates the babbitt outer layer from the cast copper-lead, to prevent a metallurgical combination of the two layers, which would destroy them both.

Choosing a replacement bearing actually is easy. When in doubt, buy the next heavier-duty bearing; it won't cost much more. On older cars, the sintered copper-lead is adequate. On late-model cars with up to medium powered engines, the aluminum alloy design will do. On high-performance engines, buy the cast copper-lead (such as a Clevite 77.)

Installation of replacement bearings certainly isn't in the category of minor tuneup, but it is not a job that is necessarily out of the question for the weekend mechanic. To decide whether or not it's a job you can do, check to

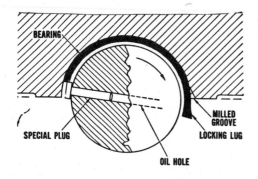

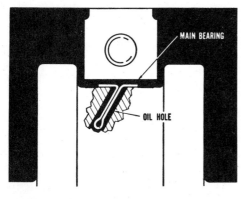

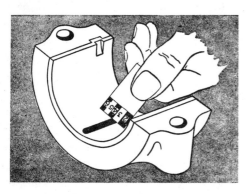

Top: Main bearings can be removed and replaced without taking out the crankshaft. Simple way is to use roll-out pins, which have a stem that fits into crankshaft journal oil hole and a head that rolls the bearing shell in or out. Middle: Cotter pin can be bent to serve as roll-out pin. Above: Checking bearing clearance with Plasti-Gage determines whether undersize bearings are needed.

see how the oil pan comes out, as this is the part of the job that can be the most "brutish."

If part of the front suspension must be dropped to take out the oil pan, the job is going to be quite difficult under backyard conditions. The trouble comes when you try to bolt everything back in place, as it gets difficult to line up things.

If you have a pair of small hydraulic jacks (which sell for about $10 each) you can use them to keep the front suspension jacked up, and to assist in realigning everything when the job is ready to go back together. You'll definitely need a helper for the job.

If the engine has to be jacked up off its mounts to provide clearance for pulling the oil pan, another potential difficulty exists. You will need a floor jack to lift the engine, and probably a pair of safety stands to brace the engine in place. If you've got this equipment in your garage, you may be able to get the pan off. Once the job is done, the engine has to be raised off the safety stands (which then are removed) onto the hydraulic jack. You'll need a helper with a crowbar at this point. One man jockeys the engine up and down with the jack, while the other moves it from side to side with the crowbar, until everything lines up. It sounds difficult and often it is. The whole operation takes but a few minutes under favorable conditions, longer when conditions get tough.

The best situation is when the oil pan can be dropped simply by unbolting it and lowering it from the engine. In this case, the job is substantially easier. The category that your car fits

Crankshaft journals should be mirror-smooth.

into depends on engine, car model and year, and any breakdown would fill this book. A careful perusal of the car underbody and the engine compartment should tell you how easy or difficult oil pan removal is.

Once the pan is off, the bearing caps, bolted in place, are in plain view and usually quite accessible. Just unbolt a cap, and you've got half a bearing in your hand.

If you're trying to replace main bearings, insert a roll-out pin (which can be bought for pennies or made from a cotter pin) into the crankshaft oil hole. Turn the crank by hand and the other half of the bearing will be rolled out.

Removing a connecting rod bearing is even easier. Unbolt the cap to remove one half, and push the rod away from the crankshaft to provide clearance to pull out the second half.

Now the critical part. If the crankshaft journal is smooth, and the bearing itself is merely well worn, installa-

tion of new bearings poses no problem. If, however, the crankshaft journals are scored, installation of new bearing shells will eliminate knocks and improve oil pressure only temporarily. If only one journal is bad, it may pay to have it ground smooth with the engine in the car. This is expensive, perhaps $25 or more for a single journal, but for just one journal it's a lot cheaper and easier than pulling and dismantling the engine, and taking the crankshaft out. If a journal is ground, a standard size bearing will allow excessive clearance. You'll need an undersize bearing.

The most common situation is that some of the journals will have light scratches. In this case, installation of new bearings should prove worthwhile. There will be the elimination of knocks and improvement in oil pressure. And if a quality oil and oil filter are used, the bearing job should last long enough to pay for itself.

Important: crankshaft and connecting rod bearings must be precisely tightened, using a torque wrench (available for $10 to $12.) Ask for the tightening specifications (given in foot-pounds) where you buy your bearings. There will be different specifications for connecting rod and main bearings.

A common consideration is crankshaft journal wear. If the journals are worn more than about .002-inch, undersize bearings should be used. As a practical matter, however, if the journals are smooth, you can be sure they haven't worn significantly, and standard size replacement bearings can be used.

If you want to check, there are two ways. One is the use of Plasti-Gage, available in most auto parts houses. It consists of strips of plastic and permits very accurate measurement of bearing clearances. The plastic is laid across the bearing, which then is tightened to specifications and removed. The plastic will have been squashed to a certain width, which corresponds to a bearing clearance.

Another way is by use of a piece of feeler strip of desired thickness. Normally, the clearance with new bearing shells should be less than .004-inch (.001 to .002-inch is desirable). Get an .004 (or thinner) strip that is a bit less than the width of the bearing, and no more than a half-inch for its other dimension. Lay the strip so that the half-inch dimension is lengthwise. Torque the bearing to specifications and try to rock the crank (just an inch or so—no more.) If the crank moves easily, undersize bearings are in order. If it locks completely or drags, install standard-size bearings.

The whole job, under favorable conditions, is a one-day deal, and if you do-it-yourself, you should save at least a $75 labor charge.

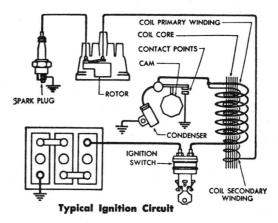

COIL PRIMARY WINDING
COIL CORE
CONTACT POINTS
CAM
ROTOR
SPARK PLUG
CONDENSER
IGNITION
SWITCH
COIL SECONDARY
WINDING

Typical Ignition Circuit

12

How the
Ignition Circuit Works

WHEN YOU TURN key of ignition switch, current flows from battery through switch to primary winding of coil through ignition points, which when closed complete the circuit to electrical ground. This creates a magnetic field in the coil.

As the engine turns, the distributor shaft turns and the distributor cam opens the points. The opening of the points causes the magnetic field in the primary winding of the coil to collapse on the secondary winding.

Because the secondary winding is much finer and has many more turns, a greater voltage is induced in the secondary.

The high-voltage electricity goes through a wire from the coil to the top of the distributor cap, through the distributor to the rotor, which spins with the distributor shaft and is designed to transfer this high voltage electricity to the correct spark plug wire, firing the plug.

The condenser is the system's shock absorber. Not all the current goes into the secondary. Some of it tries to flow through the points. However, they are open, and if the current were not given another path, it would arc across the points, burning them.

It would also create another path for the high-voltage electricity in the secondary, and some of it could bleed off and follow the arc across the points.

The condenser absorbs the current and then discharges it as the points close, preventing damage to them.

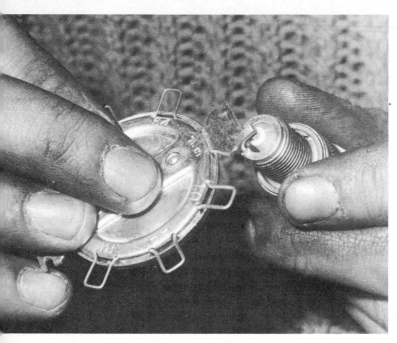

Regapping spark plugs. Only bend the side electrode. Always measure with a wire gauge. (A flat gauge gives a false reading in many cases.) Wire gauge should fit in and be withdrawable with moderate drag.

13

Sparkplug Troubleshooting

YOU CAN LEARN a lot about a car by inspecting its spark plugs.

For example, the type of deposit on the firing end of the plug can reveal how the car has been operating.

If the deposit is wet, black and oily, the car probably pumps oil, due to worn rings, pistons or cylinder walls, or worn or sticky valves. Or the ignition system may not be supplying enough power to the plug.

If, however, the electrodes and inner insulator are covered with black carbon deposits which are hard and baked on, you can suspect that too cold a plug is being used in an oil-burning engine, and you need either a hotter plug or, if fouling continues, an engine overhaul.

The plug itself may be faulty—with a badly worn electrode or even a cracked insulator. These, too, are clues to the condition of the car, and to the type of service attention it has been receiving. Once you learn how to read such clues, you can usually correct the trouble, and avoid some burdensome repair bills.

Before removing a spark plug for inspection, carefully blow any dirt out of the spark plug well. This will keep dirt from falling into the combustion chamber when the plug is taken out. Pull the wires from the spark plug terminals *gently* until the snap fitting comes free. If you jerk them, you may separate the wire from the terminal connection, and although a broken lead wire isn't visible, it will form a secondary spark gap and eventually burn through the ignition cable, causing electrical failure.

Always pull by the spark plug wire's terminal, not by the wire itself. On today's cars with resistance wire, sloppy removal almost always results in internal damage to the wire, and the engine misfires.

As you remove the plugs, first check each gasket washer. The surfaces of the washer which contact the plug and cylinder head should be bright, clean, uniform and unbroken. And the washer itself should not be completely flattened.

If the gasket washer is discolored, corroded, or irregularly marked, the plug was not tightened enough during installation. This produces an incomplete seal which allows gases to leak by, and the plug to overheat. And such overheating will cause rapid wear of the electrodes and preignition.

On the other hand, an entirely flattened washer means that the plug was tightened too much, and this will often cause a fracture in the plug shell, stretched threads, or a cracked insulator.

Flash Over. When an insulator has been cracked during installation and this crack fills up with a film of dirt and oil, you will have a condition known as "flash over." Electricity flows

All plugs normal. If all plugs have light tan or gray colored deposits and a small amount of electrode wear (not more than about .005-inch gap growth), plugs probably can be cleaned, regapped and reinstalled.

One plug fouled. If only one plug in a set is carbon fouled and the others appear normal, check the corresponding ignition cable for continuity. A compression check or cylinder leak test might also indicate mechanical trouble in the one cylinder.

directly from the top terminal to the grounded plug shell, completely by-passing the electrodes and spark gap. The plug is thus short circuited, and the only remedy is to replace the plug.

You can also have a "flash over" condition when an accumulation of dirt and oil coats the top insulator enough to allow current to pass through it. The cure here is to wipe the insulator with a cloth moistened with a gasoline or alcohol solvent which will cut the oil film.

When "flash over" occurs at the upper insulator, it may be visible in the form of a dim blue *spark discharge* around the plugs. This is sometimes confused with corona—the *steady blue light* that will appear around the base of the upper insulator, indicating a high tension field.

Inspecting the Electrodes is your next step. Here you may encounter the examples of fouling or deposit accumulation we mentioned earlier. If the electrodes are covered with a wet oily deposit, the plugs will probably give you good service after they have been cleaned and regapped. Such deposits are tell-tale signs of oil pumping in the engine, however, and you should check for worn valves or valve guides, rings, piston and cylinder walls. New rings might cut down the pumping. Or the battery or generator might be ailing to the point where not enough power is being delivered to the plug for proper ignition.

When the electrodes are coated with a hard, baked-on deposit, it's a sign that too cold a plug is being used in an oil-burning engine. You should change to a hotter plug. If such oil fouling then continues, you'll need an

All plugs fouled. These plugs may simply have been "drowned" with wet fuel during cranking. If choke is operating correctly, fouling may be engine oil. (Is car burning a lot of oil?) Fouling can be retarded by use of a hotter plug or a booster gap plug.

One or two plugs "splashed" fouled. Some plugs in a relatively new set may have splashed deposits. This may occur after a long-delayed tuneup when accumulated cylinder deposits are thrown against the plugs at high engine rpm. Clean and reinstall these plugs.

One plug badly burned. If one plug in a set has melted electrodes, pre-ignition was likely encountered in that cylinder. Check for intake manifold air leaks and possible cross-fire. Be sure the one plug is not the wrong heat range.

engine overhaul to correct the trouble at its source.

What do we mean by *cold* or *hot* plugs? To function properly, a spark plug must operate within a specific temperature or heat range. So all plugs are classified by heat ranges as well as by size, thread and reach.

The heat range of a plug is primarily controlled by internal exposed length of the center insulator, and is, basically, the speed with which the electrodes will cool after the cylinder fires. The electrodes must remain hot enough to prevent fouling, but must not get so hot that they will ignite the fuel mixture without an electrical spark (preignition.)

The problem is that combustion chamber temperatures vary greatly with the type and condition of the engine, how fast it is run and the load it is pulling. For example, when an engine fitted with spark plugs of intermediate heat range is run at slow (city traffic) speeds for a long time, the electrodes will stay cool enough to allow deposits to form rapidly.

This electrode fouling causes the plugs to misfire, and you get hard starting, poor gas mileage and a loss of power. But when the same plugs are given a high speed workout on the open road, many of the deposits may be burned away, in effect cleaning the plug. So, if you are getting spark plug miss from city driving, take your car out on the open highway and run it hard for an hour or so. Really run it up to peak engine speed and hold it there for a few seconds before you change gears. Such a "hard run" treatment may be the cheapest tune-up you can get.

Chipped insulator. If one or two plugs in a set have chipped insulator tips, severe detonation was the likely cause. Bending the center electrode during gapping can also crack the insulator. Replace with new plugs of the correct gap and heat range. Check for over-advanced timing.

Mechanical damage. A broken insulator and bent electrodes result from some foreign object falling into the combustion chamber. Because of valve overlap, objects can travel from one cylinder to another. Always clean out cylinders to prevent recurrence.

"Question mark" side electrodes. Improper use of pliers type gap tools will bend the side electrode and push the center electrode into the insulator assembly. Because of the force multiplication exerted by these tools, use them with care.

It helps to clean away the type of fluffy dry carbon deposits in the electrode and inner insulator which are caused by gas-fouling. To prevent a recurrence of such rapid fouling, you might—in addition to regular high-speed workouts—lean down the fuel mixture by adjusting the carburetor. Then, if you still get rapid fouling, even after a carburetor adjustment, it might be wise to change to a hotter range of spark plug.

White, Yellow, Brown Deposits. The most common form of deposit fouling results in white, yellow, brown or red coatings on the electrodes. These are normal by-products of combustion which result from the many additives in today's fuels and lubricants. In their original powdery form, they usually have little effect on spark plug operation. But when high speeds or heavy loads raise the engine temperature enough, such deposits melt and form a glaze coating on the inner insulator.

When hot, this glaze is an excellent conductor, and allows the current to follow the glaze instead of jumping the spark gap.

Periodic sandblast cleaning usually removes these coatings and restores the plugs to proper operation. If the deposits are compacted between the plug shell and the inner insulator, however, replace the plug. It is almost impossible to remove such compacted deposits without damaging the insulator.

The sandblast treatment, available at some service stations, is the most effective way to clean the face of the plug and the inner insulator. It won't always remove all the scale and oxide deposits from the center electrode and from the underside of the ground electrode. So, to ensure clean firing surfaces, try bending the ground electrode up slightly and cleaning both surfaces thoroughly with a flat distributor-point file.

After a cleaning, you frequently dis-

Left: All plugs overheated. When the entire set has dead white insulators and badly eroded electrodes (more than .001-inch gap per 1000 miles), the next colder heat range plug should be installed. Be sure ignition timing is not over-advanced. Right: All plugs worn. If all plugs have tan or gray colored deposits and excessive electrode wear (about .008 to .010-inch more than original gap), they probably have over 10,000 miles. Replace the entire set with new plugs of the same heat range.

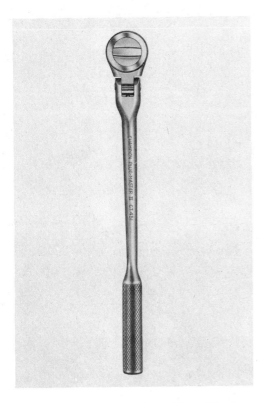

This is a Champion Plug-Master wrench, ideal for those inaccessible V-8 plugs. Handle is curved, ratchet head has universal joint.

cover other faults, such as a broken inner insulator. This may be caused by carelessness in regapping, or sustained operation with heavy detonation and preignition.

If the lower insulator is cracked and the center electrode worn to a fine point, while the ground electrode shows no sign of wear, the plug is operating too hot. The solution is to discard the damaged plug and replace it with one of a lower heat range.

Damaged plug shells are unusual. They are always the result of such mishandling as overtightening during installation. The damage generally shows up as a crack in the threads near the gasket seat, and such a plug should be promptly replaced.

Electrode Wear. Once the fouling deposits have been cleaned off the electrodes, you can check them for wear. As a rough guide, remember that a set of spark plugs, properly cared for and regularly cleaned and regapped, should

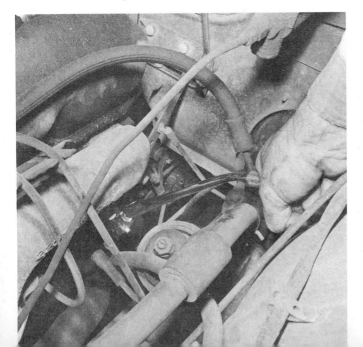

Notice how Plug-Master wrench fits in without the need for disconnecting or pulling out anything.

TO START THE FIRE

Often times we refer to the spark plug as "starting the fire" in the combustion chamber, and while this statement gets the *idea* across, it is over-simplified.

If engine *compression* is good and the carburetor is able to supply a *proper mixture* of air and fuel, then ignition may occur in one of several ways:

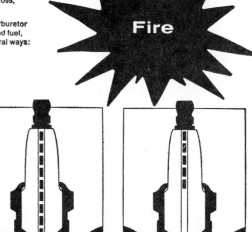

Fire

NORMAL IGNITION

When a spark occurs at the proper instant across the spark plug gap, we can say that ignition is *normal*. This requires an ignition system properly timed, and delivering adequate voltage to spark plugs in good condition.

TRACKING IGNITION

Instead of jumping the electrode gap, the spark may jump from one deposit "island" to another along the insulator nose. The fuel charge *may* be ignited, but the effect is to retard timing. Performance and economy are lost without the driver being aware of the problem.

SURFACE IGNITION

Sometimes a surface in the combustion chamber becomes hot enough to fire the fuel charge. Usually this type of ignition occurs *before* the timed spark and is called *preignition*. Deposits, overheated spark plugs, valves and sharp edges in the combustion chamber are all good sources of "hot spots." Again, the driver may not be aware of the condition, but besides losing power, extensive engine *damage* could occur.

give you good service for about 12,000 miles. Considering that the spark plug must give off from 1,000 to 3,000 sparks per minute while operating in gas temperatures as high as 4,000° F. —and also withstand explosive pressures of up to 800-lbs/psi—this is a remarkable life expectancy.

These intense pressures and temperatures, when combined with the corrosive gases in the combustion chamber, gradually wear the electrodes down to the point where the gap can't be effectively reset. Replace such plugs. Deposits may become too embedded to clean. Replace plugs once a year or every 12,000 miles, whichever comes first.

If *no spark* occurs to set off the fuel charge, *misfire* occurs. Usually, however, the average motorist can feel the engine miss and knows that service is needed.

Misfiring of the fuel charge can occur in several ways:

Misfire

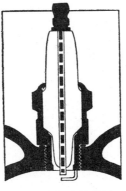

WIDE ELECTRODE GAP

When spark plug electrode gaps become worn, the ignition system may not be able to supply enough voltage to jump the gap.

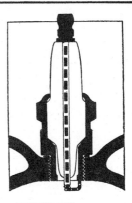

BRIDGED GAP

If deposits bridge the electrode gap, coil voltage is shorted to ground. Under this condition no spark occurs to "start the fire."

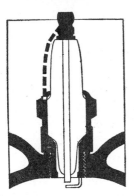

FLASHOVER

When dirt, grease and moisture are allowed to accumulate on the spark plug insulator, high voltage may short over the outside of the insulator. Hard, brittle plug boots also can encourage flashover. (Champion five-rib insulators help guard against flashover.)

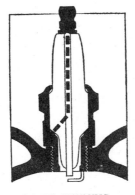

CRACKED INSULATOR

A cracked insulator may allow high voltage to leak to ground. (Be careful, when gapping plugs, not to damage the insulator with your gap tool.)

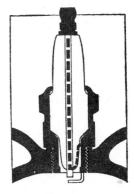

FOULED PLUGS

Some deposits that form on the insulator nose will conduct electricity. The coil, "seeing" this easier path to ground, will not build up enough voltage to jump the electrode gap.

When the plug is fairly new, and shows substantial wear, the trouble may be faulty installation, too lean a carburetor mixture, an over-advanced spark, dirty or damaged gasket seats, or a plug which has too hot a heat range.

Cleaning and Regapping. A good rule of thumb for spark plug servicing is to remove, clean and regap plugs at least once every 5,000 miles.

Always regap an old plug to the exact specifications set by the engine manufacturer. If you use a new plug, check it before installing to make sure it also meets the engine specs. Make the gap adjustment by bending the *ground* electrode. If you bend the center electrode, you'll fracture the inner insulator tip.

Always use a round wire gauge (from an auto supply store) when setting the plug gap. Because the wearing away of the electrode tends to form a concave hollow on the underside, a flat feeler gauge cannot give an accurate gap measurement.

Seating the Plug. The ideal way to ensure a correct seating of the plug is to use a torque wrench for tightening down the plugs. If you own one, and put in your own plugs, follow what the manufacturers recommend.

If you can't torque in your plugs, hand turn the plug in until it seats finger tight on the gasket. Then, using a *proper fitting* spark plug socket wrench, give it an additional ½ turn. This will produce the proper seal between the plug and the cylinder head.

Is Your Driving Average? When you go to buy a new set of plugs, remember that the manufacturer's chart gives the recommendations for *average* driving (about 40% city and 60% highway). If you are on the highway a lot, covering most of your distance at fairly high speed, you may need a plug that is a little cooler than average. If you're a "stop and go" driver, putting on most of your miles in the city at slow speeds with lots of waits at traffic lights, maybe a hotter plug will keep you going longer between tuneups.

Timing an engine. Aim light carefully to avoid parallax error.

14

Engine Tuning For Power

A GOOD TUNEUP can do wonders for a car in the areas of easier starting, smooth idle, better acceleration and higher gas mileage.

Initial Checks. To gain performance by tuning, the best place to gain is with a compression test, as explained in the chapter, "Taking Care of Your Engine."

If the compression test shows good results, the engine can be tuned. If compression is very high in some cylinders, the cause is probably a carbon accumulation. If compression is uniformly low, there are two possibilities:

1. The condition is normal. Many high-performance engines have camshafts designed for high-speed performance. Compression during cranking will not be particularly high; in fact, it may be as low as 75 psi.

2. There is wear in the engine, either worn rings or valve guides or valves. See the Chapter, "Tackling Valve and Ring Jobs" for details.

The whole point of this initial checking is: Don't expect too much from the best of tuning, unless the cylinders all have close to the same compression. Period.

Inspect the Electrical Circuits. Clean and tighten all the battery terminals and fill battery with water. Then follow the ground and starter cables and tighten the other ends to ensure that your ignition is getting all the current it requires for perfect performance. A number of domestic and imported cars have more than one ground strap connecting the engine to the frame or body. It's well worth your time to check these out for tightness and electrical conductivity.

Also check and clean and tighten if necessary, the thin-wire connections at the coil and the external thin-wire connection (if there is one) on the distributor from the coil. On many distributors, the wire goes through a rubber grommet into the distributor itself, and the cap must be removed to check its tightness.

Checking the Distributor. First disconnect one spark-plug wire at a time from the plugs and, with the engine idling, hold the terminal of the disconnected wire about ¼ inch away from a good ground such as the shell of the plug or a cylinder-head bolt. A good "fat" spark should jump regularly from wire to ground. If the wires have rubber protectors over the ends which cannot be slid back, place a key in the end of the terminal to make contact with the end of the wire and let the spark jump from the key to the ground.

To avoid getting a shock when testing each spark plug wire, have some-

Left: Spark check on plug wires with recessed terminals can be made by inserting key into terminals as shown. Right: Check thin wire terminals at coil for tightness.

one start and turn off the engine each time you disconnect a wire, or use pliers with insulated handles to place the key into the rubber socket.

If you get a very weak spark or none at all from one of the wires, it could be due to a wet or dirty distributor cap, a worn or burned rotor or the wire itself, which may have worn spots in the insulation or make poor contact in the cap.

Take off the distributor cap without disconnecting any wires. On most cars the cap is held by two spring clips. On many late-model cars it is held by two spring-loaded locking rods with screw-slot heads.

To undo the locking rod type, press down with the screwdriver and turn to twist the locking rod out of its engagement point in the distributor body.

Wipe the cap clean, both inside and out with a dry cloth. Carefully inspect the inside of the cap for cracks or carbon deposits along a crack extending from one contact point to another. Carbon deposits, particularly on caps having a smooth inner surface, can conduct electricity and cause engine "miss."

Either replace the cracked cap with a new one or, for an emergency repair, scrape off the carbon along the crack with the point of a knife blade. Seal the scraped-out crack with lacquer or a dab of nail polish to prevent future carbon deposits.

While you have the distributor cap off, remove the rotor, and carefully inspect the tip. If it is burned and pitted so that the edge is irregular, replace it with a new one. Any attempt to file

Left: Distributor cap held by locking rods can be released with screwdriver. Press down on rod and turn to release. Right: Carefully inspect interior of distributor cap for cracks.

Removing rotor. On GM cars with V-8 (illustrated), rotor is held by two screws.

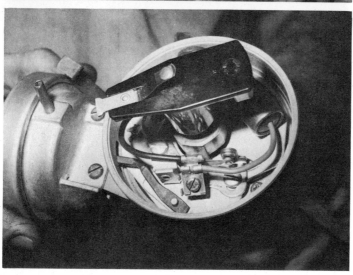

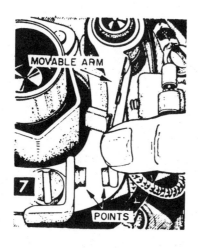

Above: Typical Ford and Chrysler distributor. This type of rotor is just pulled off. Notice adjusting screw just below points, and the elongated hole in the ignition point through which it goes. To adjust points, loosen lockscrew and this adjusting screw, and move fixed point toward or away from distributor cam to adjust points gap. When gap is correct, as measured by feeler gauge, tighten the two screws. Left: Points can be inspected for burning by spreading them apart with finger.

the edge clean would increase the gap between rotor and cap terminals and interfere with delivery of a good hot spark to the plugs.

Distributor point failure is sometimes due to oil being thrown on the point contact surfaces by the rotating cam. If you notice a black oily smear on the point support plate, called the breaker plate, it is evidence that oil is getting on the points and interfering with engine performance.

If the distributor has not been cleaned in tens of thousands of miles, some oil accumulation is to be expected and can be cleaned off. However, under normal circumstances, the oil is evidence of a worn bushing around the distributor shaft.

The only cure is to have a new bushing installed at a machine shop or to install a rebuilt distributor. (This is the simplest and quickest procedure.)

Installing Points. With the rotor off and out of the way, spread apart the points with a screwdriver and inspect the little discs which make and break the ignition circuit to create the high-voltage electricity for the spark plugs.

If they are pitted or burned, they should be replaced. Points normally last 10,000 to 15,000 miles, but in short trip driving, they may burn more quickly. If points fail in very low mileage, such as 4,000 or so, this indicates that something is wrong.

Reasons for Burnt Points. You'll be wise to do more than merely replace badly burned contact points. Check for the cause among these six common troubles:

1. Coil resistance unit not properly connected into the circuit between ignition switch and the coil positive.

2. Defective condenser.

3. Points do not open widely enough.

4. Oil vapor may seep into the distributor and get on contact points to cause arcing and rapid burning. A smudge line on breaker plate under the points is a clue to this.

5. High voltage condition may cause excessive flow through points and produce a blue scale on the points.

6. Radio capacitor connected to distributor terminal may cause excessive pitting.

Replacing the points varies slightly according to the make of car. To start, become familiar with the action of the points by watching them as someone cranks the engine.

You will see the points open and close. They will open as a little fiber block on the point assembly comes up against high spots on the distributor shaft. (This section of high spots is called the cam and the high spots themselves are called lobes.) The points will close as the fiber block comes off a high spot.

Actually only one point moves (out and back). The other is stationary.

Each of the lobes is shaped exactly the same (except on Volkswagen and Buick V-6 engines), so the points are separated exactly the same distance each time. That distance is measured with a feeler gauge and should be at factory specifications.

Removing the points is very easy. If there is a wire connected to the points, disconnect it. Then look for a

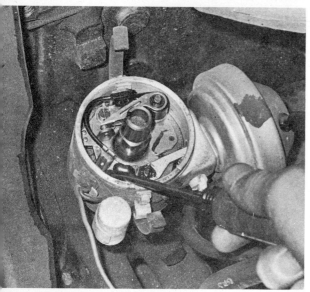

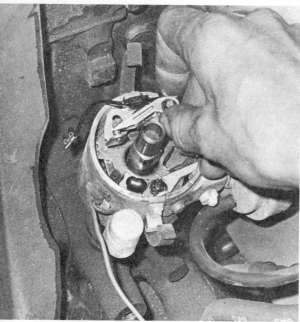

lockscrew holding the points to the distributor breaker plate under them. If there is more than one screw, the larger one is the lockscrew. Remove it and its lockwasher, and you can lift the points up and out.

Install the new points in the same position, but don't tighten the lockscrew except on General Motors V-8 distributors, as explained later.

The points now must be adjusted.

On all but General Motors V-8 distributors, there is a special tool to simplify point adjustment. It consists of a special ring that fits over the distributor cam and a special feeler gauge that is actually thinner than the size stamping says it is.

The point gap is measured in thousandths of an inch when the fiber block is at a high spot of the distributor cam, and this means the highest point. To get the distributor shaft properly lined up requires cranking the engine in very short bursts—a sometimes time-consuming feat.

The ring simulates the condition and the feeler gauge that is provided with the ring is thinner to compensate for the thickness of the ring.

On GM V-8 distributors, the mechanical advance mechanism is at the top of the distributor and there is no way to fit a ring over it. You will have to either crank the engine or use the special technique explained later.

To measure a point gap, insert the correct size stamped on the gauge feeler gauge between the points' contact faces. If the gauge can be inserted and withdrawn with light drag on it, the gap is correct. If the gap is too wide or too narrow, it must be changed.

Top: Removing points on this typical distributor starts with disconnecting push-on connector with screwdriver as shown.
Above: Remove adjusting and lock screws and just pull the points out, as shown.

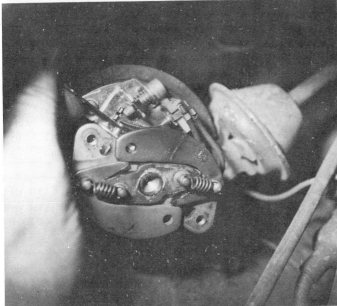

Above: On GM V-8s, point gap is set with engine running. Lift up window on distributor cap as shown, and insert allen wrench. Left: Point gap is adjusted by inserting feeler gauge between points with rubbing block on cam lobe, or special ring inserted.

The adjustment is made by moving the stationary point in toward the distributor cam. Sometimes there is an eccentric screw that does this when turned. Other times there is a screwdriver slot in the breaker plate and the stationary point plate and you just twist the screwdriver to increase or decrease the gap.

Once the gap is correct, tighten the lockscrew.

On GM cars with the mechanical advance at the top of the distributor, the following technique will work:

There is an Allen-head adjusting screw at the side of the points and all you have to do is have someone crank the engine while you turn it, until you can see a small gap (about the thickness of a matchbook cover). With this gap, the engine should start, even if it runs poorly.

Refit the rotor and distributor cap, which has a little metal window in its side. This window can be lifted while the engine is running to permit adjustment of the points.

Note: on GM cars with the windshield antenna, there is a metal shield around the points to prevent them from interfering with radio reception. This shield, a two-piece assembly, should be refitted.

With the engine running, turn the Allen wrench slowly clockwise until the engine just starts to misfire, then turn it one-half turn counterclockwise to complete the adjustment. (If the engine is running roughly when you first start it, turn the screw first one way, then the other, until it smooths out.)

After the ignition points are adjusted, they should be double-checked with a dwellmeter, which is available in a combination unit with a tachometer for as little as $15.

The dwellmeter measures the number of degrees that the ignition points are closed. It is the opposite of the point gap, but it also is an important measurement.

For it is when the points are closed that the magnetic field builds up in the coil. If the points aren't closed long enough, the magnetic field will not be strong enough, and when it collapses, the spark it produces will be weak. This is particularly true at high engine speed.

If the points are adjusted for the correct gap, the dwell reading should also be within specifications—but not always, hence the desirability of a dwell check.

Car makers provide an acceptable range of both point gap and dwell readings and you may have to modify the point gap to get the dwell that is necessary.

The dwellmeter is easily connected —one wire to the "CB" or minus terminal of the coil, the other to a good ground. Then the engine is started and run.

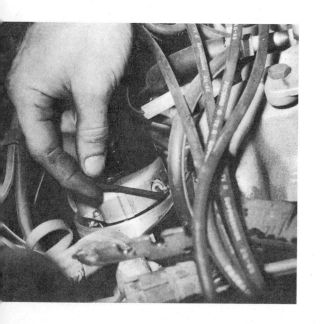

Distributor cap has been removed to show how allen wrench fits into adjusting screw on GM V-8 distributors. This distributor has radio interference shield, explained in next photo.

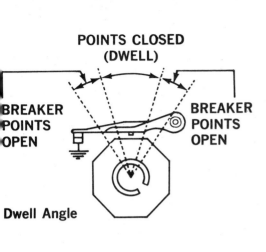

POINTS CLOSED
(DWELL)

BREAKER
POINTS
OPEN

BREAKER
POINTS
OPEN

Dwell Angle

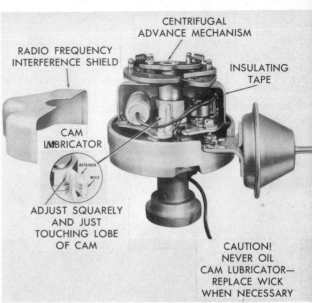

CENTRIFUGAL
ADVANCE MECHANISM

RADIO FREQUENCY
INTERFERENCE SHIELD

INSULATING
TAPE

CAM
LUBRICATOR

RETAINER
WICK

ADJUST SQUARELY
AND JUST
TOUCHING LOBE
OF CAM

CAUTION!
NEVER OIL
CAM LUBRICATOR—
REPLACE WICK
WHEN NECESSARY

Left: Explaining the meaning of the word "dwell," which is the period of time, in degrees that points are closed. Right: GM cars with windshield antenna have radio interference shield (a two-piece unit) around points. It must be removed to install new points.

At the same time you should make a dwell-holding test, that is, see if the dwell reading remains the same as engine speed increases. Slowly increase engine speed from idle to 1500 rpm and then slowly let it drop back to idle. Never exceed 1500 rpm.

If the dwell varies more than three degrees, the distributor is worn and should be removed for service. See the distributor removal section that follows.

A final check of the distributor is made when setting ignition timing. At that time, the mechanical and vacuum advance units are tested with a timing light.

Distributor Removal. No matter how well you adjust the points, a dis-

tributor to the coil at the distributor end.

Crank the engine until the rotor points to a convenient reference point tributor may not give good performance if considerably worn or inadequately lubricated. A worn shaft or bushing may cause the points to open unevenly. An overgreased distributor may pick up enough dirt to interfere with operation of advance mechanisms.

With such troubles, the distributor must be removed. This isn't difficult; putting back the distributor is another matter, particularly on Ford products.

If you must remove the distributor, here are recommended precautions.

Remove the distributor cap.

Disconnect the wire from the dis-

Dwell is checked with special meter, which is normally combined with a tachometer and called a dwell-tachometer. One lead of meter goes to distributor minus (or "CB") thinwire terminal, other goes to a good ground on engine.

on the engine, or perhaps a time of day on an imaginary clock.

With chalk, mark points on the engine alongside the distributor that align with some portion of the distributor body, such as a cap spring clamp.

Disconnect the vacuum hose or tube.

Slacken the distributor lock. It may be a pinch-clamp or a simple hold-down bolt and bracket.

Twist the distributor body as you pull on it, to break any stickiness.

When you install a new or rebuilt distributor, mark the body as you did on the old distributor, and when you get it in, the engine will start.

Timing may or may not be precise, but adjusting timing is a lot easier when the engine is running.

Now let's look at the condenser.

The Condenser Is an Integral Part of the ignition system. Without it the points would be pitted, burned, and

worn in a few days. There's an easy explanation.

In order to force the electrical current to jump the air gap between the spark plug case and the electrode, the relatively insignificant current from the battery must be built up to 20,000 volts or more. The buildup takes place in the primary and secondary windings of the coil. The low voltage battery current flows into the primary winding of the coil, setting up a magnetic field in the coil. When the voltage is abruptly stopped, the magnetic field collapses and induces a higher voltage in secondary coil windings.

The low voltage is stopped by the opening of the distributor contact points. The moment the points separate, the current stops flowing from battery to coil. Collapse of the magnetic field not only keys the needed high-voltage induction in the secondary windings of the coil, but also induces, as a by-product, a higher voltage in the primary circuit, a voltage high enough to jump the point gap. If this were allowed to happen, the contact points would soon become useless, and the arcing would drain needed power from the higher secondary voltage.

The condenser saves voltage and points by acting much like a refrigerator. It offsets the unwanted build-up by storing the surge of electrons. The electrons are crowded into the condenser where they continue to build up. As they work, they set up a reverse direction to their flow pattern. Because the points are still open, the flow is toward the grounded side of the condenser. At a point, the buildup collapses and reverses, building up toward the insulated side of the condenser, then the flow and buildup reverses again and again.

Each time the flow is reversed, the magnetic field it creates collapses, then builds up in the opposite direction continuing from side to side until the electrons are dissipated or stopped by closing of the points. The condenser thus helps retard the flow by impeding or blocking the electrons and keeping them where they can do no damage.

Inside Your Condenser are four strips, two of metal foil and two of insulating paper. Almost 15 feet long, they are rolled tightly (metal foil sheets are slightly narrower than the insulation to prevent leakage of electrons around the edges) and the roll is placed in a metal case. The case is hermetically sealed to shut out moisture—the enemy of a condenser.

One foil strip is connected to the cap of the condenser and an exterior terminal. The second is connected internally to the condenser case. A pigtail soldered to the outside terminal connects to the primary distributor terminal, placing the condenser in parallel. The case acts as ground so the condenser is wired across the circuit.

Automotive condensers are rated in microfarads. It is important to replace a worn condenser with one of the proper rating for your car. For average driving conditions, a condenser rated between .18 and .25 microfarads is right, but if you drive at high speeds over open roads, try a slightly lower capacity condenser. If you drive most ofen at low city street speeds, try one of higher capacity.

Although the condenser in your car is a reliable, long-lasting item, trouble could strike when least expected. A weak or leaking condenser usually has absorbed enough moisture to weaken the insulating papers and can no longer hold the buildup charge it was designed to handle. A condenser with poor insulation can drain enough energy from an ignition system to lower the secondary voltage substantially. A weak or intermittent spark at the plugs can be a disastrous result.

Signs of Trouble may go unnoticed except when the engine is hot. It is unlikely a leaking condenser would cause misfiring at low or medium speeds, except under conditions which cause it to heat.

Frayed pigtail, broken terminal, or loose insulation can all increase point wear. Under severe conditions, they can render the points useless. If you're experiencing ignition trouble, burned points, hard starting, check the condenser. Remove it from the distributor. Check for broken leads, frayed or loose insulation, corroded terminals, signs of moisture, or poor ground at the mounting.

Some Simple Tests. Condensers are generally tested on equipment giving three readings: microfarads, leakage, and series resistance. But test equipment costs money and condensers cost but a few pennies. You'll be money ahead if you make these few simple tests; then if the condenser seems faulty or if you're in doubt, replace it and test again.

A condenser can be tested for excessive leakage (short) by charging it from a spark plug as the engine is turned over. Be sure the spark used for

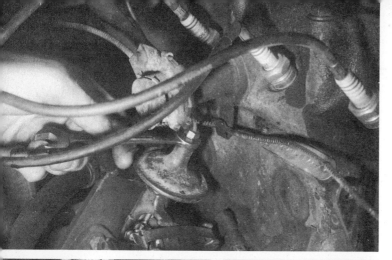

Distributor removal starts with disconnection of vacuum line. On many cars it's a hose that can be pulled off; on this one it's a tube.

Next, loosen distributor lock. On most cars, it's a bolt and bracket to engine. On this car it's a pinch-bolt.

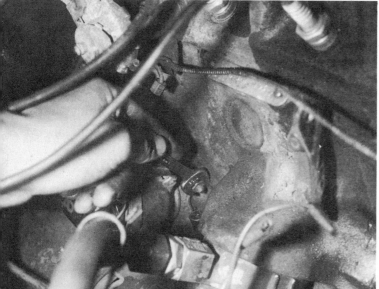

Below left: Pull distributor out with twisting motion to break it free. Below: Condenser can be tested for grounding with test lamp. Disconnect condenser lead and attach alligator clip of lamp to it. Turn on ignition and touch prod of test lamp to ignition points terminal. If lamp lights, condenser is internally grounded and should be replaced.

the test has a gap no greater than .030. The small gap will limit the voltage involved.

Ground the condenser case to the cylinder head or block, then touch it to the plug terminals. Remove the plug, turn off the engine, and wait one minute. With a *well-insulated* screwdriver, short the condenser terminal to the outer case. One heavy spark should result. If the condenser will not hold such a charge for one minute, it should be replaced.

Caution: Charged in this manner, a condenser can give you a severe shock. A plug gapped to .030 inch and operating in low compression with the engine at idle will develop about 300 volts. This is not enough to injure the condenser insulation, but plenty "hot" if you touch it. Be sure the screwdriver is well insulated before you short the condenser.

A safer test is to check the condenser with the coil. Remove the high tension lead from the coil terminal and fit a 12-inch jumper wire to the terminal. Now make certain you are properly insulated from the jumper wire, then turn on the ignition switch and hold the open end about ¼ inch from the cylinder head as the engine is cranked. If a spark leaps across the gap regularly, coil and condenser are OK. If there is no spark, or if it is weak or irregular, either the coil or condenser are at fault.

Replace the condenser and repeat the test. If there is still no spark, the trouble lies in the coil. If the spark now jumps the gap, the condenser was at fault and the trouble has been fixed.

Another test of a condenser is for internal grounding. Disconnect the condenser wire and connect a test lamp or jumper wire to it. Touch the other end of the test lamp or jumper wire against the battery's starter terminal. If the test lamp should light, or the jumper wire should spark, the condenser is defective, and should be replaced.

Setting Ignition Timing. For this you will need a power timing light. There are inexpensive versions (about $10 to $12) that plug into a household outlet, and for weekend mechanics they are adequate.

Totally inadequate is the neon bulb timing light available for about $5 to $7. It just is not bright enough, and on today's cars you can't get it close enough to the timing marks without risk to your hands.

Timing is set with the engine at idle or another specified speed, and with the vacuum tube or hose on the distributor disconnected and plugged. Factory timing specifications are based on the disconnected vacuum tube or hose, and you should not try to do the job any other way.

Slacken the distributor locknut, lockbolt, pinch-clamp or whatever is used. Connect the timing light and start the engine. The light will start flashing.

Aim the light at the timing marks, which are on the crankshaft pulley or vibration damper and a stationary part of the engine adjacent to it.

If timing is off the mark, turn the distributor body until the marks line up. If you can't see the marks, stop the engine and take a look with a flashlight. You may have to short-burst-crank the engine to find the mark on the pulley.

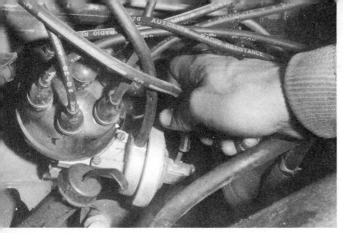
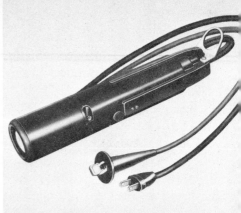

When setting ignition timing, always disconnect vacuum line from distributor and plug the line. (A golf tee makes a suitable plug.) This is an AC timing light. It plugs into household current and costs $10 to $12, much less than a 12-volt timing light.

If the marks are covered with road film (and they shouldn't be if you keep your engine clean), wipe them off. You may find several marks, and you will have to check manufacturer's specifications to find out which are the correct ones for your car. If necessary, mark them with chalk.

Once you have the distributor body positioned so that the marks line up, tighten the locking arrangement (bolt, nut, clamp). Now speed up the engine and the timing should advance. If it does not, the mechanical advance mechanism in the distributor is defective. On General Motors V-8s, the mechanical advance is above the points (just below the rotor) and you can easily see if a spring has come off, or stretched. On other distributors the breaker plate must be removed.

Keep the timing light on the marks and reconnect the vacuum tube or hose. With the engine running at idle speed or slightly above, the timing should advance as soon as the tube or hose is back on. The advance in tim-

ing will also cause the engine to speed up a bit. If the timing does not change, the vacuum advance unit is stuck and should be replaced. This can be done on the car in most cases.

Wiring. From the coil to distributor, and from distributor to spark plugs is a mare's nest of most important wiring. These high tension wires should be firmly soft. If they are hard, cracked, or gooey with oil, replace them all. Cost is low for a new set of high tension wiring, and the results are well worth your trouble. A little cleaning fluid on a clean rag does a good job of wiping off the top of the coil, so electricity can't sneak out of the wires and lose itself to ground.

Spark plugs can tell you a lot about your engine. And this book has a lot to tell you about spark plugs. See the chapter, "Sparkplug Troubleshooting."ing."

Nuts and Bolts are next. Use a good set of wrenches to tighten all the manifold (both intake and exhaust) carburetor attachment, and other odds and ends of hex-headed objects you can find. After thousands of miles of vibration they loosen. Leaking intake manifolds could burn plugs or valves, as well as destroy efficiency of the fuel mixture.

Cylinder head bolts also should be tightened, but this job must be done with a special wrench, the torque wrench, which is described in the chapter, "How Tight Is Tight?"

As you well know, exhaust fumes are both dangerous and stinky, which makes a tight exhaust manifold a blessing and a necessity.

Other steps in tuning for power are:

1. Adjusting valves, described in Chapter 7, "Valves: Tapping for Service."

2. Servicing the heat riser, described in Chapter 19, "The Heat Riser."

3. Replacing or servicing the air filter, described in Chapter 2, "How to Change Your Car's Filters."

4. Servicing the hardware installed for smog control, described in Section IV, "Pollution Control Devices."

The final step in any tuneup is a road test.

Road Testing the Car is done in the following sequence: In High, run along a level road at some 10 mph. The engine should pull evenly, without surge or hesitation. Should it not be smooth, work the idle mixture needles until you have a perfect idle.

Gradual acceleration resulting from a slow even pressure on the throttle is the next check. During this one, you should have even acceleration, without hesitation or leaping forward. Try this several times, paying close attention to evenness of the speed increase. You will then notice that between 40 and 60 mph there will be a sudden surge forward, though you have not moved your foot that much. Action in the engine room comes from opening of the power valve(s) or secondary throttle blades. All of this is controlled by engine vacuum and position of your foot.

There's more fun to the third checkout. While running 20 to 25 mph, floor the throttle. Here you want a smooth, even increase in speed. Again, lack of flat spots is the most important thing. Should the engine seem to gasp once or twice when you floor the throttle, try moving the accelerator pump lever to another hole. This modifies the amount of fuel pumped into the engine and is an adjustment worth making. Make this test several times so you'll have a good idea how well an engine can run. Then as performance changes when the engine ages, you'll be in a better position to determine when another tuning is needed.

The last test is to hold the throttle in a steady position at 40 to 50 mph on a flat road. Here is where smoothness is the top dog. The engine should keep you rolling at an even pace. If not, the carburetor float level may be off, or the vacuum line to the distributor could be leaking enough to cause spark advance to wander.

One thing is certain—after you've spent the necessary four hours making a thorough tune-up, you will have an engine that outperforms most others of its type. It will also run smoother and be more pleasant to drive, while giving you better fuel mileage than ever before.

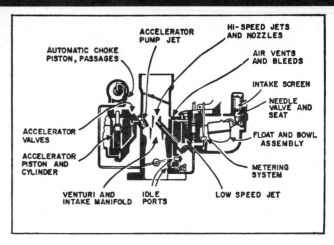

Cutaway of a simple one-barrel carburetor.

15

Put New Life in Your Carb

A LIST OF malfunctions caused by a sick carburetor reads like a "Who's Who of Auto Ailments." It includes hard starting, flooding, delayed acceleration, poor gas mileage, stalling, rough running, fouled spark plugs, and gas leaks at the carburetor.

Not all of these problems, however, result only from an ailing carburetor. For this reason you should make sure spark plugs, ignition parts, compression, and timing are all in good condition before beginning carburetor service. In short, make sure your engine is correctly tuned, because your carb depends on proper operation of the rest of the engine.

Make No Mistake about one thing, a carburetor would probably function properly forever if it were not for dirt that is present in the air sucked into it and in the gas. This dirt builds up in

the carb and causes the engine to lose power while drinking up an increasing amount of gas. Or, dirt can strike suddenly and cause the engine to stop running without warning. In either case, the results are the same: loss of power, engine sputter, stalling, and wasted gas.

There are several ways to remove this dirt. First, a cleaner can be added to the gas tank. If this cleaner is added three or four times a year from the time the car is new, it does a fairly effective job. The cleaner enters all parts and orifices of the carb and cleans them out while driving.

Another way to keep your carb clean is to introduce the solvent directly into the carb through a gravity-feed kit. One such kit is made by the Gum-out Division of Pennsylvania Refining Co., and can be purchased at most auto supply outlets or accessory stores.

Gumout kit attached to fuel inlet of carburetor. Fuel line has been disconnected and plugged.

Run engine at various speeds with kit attached, actuating throttle linkage at carburetor.

How the Idle System Works

THE idle system consists of the idle tubes (5), idle passages (3), idle air bleeds (1), idle adjustment needles (7), and idle discharge holes (6).

In the curb idle speed position, the throttle valve (9), is slightly open, allowing a small amount of air to pass between the wall of the carburetor bore and the edges of the throttle valve.

The idle needle hole (8) is in the high vacuum area below the throttle valves while the fuel bowl is vented to atmospheric pressure.

The fuel is drawn from the bowl through the main metering jets (4) into the main well. The fuel is metered by the idle fuel metering orifice at the lower tip of the idle tube (5) and travels up the idle tube. When the fuel reaches the top of the idle tube, it is mixed with air through two idle air bleed holes (1). This mixture moves through the horizontal idle passage through a restriction (2) and down the vertical idle passage to the four idle discharge holes (6) located just above the throttle valves where more air is added to the mixture. It then passes through the idle needle holes (8) and into the bore of the carburetor.

In addition to this mixture of fuel and air, air enters the bore of the carburetor through the slightly opened throttle valve. For smooth operation, the air from the bore and the air-

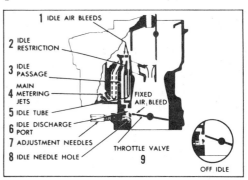

1 IDLE AIR BLEEDS
2 IDLE RESTRICTION
3 IDLE PASSAGE
4 MAIN METERING JETS
5 IDLE TUBE
6 IDLE DISCHARGE PORT
7 ADJUSTMENT NEEDLES
8 IDLE NEEDLE HOLE
FIXED AIR BLEED
THROTTLE VALVE 9
OFF IDLE

fuel mixture from the idle needle hole must combine to form the correct final fixture for curb idle engine speed.

The position of the idle adjusting needle (7) regulates the amount of air fuel mixture admitted to the carburetor bore. Except for this variable at the idle adjustment needle, the idle system is specifically calibrated for low engine speeds.

As the throttle valves are opened, a pressure differential change occurs. Opening of the valve progressively exposes the idle discharge holes (6) to manifold vacuum and the air flow, with the result that they deliver additional air-fuel mixture for off-idle engine requirements.

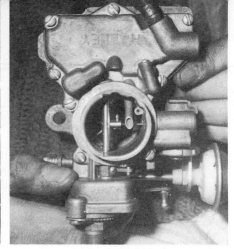

Left: Replacement of carburetor begins with disconnection of fuel line. For details, see chapter, "Replacing Engine Parts." Right: Disassembly of carb begins with removal of eight screws on top. After they are out, top of carburetor can be removed.

It contains adapters, a flexible hose line, and a container of cleaner.

To use this cleaner, disconnect the gas line at the carb, then block off the flow of gas through the line with the universal block-off fitting provided with the kit. Attach the hose to the carb at the gas inlet port, using the adapter that fits the hole. Start the engine and run it at various speeds. Every so often, place the palm of your hand over the carb to block off air and force the cleaner into all gas and air passages.

The most effective method to really clean the carb when the other ways don't correct the ailment is to take it off the intake manifold, disassemble it, and clean each part. This way you can inspect each part, change if necessary, and make internal adjustments.

Modern carburetors are somewhat complex. Unless you have a reasonable amount of experience, you should buy a rebuilt. With experience, however, you can tackle a one-barrel or even a two-barrel carburetor, as explained in this chapter. If you feel extremely confident, you might even try a four-barrel, as explained in the chapter, "How to Rebuild a Four-Barrel Carburetor."

The illustrations in this chapter are based on a one-barrel carburetor. Most one-barrels are reasonably simple and similar.

A carburetor rebuilding kit often contains rather complete information to guide you over any difficult items.

Prices of carburetor kits vary by several dollars, and the only way to decide on the best buy is to find out what each kit contains. More expensive kits contain instructions, a gauge for measuring the all-important float level, and internal replaceable parts, including gaskets, jets, accelerator pump, power valves, and needle and seat valve. Cheaper kits may only contain gaskets and a needle and seat valve.

The most complete kits are only about $15 for a four-barrel, which is about a third of the price of a quality

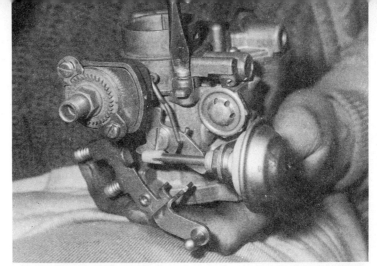

Top: Hold carburetor vertical while removing.

Center: Float is disconnected by removing hinge pin. Directly under float tab is the needle and seat assembly, which controls fuel inlet.

Right: This is accelerator pump, which should be removed. Job starts with pulling of a cotter pin on this particular carburetor; on others a C-clip is used.

rebuilt. So if you're doing it yourself, don't skimp.

When buying your kit, refer to the name and model number of your carb (found on the nomenclature plate attached to it). If you can't find this plate, give the salesman the make and year of your car, type of engine (six or eight cylinders), and kind of transmission (manual or automatic).

To Aid in Diagnosing the cause of your malfunctioning carb, remove it from the engine without draining fuel from the bowl. You can check the bowl for dirt and find out if the float has a hole in it.

Remove the fuel inlet nut with an open-end wrench, then use the needle-nose pliers to disconnect the spring clips that hold the throttle linkage. Loosen any vacuum lines, then remove the carb from the engine by taking out the nuts that connect the throttle body to the intake manifold.

Disconnect the accelerator pump from its external linkage, then unscrew

the cover fasteners and lift the cover from the bowl. Discard the gasket separating the cover assembly from the lower part of the carb.

Disconnect the float by removing the hinge pin. (On some carbs, the float is hinged to the cover, on others it is hinged to a flange inside the fuel bowl.)

Performance of All Parts of a carb is influenced by the fuel supply in the float bowl. This fuel level must remain constant despite varying speeds of the engine and demands on the carburetor. When the car is driven at high speed, the greater rate of fuel consumption causes the float to lower, the needle valve to open, and more fuel to enter the bowl.

As the throttle closes when the engine idles, thus reducing the demand for fuel, the rising float closes the needle valve, stopping the flow of fuel.

The smallest drop of dirt on the needle valve or a sticky float can cause

Left: Pull accelerator pump out completely. Caution: there are balls inside that are part of check valve assembly. Invert carb very slowly so you can see where they come from, along with any other parts that might fall out. Right: Needle, held in fingers, is removed from seat. On this carb, seat is not replaceable as it is built into top of carb. On most carbs, it is a replaceable screw-in fitting.

the carb to flood, resulting in a rich mixture that wastes fuel and causes hard starting.

Check the float by shaking it close to your ear: if there is a sloshing sound, it has a leak and should be replaced. Inspect the lower surfaces of the float bowl to see that the small sealing beads are not damaged, because this can result in air or fuel leaks at that point. Don't try to solder the opening, because it will make the float heavier.

A float that is thrown off balance by anything inside it or any extra weight will lie low in the bowl and keep the needle valve open for a longer period. This lets too much gas into the bowl, resulting in an over-rich mixture.

Free the accelerator pump plunger from the pump arm by removing the pin or clip that retains it. Pull the pump plunger straight out and discard it. (When installing a new plunger, soak its leather seal first in light engine

oil for about 10 minutes. This will ease the process of fitting it into its bore).

Remove the power valve, which is normally held by screws. (On multi-barrel carbs, there are more than one power valve.) Take off the choke assembly.

Dunk the carburetor in a medium-duty solvent and agitate it every few minutes for a total of thirty minutes. Do not attempt to dry a carburetor with compressed air; allow it to air-dry instead. (Some carbs have an ignition advance or fuel control diaphragm in the carburetor and this could be damaged by compressed air.)

Install a new power valve, gaskets, jets, idle mixture needles, needle and seat valve, and accelerator pump. The only tools you will need are screwdrivers, needle-nose pliers and perhaps a wrench to change the seat part of the needle and seat valve.

When Reassembling, screw the idle mixture and adjusting needles and

Left: Carburetor should be cleaned in a suitable solvent, agitating periodically. Use of a brush to wash away dirt also is good practice. Right: Measuring float level may be done with machinist's ruler, in this case attached to feeler gauge. This float top is perfectly level with top of carb (cover inverted), so measurement can be taken anywhere. On other carbs, measurements are different for heel and toe of carb.

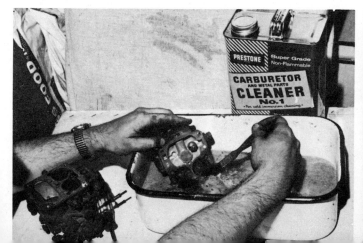

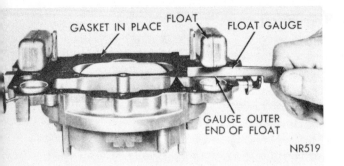

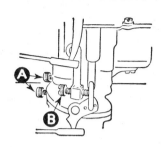

Above : On this four-barrel carb, float level measurement is made with gasket in place and gauge at outer end of float (toe end).

Above: Two and four barrel carb has two mixture screws, labeled "A," in addition to throttle stop speed screw (also called idle speed screw) labeled "B."

In addition to idle mixture screws and idle speed screw, carburetor also has a fast idle screw, which should not be confused with them. Fast idle screw rides against a metal or plastic curved or stepped surface called the fast idle cam. Fast idle speed should be 1,500 to 1,800 rpm when engine is running immediately after a cold start. If it is not within that range, turn the fast idle screw (clockwise to increase speed, counterclockwise to decrease).

Once you have your carb clean and running right, keep it that way by spraying all external linkage with automatic choke cleaner.

springs into the throttle body until finger-tight, then back out 1½ turns as a preliminary idle adjustment. Put a new throttle body gasket in position and tighten screws evenly and securely.

Every carburetor has some unique design features. On some carbs, the accelerator pump has an external linkage with several holes for seasonal adjustment. On others, the power valve is removed from the outside of the bowl. To prevent fuel from percolating when the engine is shut off after operation in hot weather, some carbs have a special spring-loaded vent.

If your carb has some unrecognizable features that require special attention or parts replacement, maintenance information should be contained in the instructions in your rebuilding kit.

As a carburetor ages, the float level rises naturally. This is due primarily to wear of the float lever pin. As the float rises higher to shut off fuel entering the float bowl, the carb tends to give a richer mixture to the engine. If necessary, adjust the float by bending the tang at the rear of the float, then visually check alignment. Decrease float drop by bending it toward the needle seat, or away from the seat to increase.

All Types of Carburetors—no matter how many barrels—have only one throttle adjusting screw. Two- and four-barrel units, however, have two idle adjustment screws—one for each idle system.

Warm the engine to operating temperature and have the choke valve completely open when adjusting. Start the engine and let it idle. If it stalls, turn the throttle screw in until the engine is running steady without any foot pressure on the accelerator.

The idle mixture should be adjusted to give a smooth idle. Missing is a sign of too lean an idle mixture while rolling or loping indicates too rich a mixture. Turning the screw in leans the mixture. It may be necessary to readjust the idle speed and mixture after the air cleaner is installed.

(Note: late model smog-controlled cars usually have a plastic limiter that restricts the movement of the mixture screw. An acceptable mixture adjustment should be possible within its limits.)

Turn the idle adjusting screw in slowly until the engine is about to stall. At this point, turn the screw out about a half-turn. If the engine seems to race, turn the throttle adjusting screw out slowly until the speed comes down. Once you touch the throttle adjusting screw, you must find the best adjustment for the idle adjusting screw.

Best Way to Check Out your work, if you don't have a tachometer, vacuum gauge, and exhaust analyzer, is by sight, sound, and feel.

Listen to the engine to determine if it is operating at an even and smooth speed. The exhaust sound coming from the muffler should sound like the engine is firing steadily. Check for excessive vibration by seeing how the engine rests on the mounts, and feel the fender.

Cars with automatic transmissions should be adjusted with the least pull on the engine. Be sure the handbrake is set and transmission is in **DRIVE** position when you adjust the idling and throttle screws.

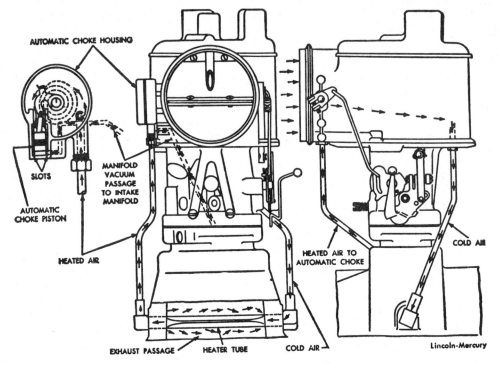

AUTOMATIC CHOKE HOUSING

MANIFOLD
VACUUM
PASSAGE
TO INTAKE
MANIFOLD

SLOTS

AUTOMATIC
CHOKE PISTON

HEATED AIR

HEATED AIR TO
AUTOMATIC CHOKE

COLD AIR

EXHAUST PASSAGE   HEATER TUBE   COLD AIR

Lincoln-Mercury

Drawing shows how the typical in-carburetor piston choke works.

16

Keep Your Automatic Choke Automatic

WHEN THE ENGINE in your car is running at normal temperature, each part of gasoline has to be mixed with about 14 parts air in order to burn in the cylinder combustion chambers. But, when the engine is cold, it needs a richer mixture—more fuel and less air. The choke helps control this mixture.

It is likely, when starting a cold engine, that much of the fuel entering into the carburetor throat is in the form of small drops, and only a small portion of these will be properly vaporized by the time the mixture reaches the cylinder. By enriching the mixture and increasing the proportion of fuel to the proportion of air, sufficient vaporized gasoline can be delivered to the combustion chamber to start your engine and keep it running until the engine warms up enough to work on a normal fuel-air mixture.

Temporary changes in the fuel-air mixture are regulated by the choke plate in the carburetor throat. As the choke plate is closed, more fuel and less air is allowed down the throat.

The Manual Choke. On most older cars and even many late-model economy and sports cars and trucks, temporary choke adjustments are accomplished manually by a pull knob on the dash. Pulling the knob out closes the choke, pushing it in opens the choke.

But manual choking has always been a problem. It is simply too easy to overchoke the carburetor. The threat of overchoking has been removed by the automatic choke, a device which has been put on most cars since the late '40s and early '50s.

The Automatic Choke is a unit which reacts to the engine temperature, by a temperature-sensitive metal coil, which opens and closes the choke plate in response to the action of the metal.

Automatic chokes today utilize some variation of the temperature-sensitive metal coil, and couple a vacuum-controlled piston or vacuum-controlled diaphragm to the choke plate linkage. Until the thermostatic coil becomes warm, its tension is relatively high so that neither the suction effect in the carburetor nor intake manifold is sufficient to overcome the tension, or the tension is high enough to overcome the downward pull of the piston. As the thermostatic metal warms, its tension decreases.

The vacuum-controlled piston or vacuum-controlled diaphragm or piston is connected to the choke linkage in such a way as to oppose the thermostatic coil. The coil tries to keep the choke plate closed; the diaphragm or piston,

Keeping automatic choke's external linkage and choke plate clean is a preventive maintenance job that takes just seconds with an aerosol solvent.

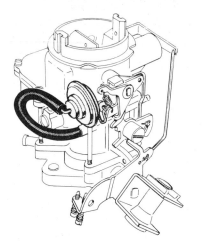

This is carburetor with vacuum diaphragm to pull open the automatic choke, instead of the in-carb piston.

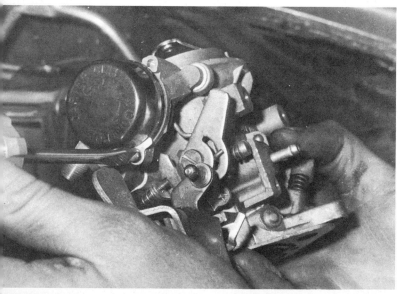

In-carb piston is accessible through plastic cover, which is held by screws. Before disturbing, note alignment mark on top of cover and what it matches up with on carb body.

Cover off (note thermostatic coil in cover). Now remove gasket. Rod projecting from gasket is linked to vacuum piston. When cover is on, rod engages thermostatic coil.

which is being drawn by engine vacuum, tries to pull it open.

As the thermostatic coil tension decreases, the diaphragm or piston pulls on the choke linkage, gradually opening the choke.

The thermostatic coil can be located in either of two places: a cast well in the intake manifold, or in the carburetor itself.

If the coil is in the intake manifold well, there is a rod from the coil up to the carburetor, to the choke linkage.

Current design practice is to use a vacuum diaphragm with the well choke and a piston with the in-carb unit.

The vacuum diaphragm is mounted on the outside of the carburetor, where it can easily be checked and replaced. It is connected to the carburetor base or intake manifold (the source of vacuum) by a short hose.

The piston is inside the choke assembly, just back of the thermostatic coil. A passage in the carburetor runs from the back of the piston to the intake manifold, the source of vacuum.

The hose or tube you see on the outside of the housing for the in-carburetor coil choke is a heat tube. It runs to the intake manifold, and is the source of heat for the thermostatic coil.

Problems With an Automatic Choke. An automatic choke is anything but a foolproof item. Among the things that can go wrong are:

1. sticking linkage.
2. improper adjustment
3. weak thermostatic coil
4. seized thermostatic coil
5. stuck vacuum piston or defective vacuum diaphragm
6. clogged heat tube (in-carburetor coil chokes only)

If the choke fails to close or opens too soon, the car will be very difficult, if not impossible, to start. If the choke sticks closed, the engine will stall and when it does run, the mixture will be overly rich—overchoked.

Left: Pen points to vacuum piston bore. Work piston back and forth, and unless it's absolutely free, spray with solvent until it is. Right: When you put the choke together, make sure cover mark is properly aligned with marks on carb body.

To replace well choke, start by disconnecting link. This one is held by push-on clip.

Rod slides out of well choke thermostatic coil. On cars so equipped, you could bend rod to change adjustment, but if choke coil is weak, replacing it is the thing to do.

Overchoking is a very serious problem. Large quantities of raw gasoline enter the combustion chamber and the excess washes the oil from the cylinder walls, creating unnecessary cylinder wall wear. The extra fuel can flow past the rings and dilute the oil in the crankcase. Diluted crankcase oil may cause rapid wear of bearings and other fast-moving engine parts.

If you suspect trouble with the automatic choke, check its operation before you remove or replace it. Remove the air cleaner from the carburetor so you can see the choke plate in the carburetor throat.

When the engine is cold, the choke plate should be closed. Start the engine. The choke plate should open slightly and, as the engine warms, should open gradually. When the engine reaches the proper operating temperature, the choke plate should be fully open.

If the choke plate opens too soon or too slowly, you can compensate by adjusting the position of the thermostat spring cover. If the choke plate seems extremely slow opening, try this check before you remove the automatic choke. Accelerate the engine quickly, then release. The choke plate should remain in full open position. Close the choke plate with your finger, then release it. It should open immediately. If it does not, the trouble may be caused by a bent or sticky choke plate shaft or a vacuum piston or diaphragm rather than the automatic choke.

Adjustment. If the automatic choke opens too soon or too late, you should be able to make an outside adjustment rather than complete repairs.

Most automatic chokes of the in-carburetor coil type are provided with a system of cover adjustments to control the thermostat spring reaction to engine temperature. By loosening three screws enough to move the choke cover, you can turn the cover left or right and change the spring reaction.

On most covers you will find an arrow marked "lean" pointing to the left. If you move the cover to the left, or to lean position, you will cause the choke to open at a lower engine temperature. If you turn the cover to the right, you will cause the choke to open at a higher engine position. The proper adjustment of the choke for your engine normally is at the mid position, or one line "rich." But if your car experiences any starting problems, check manufacturer's specifications. On some cars the specifications were as high as four lines rich for very cold weather.

The well choke normally requires no adjustment. If you experience hard starting and cold stalling that seems to be accompanied by an early-opening choke, there is an adjustment on some Chrysler Corp. cars.

Undo the screw or screws that hold the well cover, disconnect the rod from the coil to the choke plate and take out the thermostatic coil assembly.

There is a locknut that holds two coil tension indexing plates together. Like the other type of automatic choke, this one has markings. One plate has a notch, the other has calibration lines. If you loosen the locknut, you can realign the marks to increase spring tension, which will lengthen the time required for the choke to open fully.

The normal adjustment is to align the notch with the center calibration line or one line toward more tension. If the choke fails to perform with this adjustment, the coil should be replaced.

Regardless of type of choke, this cannot be overemphasized: a thermostatic coil adjustment is not a cure-all for a weak coil.

Note: On some Chevrolets, the rod from the well coil goes into an elongated hole on the choke linkage. With the choke closed, the top of the rod should be even with the top of the elongated hole on six-cylinder engines. On virtually all V-8s with an elongated hole, the rod should be even with the bottom of the hole.

All moving parts of the automatic choke should be dry and free of dirt. Never oil linkages, for oil collects dirt and causes the parts to stick and eventually bind.

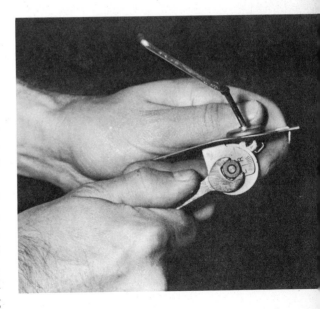

On Chrysler products, you can loosen nut and adjust coil tension. "L" means lean, "R" means rich, and refers to mixture.

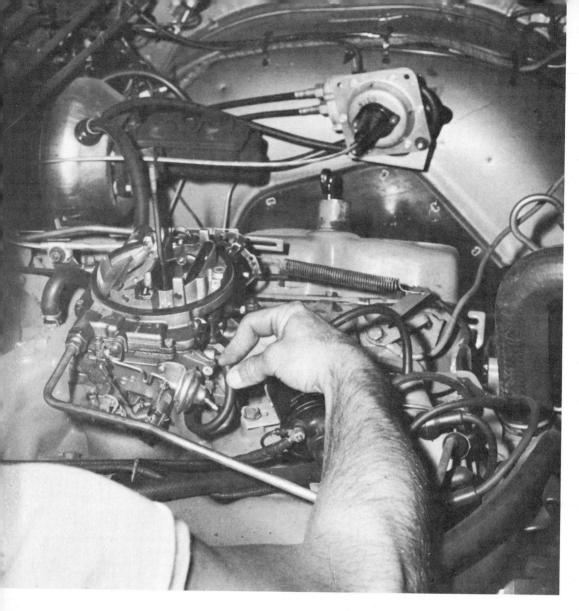

Checking for vacuum with engine idling and vacuum hose disconnected from choke vacuum diaphragm.

The best "tool" for automatic choke service is an aerosol can of choke solvent. As part of every tuneup, spray the external choke linkage clean. Remove the plastic cover on in-carburetor coil chokes and spray the solvent onto the piston and into its bore. Check the piston, which should move back and forth completely freely.

With vacuum diaphragms, the only service is to check the operation of the unit. With the engine cold, start the engine and watch the diaphragm. If it is functioning, it will pull the link to which it is attached and crack open the choke. (The piston does the same thing.)

The cracking open of the choke by the diaphragm or piston gives an engine that has just been started enough air to run at fast idle.

If the vacuum diaphragm does not pull the link, pull off the hose and feel for vacuum. (Engine must be running.) If there is little or none, the hose is clogged or leaking, both very remote occurrences.

More likely, there is vacuum and the diaphragm has become porous, and the assembly must be replaced. This is a simple job since the assembly is held by screws.

The diaphragm or piston must crack the choke open only a specified amount. If the opening is too small, the engine will die for lack of air. If the opening is too great, the fuel mixture will be too lean and the engine will also stall out.

The initial opening of the choke is measured at its widest point, using a drill bit as a feeler gauge (the drill should just fit in). The specification is referred to as the "choke vacuum kick" and varies according to carburetor.

The adjustment on carburetors with external diaphragms is on the link to the choke, which has a U-bend in it. Decreasing the bend lengthens the link and reduces the choke opening. Increasing the bend shortens the link and increases choke opening.

Just disconnect the link and make the appropriate bends with your fingers at the "U."

On in-carburetor coil chokes, there is a link from the choke plate shaft down to the thermostatic coil housing in which the vacuum piston is located. This link will normally have some form of threaded swivel on it to effectively change the length of the link. Lengthening the link reduces choke opening; shortening the link increases it.

Some Ford products with a water-heated choke (you will see the hoses going into it) have an internal diaphragm choke. On this design, there is a diaphragm housing on the side of the choke and an adjusting screw (normally with a cap over it). To adjust this design, remove the cap and turn the adjusting screw in or out as required.

17

How to Rebuild a Four-Barrel Carburetor

FOUR-BARREL CARBS are a lot simpler than most people believe. All it takes to rebuild a four-barrel carb is patience, care, carb solvent and a rebuild kit. Several manfacturers make rebuild kits for four-barrel carbs. Make sure that the kit you buy has complete diagrams and specifications for the carb that is on your engine.

Most carbs can be identified by telling the dealer who sells the rebuild kits the make, model and year of your car and what engine you have, as well as if the car has a stick or auto trans. Most carbs also have code tags attached with all the vital info stamped on them so that identification is simplified.

Rather than give detailed specs for any one carb we have gathered up material that shows how the Carter AFB four barrel carb works and how to make adjustments on it. To round out our coverage and give GM owners assistance, we also have a view of a typical 4GC Rochester four barrel carb and instructions on how to perform adjustments on it. Special tools are helpful but not really needed. If you have a good eye and measure carefully you can do a top notch job.

Before you take the carb off the engine (you should not attempt to rebuild the carb on the engine) clean the carb of grease and grime. Kerosene and a paint brush will do an excellent job of cleaning the outside of the carb. To clean the inside of the carb you will need special solvent. Some of the well-known brands are Gumout, Carb Master, Bendix Carb Cleaner and Gunk.

Be careful when you disassemble the carb that you do not lose any parts. Soak all of the parts, except plastic, rubber or gasket material, in the solvent until the parts are clean. Be careful not to let your hands soak in the carb cleaner as it is a very powerful solvent and will irritate your hands. Most smart mechanics take the parts out of the solvent and flush them with kerosene to make sure that the parts are clean and that they can be handled without irritation. Do not use gasoline to clean the carb as it is very explosive. Be careful when using the carb cleaner. Use it outside or where you have adequate ventilation. Empty coffee cans with the snap-on plastic top make excellent cleaning tanks for carb cleaner.

If compressed air is available, it is a good idea to blow out all of the carb passages to make sure that they are clean.

It is not a good idea to take out the main jets as they often vary from the primary and secondary barrels and sometimes from the right to left side.

The purpose of the float circuit is to maintain an adequate supply of fuel at the proper level in the bowl for use

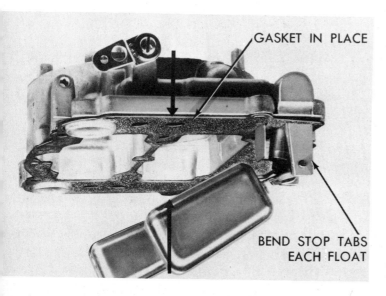

GASKET IN PLACE

BEND STOP TABS EACH FLOAT

Float drop setting. Holding air horn in an upright position, measure distance from top of floats at outer end to the air horn gasket as illustrated (see arrows). This measurement should be ¾-inch. To check float level, invert and measure from top of float to gasket, which should be ⅞₂ inch at outer end. If float drop adjustment is necessary, bend stop tabs on float levers (toward needle seat to reduce drop, away from seat to increase drop). If float level adjustment is necessary, bend float arm.

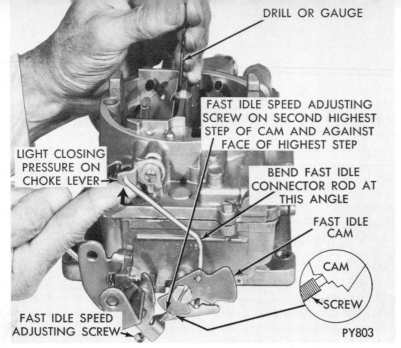

DRILL OR GAUGE

FAST IDLE SPEED ADJUSTING
SCREW ON SECOND HIGHEST
STEP OF CAM AND AGAINST
FACE OF HIGHEST STEP

LIGHT CLOSING
PRESSURE ON
CHOKE LEVER

BEND FAST IDLE
CONNECTOR ROD AT
THIS ANGLE

FAST IDLE
CAM

CAM

SCREW

FAST IDLE SPEED
ADJUSTING SCREW

PY803

Fast idle speed cam position. Fast idle speed is set with engine running, but cam position adjustment can be made off the car, assuring that the speeds of each cam step occur at the proper time. With fast idle speed screw in contact with second highest speed step on cam, move choke valve toward closed position with light pressure on choke shaft lever. Insert #28 drill as shown and there should be light drag. To adjust, bend connector rod.

by the low-speed, high-speed, pump and choke circuits. There are two separate float circuits. Each supplies fuel to a primary low-speed circuit and a primary and secondary high-speed circuit.

Setting the floats to specifications assures an adequate supply of fuel in the bowls for all operating conditions. Special consideration should be given in service to be sure the floats do not bind in their hinge pin brackets or drag against inner walls of bowl.

The intake needle seats of the Carter carb are installed at an angle to provide the best possible seating action of the intake needles. Intake needles and seats are carefully matched during manufacture. Do not use the left needle in the right seat or vice versa. To avoid unnecessary bending, both floats should be reinstalled in their original positions and then adjusted.

The bowls are vented to the inside of the air horn and, on certain models, also to atmosphere. A connecting vent passage effects a balance of the air pressure between the two bowls. Bowl vents are calibrated to provide proper air pressure above the fuel at all times. Baffles are used in the bowls to provide a stable fuel supply for the primary and secondary main jets.

The carburetor bowl and the intake strainer screen should be clean and free of dirt, gum or other foreign mat-

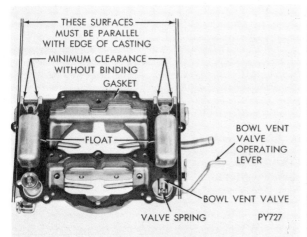

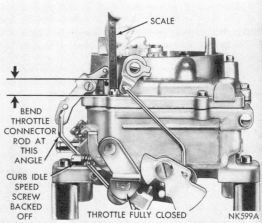

THESE SURFACES MUST BE PARALLEL WITH EDGE OF CASTING

MINIMUM CLEARANCE WITHOUT BINDING

GASKET

FLOAT

BOWL VENT VALVE OPERATING LEVER

VALVE SPRING

BOWL VENT VALVE

PY727

SCALE

BEND THROTTLE CONNECTOR ROD AT THIS ANGLE

CURB IDLE SPEED SCREW BACKED OFF

THROTTLE FULLY CLOSED

NK599A

Left: Float alignment setting. Each float should be parallel to outer cage of air horn casting. If not in alignment, bend float lever by applying pressure to end of float shell with thumb. Right: Accelerator pump adjustment. Move choke valve to wide open position. Back off idle speed screw until throttle valves are fully seated. Measure from top of air horn to top of lever (should be $\frac{7}{16}$-inch). To adjust, bend connector rod.

ter. To assure a positive seal, the gasget surface of the castings must be free of nicks and burrs. An air or fuel leak at these points can result in a mileage complaint and cutting out on sharp turns or sudden stops. A new air horn gasket should be used when reassembling.

Low speed circuit. Fuel for idle and early part throttle operation is metered through the low speed circuit. The low speed circuit is located on the primary side only. Gasoline enters the idle wells through the main metering jets. The low speed jets measure the amount of fuel for idle and early part throttle operation. The air by-pass passages, economizers and idle air bleeds are

carefully calibrated and serve to break up the liquid fuel and mix it with air as it moves through the passages to the idle ports and idle adjustment screw ports. Turning the idle adjustment screws toward their seats reduces the quantity of fuel mixture supplied by the idle circuit.

The idle ports are slot shaped. As the throttle valves are opened, more of the idle ports are uncovered, allowing a greater quantity of the gasoline and air mixture to enter the carburetor bores. The secondary throttle valves remain seated at idle.

All by-passes, economizers, idle ports, idle adjustment screw ports, as well as the bore of the carburetor must be clean and free of carbon. Obstructions will cause poor low speed engine operation. Worn or damaged idle adjustment screws or low speed jets should be replaced.

The low speed jet, air bleed, economizer and by-pass bushings are pressed in place. Do not remove in servicing. If replacement is necessary, use a new venturi assembly. To insure proper alignment of the low speed mixture passage, the primary venturi assemblies were designed with interlocking bosses so they can only be installed in the proper locations. (When the primary venturi assemblies are placed in the wrong side of the carburetor, they will not fit all the way into the casting.)

Air leakage at the gasketed surface surrounding the low speed mixture passages or between the flange and manifold may cause poor idle and low speed operation. Tighten venturi assemblies securely. Always use new gaskets.

To assist in quick hot engine starting on some models, fuel vapor accumulated in the primary and secondary bores is vented to atmosphere through vent passages above throttle valves.

Fuel for part throttle and full throttle operation is supplied through the high speed circuit. On the primary side, the position of the step-up rod in the main metering jet controls the amount of fuel admitted to the nozzles. The position of the step-up rod is controlled by manifold vacuum applied to the vacuum piston.

During part throttle operation, manifold vacuum pulls the step-up piston and rod assembly down, holding the large diameter of the step-up rod in the main metering jet. This is true when the vacuum under the piston is strong enough to overcome the tension of the step-up piston spring. Fuel is then metered around the large diameter of the step-up rod in the jet.

Under any operating condition, when the tension of the spring overcomes the pull of vacuum under the piston, the step-up rod will move up so its smaller diameter or power step is in the jet. This allows additional fuel to be metered through the jet. The step-up rod does not require adjustment.

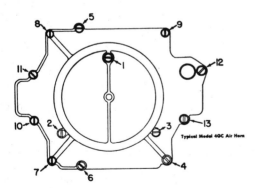

Typical Model 4GC Air Horn

Proper tightening of carburetor air horn screws is essential to good operation. Loose screws or air horn warpage due to excessive screw tightness can cause poor mileage and momentary flooding. First tighten each screw just enough to compress the lock washer, then follow same order and tighten each screw ½ turn more. Here is the tightening sequence for Rochester carb.

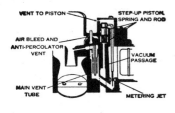

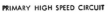

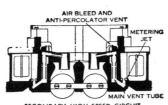

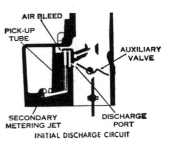

PRIMARY HIGH SPEED CIRCUIT

SECONDARY HIGH SPEED CIRCUIT

INITIAL DISCHARGE CIRCUIT

On the secondary side, fuel for the high-speed circuit is metered at the main metering jets (no step-up rods used). The main vent tubes on primary and secondary sides mix air drawn through the high speed air bleed with the fuel before it passes out of the nozzles.

A clogged air bleed or main vent tube may cause excessively rich mixtures. The high speed bleed and main vent tubes are permanently installed. If replacement is necessary, use a new venturi assembly.

The high speed bleeds also act as anti-percolator vents when a hot engine is stopped or at idling speed. This will help vent fuel vapor pressure in the high speed and idle well before it is sufficient to push fuel out of the nozzles and into the intake manifold.

On models with auxiliary valves, initial discharge ports are incorporated to assist the starting of the fuel flow in the secondary high-speed circuit. These ports are located next to the venturi struts. When the auxiliary valves start to open, the vacuum at the discharge ports pulls fuel into the pick-up tubes. Air bleeds serve to break-up the liquid fuel and mix it with air as it moves through the passages to the initial discharge ports where it is discharged into the air stream. As the auxiliary nozzles deliver additional fuel, less fuel flows from the initial discharge ports.

The secondary throttle valves, on some models, are vacuum controlled. This feature provides the added capacity of the second carburetor only when the engine is able to make use of this capacity. When the accelerator is fully depressed, the secondary valves are cracked open manually a few degrees. Air passing through the primary venturis determines the amount of vacuum applied to the secondary throttle operating diaphragm, by way of the pri-

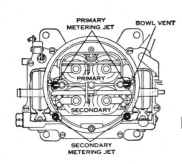

SECONDARY METERING JET

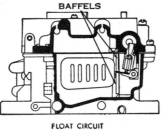

FLOAT CIRCUIT

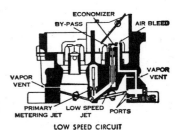

LOW SPEED CIRCUIT

mary vacuum pick-up port. When the vacuum is strong enough to overcome the diaphragm spring, the secondary valves open. A vacuum pick-up port, located in the secondary venturi, supplies vacuum to overcome the partial loss of vacuum at the primary pick-up port, when the secondary valves open. A mechanical over-riding linkage insures that the secondary valves will always close with the primary valves.

Some models use offset valves above the secondary throttle valves. These are called "auxiliary throttle valves." Counterweights are located on the ends of the auxiliary throttle shaft. The auxiliary valve counterweights operate in a recess inside the carburetor body. Throttle valves in the secondary side remain closed, until the primary valves have been opened a predetermined amount. Air velocity through the carburetor controls the position of the auxiliary valves. The auxiliary valves open when the force of the air against the offset valves is able to lift the counterweights.

When the accelerator is fully depressed, only the primary high-speed circuit will function until there is sufficient air velocity to open the auxiliary valves. When this occurs, fuel will also be supplied through the secondary high-speed circuit.

The accelerating pump circuit, located in the primary side, provides a measured amount of fuel necessary to insure smooth engine operation on acceleration at lower car speeds. When the throttle is closed, the pump plunger moves upward in its cylinder and fuel is drawn into the pump cylinder through the intake check. The dis-

charge check is seated at this time to prevent air being drawn into the cylinder. When the throttle is opened, the pump plunger moves downward, forcing fuel out through the discharge passage, past the discharge check, and out of the pump jets. When the plunger moves downward, the intake check is closed, preventing fuel from being forced back into the bowl.

At higher car speeds, pump discharge is no longer necessary to insure smooth acceleration. When the throttle valves are opened a predetermined amount, the pump plunger bottoms in the cylinder eliminating pump discharge.

During the high speed operation, a vacuum exists at the pump discharge ports. To prevent fuel from being drawn through the pump circuit, the pump jets are vented on some models by a cavity between the pump jet restrictions and discharge ports. This allows air instead of fuel to be drawn through the pump discharge ports.

Be sure the pump plunger leather is in good condition and the intake and discharge checks and pump jet are free of lint, gum or other foreign matter. To facilitate service, the intake check ball and seat may be inspected and replaced by removing the screw plug in the face of the flange without complete disassembly of the carburetor.

The Climatic Control circuit of the Carter AFB carb, located in the primary side, provides the correct mixture necessary for quick cold engine starting and warm-up. When the engine is cold, tension of the thermostatic coil holds the choke valve closed. When the engine is started, air velocity

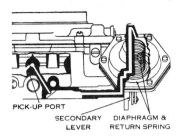

PICK-UP PORT

SECONDARY LEVER   DIAPHRAGM & RETURN SPRING

VACUUM OPERATED SECONDARY

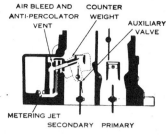

AIR BLEED AND ANTI-PERCOLATOR VENT   COUNTER WEIGHT   AUXILIARY VALVE

METERING JET

SECONDARY   PRIMARY

AUXILIARY VALVE OPERATION

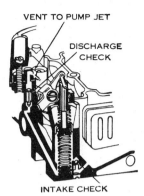

VENT TO PUMP JET

DISCHARGE CHECK

INTAKE CHECK

PUMP CIRCUIT

against the offset choke valve causes the valve to open slightly against the thermostatic coil tension. Intake manifold vacuum applied to the choke piston also tends to pull the choke valve open. The choke valve assumes a position where tension of the thermostatic coil is balanced by the pull of vacuum on the piston, and force of air velocity on the offset valve.

When the engine starts, slots located in the sides of the choke piston cylinder are uncovered, allowing intake manifold vacuum to draw warm air through the Climatic Control housing. This air is heated in a tube running through the exhaust cross-over passage, or a manifold stove. The flow of warm air heats the thermostatic coil and causes it to lose some of its tension gradually, until the choke valve reaches full-open position. If the engine is accelerated during the warmup period, the corresponding drop in manifold

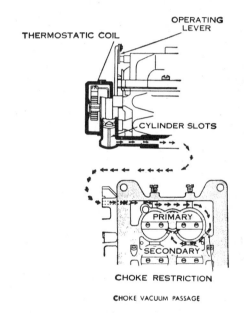

THERMOSTATIC COIL   OPERATING LEVER

CYLINDER SLOTS

PRIMARY

SECONDARY

CHOKE RESTRICTION

CHOKE VACUUM PASSAGE

DASHPOT ARM

UNLOADER LUG

DISCHARGE CHECK

CONNECTOR ROD

DISCHARGE RESTRICTION

DASHPOT

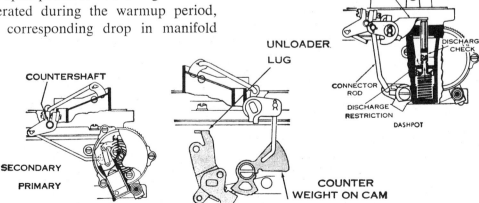

COUNTERSHAFT

SECONDARY

PRIMARY

COUNTERSHAFT LINKAGE

COUNTER WEIGHT ON CAM

FAST IDLE AND UNLOADER LINKAGE

vacuum allows the thermostatic coil to momentarily close the choke, providing a richer mixture.

On some models, to combat engine stalling during warm-up on cool humid days, caused by "carburetor icing," heated air from the choke housing is circulated through the passage in the base of the carburetor flange. The heat transferred helps eliminate ice formation at the throttle valve edges and idle ports.

On some models, to permit lower overall height, a choke countershaft over the secondary bores connects the choke linkage to the choke valve.

The choke shaft and fast idle cam must operate freely without any tendency to stick or bind. Remove gum or dirt accumulation on the choke operating parts.

During the warm-up period, it is necessary to provide a fast idle speed to prevent engine stalling. This is accomplished by a fast idle cam connected to the choke linkage. The fast idle adjusting screw on the throttle lever contacts the fast idle cam and prevents the throttle valves from returning to a normal warm engine idle position, while the Climatic Control is in operation.

If during the starting period the engine becomes flooded, the choke valve may be opened manually to clean out excessive fuel in the intake manifold. This is accomplished by depressing the accelerator pedal to the floor mat and engaging the starter. The unloader projection on the throttle lever contacts the unloader lug on the fast idle cam and in turn partially opens the choke valve.

An internal dashpot is incorporated on some models to slow the closing of the throttle, to prevent stalling on quick deceleration.

When the throttle is opened, the plunger spring pushes the plunger upward. The intake check opens allowing fuel to fill the cylinder below the plunger. When the throttle is closed, the plunger is pushed downward. The intake check is closed and fuel is forced through the discharge restriction, delaying the closing of the throttle valves.

Be sure the plunger leather is in good condition and the intake check and discharge restriction are free of lint, gum or other foreign matter. The plunger shaft must operate freely in its guide in the air horn.

It may be necessary to adjust the dashpot on the car due to engine-transmission combinations and individual driving habits. Be sure dashpot arm does not contact air horn next to plunger shaft at idle. This condition may cause inconsistent idle speeds.

Exploded illustration
shows fuel pump compo-
nents.

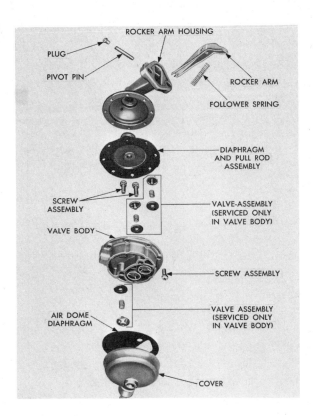

ROCKER ARM HOUSING

PLUG

PIVOT PIN

ROCKER ARM

FOLLOWER SPRING

DIAPHRAGM
AND PULL ROD
ASSEMBLY

SCREW
ASSEMBLY

VALVE-ASSEMBLY
(SERVICED ONLY
IN VALVE BODY)

VALVE BODY

SCREW ASSEMBLY

VALVE ASSEMBLY
(SERVICED ONLY
IN VALVE BODY)

AIR DOME
DIAPHRAGM

COVER

18

Fixing Your Fuel Pump

ONE OF THE easiest of all parts in your car to understand and trouble-shoot is the fuel pump. It is also one of the most important because a faulty pump will cause your engine to run ragged or not at all.

Fuel pumps used in today's cars are primarily (Vega and some sports cars excepted) of the mechanical dia-phragm type. This diaphragm creates pressure inside the pump by pulsating back and forth.

The only difference in mechanical fuel pumps is that some have a vacuum booster section combined with a fuel pump section, while others consist only of the fuel pump.

In combination pumps, the vacuum booster section has nothing at all to do with the fuel system. Its purpose is to operate the windshield wipers by controlling vacuum pressure from the intake manifold. To do this, it is oper-ated by the same pump arm that controls the fuel portion of the pump.

There is one other difference in fuel pumps used in today's cars. Some have the fuel filter built right in, while others have a separate filter tapped into the fuel line between the pump and the carburetor.

Pump Troubles. Fuel pump troubles are limited to four. Either the pump: 1. pumps too little gas; 2. pumps too much gas; 3. leaks gas; or 4. leaks oil.

An oil leak usually is a simple matter to correct by tightening the nuts or screws that hold the pump, or pulling the pump and replacing the gasket.

A gas leak may be coming from the main chamber, which may be cured by tightening the cover screws, or from loose inlet or outlet fittings, which may be corrected by tightening. If tightening fittings doesn't cure a leak at them, they must be replaced.

If your engine refuses to run, or it coughs and falters, the trouble may be that too little fuel is being supplied to the carburetor by the pump. If, on the other hand, your engine is hard to start, idles rough, or you see gas dripping from the carb, the pump may be supplying too much gas or the diaphragm may be ruptured.

Any of these troubles can be caused by any one of a number of other things besides the fuel pump. However, it's a good idea to check the pump first since it is an easy job to do and you can pinpoint the cause of the problem immediately without having to go through a time-consuming inspection of other parts. A bad carburetor, for example, can also cause the kind of trouble just described, but to determine whether it is the cause entails a complete carburetor disassembly.

Test Pressure. A fuel pump is always tested with the pump on the car. The best way to check it is with a fuel pump analyzer (also called a vacuum or pressure tester). This tool records the pressure at which the pump is operating.

Fuel pumps push a large volume of gas per hour to the carburetor when the engine is operated at normal highway speed. The gas flows at a pressure of from as low as $2\frac{1}{2}$ pounds per square inch (psi) to as high as 8 pounds depending on the car.

To accurately check your fuel pump with the gauge, it is necessary to know the exact pressure limits of the pump; check your car's service manual.

To test the pressure limits of your pump, disconnect the fuel line at the carburetor. Attach the proper-sized adapter which you will find in your pressure tester kit, into the line. Screw the pressure gauge hose into the adapter.

Start the engine and let it idle. The gauge should read somewhere within the limits. If so, turn the engine off. The needle on the gauge should remain constant or drift back very slowly toward zero. If it drops back suddenly, something is wrong with the pump.

If the reading is lower than that specified, it means the pump is not pushing out enough gas. If higher, the pump is delivering too much gas.

If pressure is too low, it usually means that one part of the pump is badly worn, several parts are slightly worn, diaphragm is ruptured, valves are dirty, or the valve seats are clogged.

Fuel pump volume test should always follow pressure test.

If pressure is too high, the trouble is probably a tight fitting diaphragm, one that is too strong, or a pump link which is frozen to the rocker arm.

Check Fuel Delivery. In addition to the pressure gauge test, you should also make a fuel capacity test to determine if the pump is delivering the correct amount of fuel to the carburetor. More than likely, if the pump pressure records correctly, the amount of fuel it is delivering is okay. But a malfunction other than the fuel pump can cause fuel capacity to be cut down.

Generally, the pump in a passenger car delivers from ¾ to a full pint of fuel to the carburetor every minute. To test for capacity, disconnect the fuel line at the carburetor and hold a pint measuring cup beneath the open end of the line. Let the engine run a minute to determine whether the proper amount of fuel (¾ to 1 pint) is being delivered.

If the pump isn't delivering enough fuel, the cause of the trouble might lie in the gas tank, in the fuel line system, or in the filter, as well as in the pump itself. First make sure there is gas in the tank.

Replacement Alternatives. Once you have determined that the pump is faulty, you have one of two avenues open to you. If you do your own mechanical work, it would be less expensive to try and rebuild the old pump. If, however, a mechanic does your work, you would be better off installing a new pump since cost of a rebuilt is only a few dollars less than the price of a new one.

There are two types of repair kits available. One is an inexpensive kit which contains a new diaphragm (since this is the most likely part of a pump to go bad), valves, and gaskets. The other is a repair kit which contains all parts for a complete overhaul.

Before purchasing a kit, disassemble the pump to see which part or parts are worn. If it is just the diaphragm,

Left: Rebuilding of pump should include replacement of check valve assembly, to which pen points. Right: Pump arm, to which pen points, should be inspected for wear, and if outer surface (which is in contact with camshaft) is worn, arm must be replaced. In this case, cheapest way is to get new or rebuilt pump, as replacement arms are hard to come by.

the less expensive diaphragm repair kit should be purchased.

Note: On many cars, you don't have a choice when a pump fails. Virtually all Ford products, particularly in recent years, have pumps that can only be disassembled and rebuilt in a factory. And the electric fuel pump in a Vega also is a disposable type.

Repair Procedure. Pump repair, on cars on which it still is possible, starts with pump removal, which is covered in the chapter, "Replacing Engine Parts."

Once the pump is off, discard the gasket between pump and engine.

Before taking the pump apart, remove exterior dirt with solvent and file a mark across the flanges to serve as a guide for reassembly.

Remove the screws that hold the two parts together. The cover has the check valve assembly in it. The lower part has the diaphragm, pump arm spring, pump arm and linkage.

The check valve assembly is nor-

mally held by a simple screw-down retainer. The diaphragm is mounted to a shaft, and the method of retaining this to the pump arm linkage varies from make to make, but the way to disconnect should be obvious. A pin, which can be pulled with pliers, normally retains the pump arm.

The pump arm should be inspected for wear on the side that comes in contact with the camshaft. If worn, it should be replaced.

After making the necessary replacements, reassemble the pump in the reverse way in which you disassembled it. Place it back in the engine, making sure you insert the new gasket between the pump and the engine block. You must also make sure the cam eccentric engages the pump arm in the proper way to prevent a broken arm or link, which can, in turn, cause possible engine damage. The pad of the arm, which is the arm's flat surface, must rest against the cam.

COUNTERWEIGHT VALVE SHAF[T]

VALVE SHAFT

Heat riser is located on exhaust manifold, near intake manifold joint on sixes and near exhaust crossover passage on V-8s.

19

The Heat Riser

ASK ANY KNOWLEDGEABLE weekend mechanic what a manifold heat control valve is, and he will respond with something like, "That's the formal term for a heat riser."

Everyone knows its name, even its nickname. Everyone knows it's there and some even know why it's there. But very few ever service it.

Yet checking and servicing the heat riser, on cars so equipped, should be part of every tuneup. The heat riser is on virtually all engines except some late models with the thermostatic air cleaner, and you will even find it on some late models with thermo air cleaners.

How well the heat riser functions determines how smoothly the engine will perform during the warmup period.

The heat riser is a valve assembly that regulates heating of the intake manifold during engine warmup. It does this by permitting exhaust gases to flow against a predetermined hot spot joint of the exhaust manifold and intake manifold on in-line engines and through the exhaust crossover passage of the intake manifold on V-8 engines.

When the engine is fully warmed up, a thermostatic spring (mounted externally) unwinds, and the flow of exhaust gases pivots the valve to close off the heating of the intake manifold,

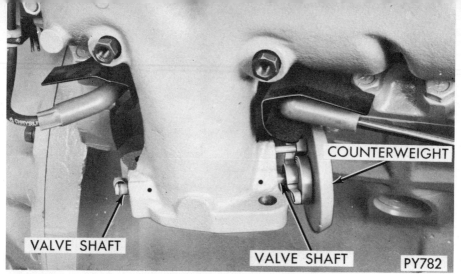

VALVE SHAFT

COUNTERWEIGHT

VALVE SHAFT

PY782

Top: Closeup of valve shows counterweight and thermostatic spring immediately to its left. Left: This Olds Toronado is one of the few cars with an easily accessible heat riser.

and prevent overheating of the air-fuel mixture.

The movement of the valve is gradual (an external counterweight keeps it from fluttering), so as the engine warms up, a smaller and smaller amount of exhaust gas—and less heat —can affect the intake manifold.

Clearly, if the valve sticks in the no-heat position, the engine will sputter along until it warms up.

If the valve sticks in the heat-on position, the air-fuel mixture will be over-

heated and warm-engine performance will drop.

The valve assembly is so designed that when the motorist floors the gas pedal and the engine still is cold, exhaust gas pressure will pivot the valve slightly toward the heat-off position, permitting the engine to gulp a cold, denser air-fuel mixture.

The thermostatic spring is at the rear of the exhaust manifold to keep it out of the air stream through the radiator. This permits the spring to react to the heat radiated from the engine, so it is sensitive to engine warmup, and if it breaks, it can be replaced without removing the exhaust manifold.

The heat riser is not mounted in a particularly convenient location, which is why it is so commonly neglected. The photograph showing how to spray the heat riser with solvent was taken on an Olds Toronado, which is an exception.

However, you can generally get to the heat riser from underneath, and it should be checked.

A simple check doesn't even require touching the assembly. Just start the engine when it is cold, and momentarily give it full throttle. The valve counterweight should move at least a half inch and then return to its normal position.

If the heat riser passes this test, it is operating properly, and requires only a preventive maintenance dousing of the valve shaft with aerosol carburetor cleaner, as illustrated.

If the heat riser fails the test, try to move it back and forth by hand (which is a good double-check even if it passes the test). Grab it by the counterweight and see if there is any binding at all. The heat riser is supposed to be absolutely free—it should be able to flop back and forth.

If it doesn't, start spraying carburetor cleaner, or an equivalent penetrating solvent, onto the valve shaft at the points it enters the exhaust manifold— if possible on both sides.

You may have to tap the counterweight back and forth with a hammer to work in the solvent and free up the shaft. The job may take 15 minutes and is tedious, but the results are worth it.

The thermostatic spring should be checked with the engine cold and warm. It should be firmly against its anchor pin with the engine cold and in the free extended position when the engine is hot.

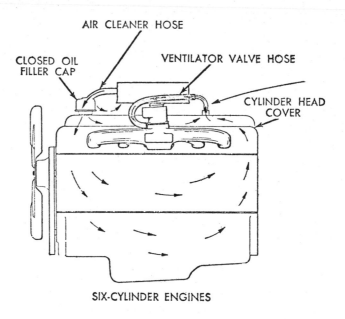

AIR CLEANER HOSE

CLOSED OIL
FILLER CAP

VENTILATOR VALVE HOSE

CYLINDER HEAD
COVER

SIX-CYLINDER ENGINES

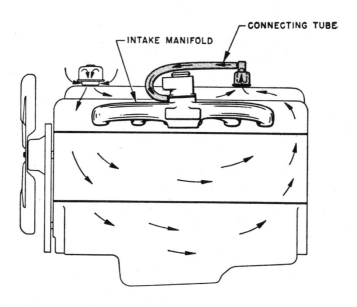

CONNECTING TUBE

INTAKE MANIFOLD

Above is most common type of PCV system. Fumes are drawn from crankcase into intake manifold for reburning. Below is another type of system. Only difference is that a filter is built into the oil filler cap.

20

Pollution Control Systems

DETROIT'S EFFORT TO curb automobile-caused air pollution has spawned a wide assortment of under-hood gadgetry.

Examples include positive crankcase ventilation (popularly called PCV), the air injection system, the thermo-statically-controlled air cleaner, a car-buretor solenoid designed to keep the critically tuned engine from running on after it is turned off, and systems that retard ignition timing at low en-gine speeds (called "vacuum chop-pers").

The first of the antipollution systems was PCV. It was introduced in the early 1960's to replace the road draft tube. With the road draft tube, gas-oline fumes in the crankcase were purged to the atmosphere. PCV in-stead reroutes the fumes from the crankcase back into the engine via the carburetor intake, and from there into the combustion chamber for burning.

The most widely used PCV systems are these: 1) Fresh air is drawn from the air cleaner through a hose into an otherwise closed oil filter cap. The air circulates through the engine, picking up fumes and exhaling them into the PCV valve. The PCV valve regulates the flow of the fumes through a hose into the carburetor air intake (at the carburetor base). Here the fumes mix with the incoming air-fuel charge and go into the combustion chamber for burning. 2) Fresh air is drawn through the filter built into the oil filler cap. This filter usually is made of wire mesh. The air flow through the engine from this point is the same as the first type.

The PCV valve is a spring-loaded device that regulates flow according to manifold vacuum (as vacuum drops, the valve opens further). Clearly, the fumes that flow through the valve de-posit soot on its working parts, and the valve in time will plug. The valve nor-

If possible, disconnect hose at air cleaner, run engine and feel for vacuum at end of hose.

If there is vacuum at other end of system, check at PCV valve. On most cars, valve sits in a grommet in rocker cover. Just pull it out.

mally must be replaced once a year, although this interval can be extended by periodic cleaning with an appropriate solvent.

There is more to servicing PCV than replacing the valve, or even cleaning it. The PCV system should be checked at every available opportunity, for on many cars it will need service at least four times a year, and preferably every two months, particularly as the car ages.

The ventilation system does not change with the age of the vehicle, so its maximum capacity for handling crankcase fumes is fixed. But as the engine wears, more and more unburned fuel blows by the piston rings into the crankcase. A worn engine can deposit three to four times as much unburned gasoline into the crankcase. Therefore, it is important to keep the ventilation system clean and operative, to handle the increasing loads imposed by engine wear.

If the system is poorly maintained, the blowby fumes will condense in the crankcase and dilute the oil, increasing engine wear. The buildup of pressure in the crankcase from the fumes actually can be sufficient to blow engine seals. As a result, suddenly the engine will start to leak oil from everywhere.

More blowby has another effect: it agitates the oil, breaking some of it into droplets, which will mix with the crankcase fumes and be blown out the inlet breather (if the pressure is high enough) or drawn through the PCV valve into the engine. The engine will burn rather large quantities of oil, particularly at higher engine speeds, when blowby reaches a maximum.

With engine running, feel for vacuum at end of PCV valve.

If there is no vacuum at end of PCV valve, place paper tag on oil filler cap neck (cap removed, engine idling). Paper should be sucked against neck and held by crankcase vacuum.

PCV service is also important for two other reasons. 1) Most new car warranties require at least periodic replacement of the PCV valve, and some require frequent checking and cleaning of the valve. 2) The engine is designed to run smoothly with a clean and properly functioning PCV system. If the system malfunctions, the engine performance will be affected; rough idle is one ailment common to engines with malfunctioning PCV.

To check out the two common PCV systems, proceed in this manner. With type 1, run the engine at idle, remove the hose from the air cleaner and place your finger over the hose end. You should feel vacuum. Note: Some PCV systems of this type have an additional filter of wire gauze in the end of the hose. If you just try to pull off the hose, without removing the filter first, you will damage the molded end of the hose. Take off the air filter cover, remove the regular element and check for the presence of this gauze filter. If it is there, clean it and refit after checking the entire system.

If you feel vacuum at the end of the hose, proceed directly to the PCV valve. On most cars, it can be pulled out of the rocker cover. Shake the valve and if it rattles, it is all right. Just clean it with special solvent, using the procedure discussed later in this section. If the valve doesn't rattle, try cleaning it, and if cleaning doesn't work, install a new valve.

If you do not feel vacuum at the end of the hose disconnected from the air cleaner, pull off the oil filter cap, and again run the engine at idle. Place a piece of paper over the oil filter tube and within a few seconds it should be sucked against the tube. If this happens, the hose to the air cleaner is plugged, probably because of contamination from heavy blowby fumes that are backing up through the system and /or plugging somewhere else in the PCV system. Replace the hose. If the engine is old, there is not much you can do about the cause of this condition except check the PCV system frequently.

At this point, let's introduce the checking procedure for the type 2 system. Remove the oil filler cap and look at the wire mesh filter. If it's dirty, clean it in solvent and let it air dry (or blow it dry with compressed air). Then make the same test as with the type 1 system, using the piece of paper over the oil filler tube with the engine idling. From this point, the checking and service procedure for both systems is the same.

If the paper is not sucked against the oil filler tube, disconnect the PCV valve from the rocker cover or engine valley cover (wherever it is mounted). Or if the valve is mounted at the carburetor, disconnect the hose connection at the rocker cover or engine valley cover.

With the engine idling, place your finger over the end of the valve or hose, and you should feel vacuum. If there is none, check the hose for plugging. If the hose is good, remove the valve completely and check for vacuum at the carburetor base. If there is vacuum

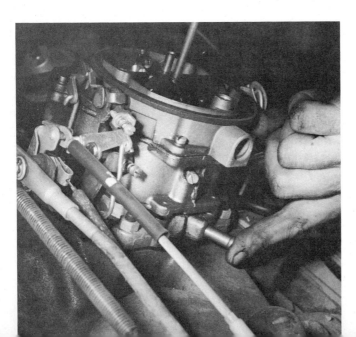

If there is no vacuum anywhere, check hose neck at base of carburetor. If vacuum is weak with engine running, neck may be clogged. Clean with a drill.

here, the valve is plugged and must be cleaned or replaced.

If there is no vacuum at the carburetor base, the carburetor vacuum passage is clogged. Remove the carburetor and clean the passage by dunking the lower end in solvent and cleaning the neck with a small drill bit. Select a drill bit that will not remove any metal, and hand turn the bit through the neck. Even if the system checks out, the valve should be cleaned. The best way is with one of the special cans of solvent designed for the job. Such cans have a tapered spout for insertion into the valve.

With the engine off, disconnect the hose or valve at the rocker cover or engine valley cover (as you did to check for vacuum). By leaving the vacuum side connected (at the carburetor base), the solvent will be drawn through the valve, cleaning it, when you run the engine.

Insert the solvent can spout into the open end of the PCV valve, and work it back and forth against the spring-loaded plunger while squirting a few shots of solvent into the valve interior. Note: if the valve is mounted on the carburetor, and merely squirting solvent into the hose doesn't clean and free up the valve, disconnect the hose

PCV valve can be cleaned with special solvent, as shown. If solvent fails to free up valve, it should be replaced. Good preventive maintenance practice is to replace valve once a year, and clean with solvent six months later.

at the other end and work the solvent in against the spring-loaded plunger.

Now start the engine and let it idle. Squirt a few more shots of solvent into the valve, reconnect it and let the engine run for a few more minutes to evaporate the solvent. PCV puts a tremendous strain on the regular air filter in most PCV systems which have the hose connected to the air cleaner. So check the air filter element frequently as part of your PCV checkout.

SERVICE ANTI-POLLUTION SYSTEMS

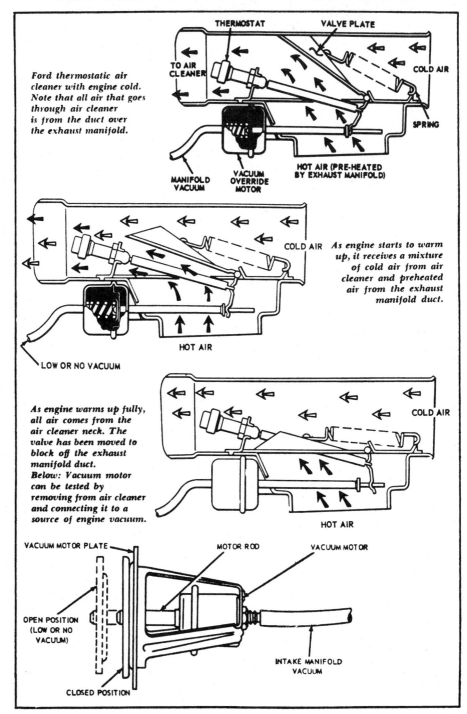

Ford thermostatic air cleaner with engine cold. Note that all air that goes through air cleaner is from the duct over the exhaust manifold.

THERMOSTAT

VALVE PLATE

TO AIR CLEANER

COLD AIR

SPRING

MANIFOLD VACUUM

VACUUM OVERRIDE MOTOR

HOT AIR (PRE-HEATED BY EXHAUST MANIFOLD)

COLD AIR

As engine starts to warm up, it receives a mixture of cold air from air cleaner and preheated air from the exhaust manifold duct.

HOT AIR

LOW OR NO VACUUM

As engine warms up fully, all air comes from the air cleaner neck. The valve has been moved to block off the exhaust manifold duct.
Below: Vacuum motor can be tested by removing from air cleaner and connecting it to a source of engine vacuum.

COLD AIR

HOT AIR

VACUUM MOTOR PLATE

MOTOR ROD

VACUUM MOTOR

OPEN POSITION (LOW OR NO VACUUM)

INTAKE MANIFOLD VACUUM

CLOSED POSITION

21

Thermostatic Air Cleaners

THE THERMOSTATICALLY-CONTROLLED air cleaner was originally conceived to improve cold engine operation, and is now part of the anti-air pollution package on Ford, GM and Chrysler products. (Chrysler uses the GM device.)

The Ford and GM units do the same thing (although in somewhat different ways). They duct intake air over the exhaust manifold to preheat it for better combustion when the engine is cold. They keep the intake air at a temperature of about 100 degrees F. until the engine warms up. Each has a vacuum override system that bypasses the duct and opens the regular air cleaner neck or snorkel on hard acceleration. When the engine warms up, all the air comes from the air cleaner neck or snorkel.

The Ford system has a thermostatic assembly that holds a valve in the air cleaner intake neck so that exhaust-manifold-heated air flows into and through the air filter. As the engine warms, heating the air in the engine compartment, the thermostatic assembly lengthens, and through linkage, pivots the valve to restrict (and finally close) the opening to the duct over the exhaust manifold. The valve also can be pivoted by a vacuum-diaphragm device that is spring-loaded. When the throttle is floored, the manifold vacuum drops, and the spring-loaded device pushes on another link to pivot the valve. But the basic action is the same in both situations: the valve closes against the exhaust manifold duct and opens the air cleaner intake neck or snorkel.

Except for this vacuum override, the pivoting of the valve is gradual, and in the middle of engine warmup, the air that goes into the carburetor is a mixture of preheated air from the exhaust manifold cut and colder air entering through the air cleaner intake neck or snorkel.

To check the system, start with the engine cold and off, and an air temperature of no more than 85-95 degrees F. The air cleaner intake neck or snorkel should be closed off by the valve. If it isn't closed, the linkage is binding or the thermostatic unit is defective.

As the engine warms up, the valve should move, closing off the duct for the exhaust manifold preheated air. If it doesn't, the thermostat is defective, the linkage is binding or the vacuum override is defective. The simplest procedure is to check the linkage first, then the vacuum device, and if they are good replace the thermostatic assembly.

Before the engine fully warms up, open the throttle. This will cause man-ifold vacuum to drop, and the spring in the vacuum device should force the valve to move and open the air cleaner intake neck. If it doesn't, check for 15 inches of vacuum at the hose connection to the vacuum device (using a vacuum-fuel pressure gauge, available for $5 or less at auto supply stores).

Low or no vacuum indicates a bad hose or connection. If vacuum is good, check the vacuum device. Remove the vacuum device from the air cleaner and connect it to a source of vacuum on the engine. (There should be one at the carburetor base, such as the PCV hose neck.) With vacuum applied, the device's link should be held against the entire assembly. Disconnect the hose and it should spring outward about a half inch. The vacuum device (called a "motor" by Ford) is not normally rebuildable. Replace it if it is defective.

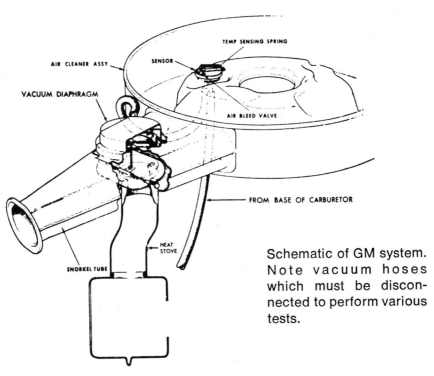

TEMP SENSING SPRING

AIR CLEANER ASSY

SENSOR

VACUUM DIAPHRAGM

AIR BLEED VALVE

FROM BASE OF CARBURETOR

HEAT STOVE

SNORKEL TUBE

Schematic of GM system. Note vacuum hoses which must be disconnected to perform various tests.

When the engine is fully warm, the valve should close off the exhaust manifold duct and open the air cleaner intake neck. Just look into the air cleaner neck and see if it is open. Note: if the vacuum device operates the linkage and moves the plate, the linkage obviously is good. If a good vacuum device fails to move the linkage, it is binding. Free up linkage by working in a good solvent. (The aerosol type used for carburetor linkage is ideal for this purpose.) If the linkage is free and the vacuum device works outside the air cleaner, any defect in the system can be traced to the thermostatic unit.

The GM system, like the Ford, uses a pivoting valve in the air cleaner intake neck and the valve is connected by linkage to a vacuum diaphragm device. But here the similarity ends. The GM system incorporates a temperature sensor inside the air cleaner housing. When the engine is off, a spring inside the vacuum diaphragm device holds the valve against the exhaust manifold air duct. When the engine is started cold, vacuum passes through the sensor into the vacuum diaphragm device, opening the exhaust manifold air duct and closing off the air cleaner intake neck. As the sensor heats up, it bleeds off vacuum to the atmosphere, and the pressure of the spring against the diaphragm inside the vacuum device moves the valve to close the exhaust manifold air duct.

On GM cars with double-snorkel air cleaners and four-barrel carburetor, only one snorkel has the temperature sensitive arrangement and one duct over the exhaust manifold. The other has a vacuum diaphragm controlled

Top: Pivoting valve of GM system. Valve should be open (as shown) when engine is warm and running. When engine is cold, valve should close air cleaner snorkel. Above: Air cleaner element removed. Vacuum sensor is at upper left, near center depression in air cleaner base.

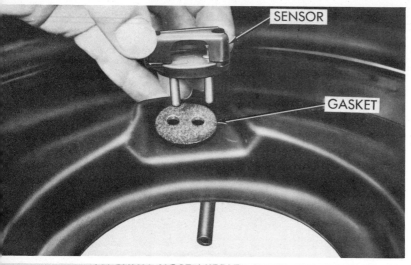

SENSOR

GASKET

Removing vacuum sensor from GM system (on Chrysler products).

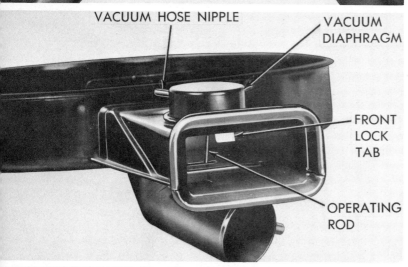

VACUUM HOSE NIPPLE

VACUUM DIAPHRAGM

FRONT LOCK TAB

OPERATING ROD

Closeup of vacuum diaphragm assembly from Chrysler products.

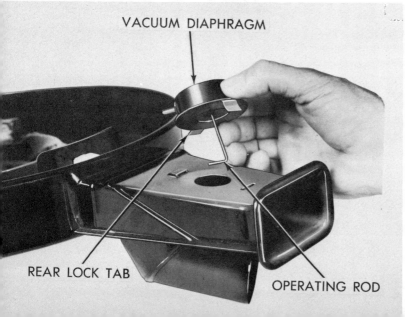

VACUUM DIAPHRAGM

REAR LOCK TAB

OPERATING ROD

Removing vacuum diaphragm from Chrysler products.

valve and it closes off the snorkel. When the throttle is opened, manifold vacuum drops and a diaphragm spring forces open the valve to admit additional air for higher performance. The second snorkel works this way whether the engine is hot, cold or in-between.

To check the GM system, proceed as follows: With the engine cold and not running, the air cleaner intake neck should be open. Start the engine and one valve should close. As the engine warms up, that valve should move and cover the exhaust manifold air duct (which you will not be able to see), opening the air cleaner intake neck (which you will be able to see).

Before the engine fully warms, open the throttle, which will cause manifold vacuum to drop. The thermostatically-controlled valve should open (so should the other snorkel's valve on double-snorkel setups).

If the valve is in the wrong position with the engine off, the cause is binding linkage or a defective spring in the vacuum device. If the valve fails to close the air cleaner intake neck when the cold engine is started, check for at least eight inches of vacuum at the end of the hose that connects the carburetor base or intake manifold to the sensor in the air cleaner. Less than this amount of vacuum indicates a defective hose or connection.

If vacuum is good at the sensor, check it at the vacuum device hose connection. If it is low, check the hose, and if this is good, replace the sensor. Adequate vacuum at this hose, combined with failure of the valve to move when the engine is started, indicates a leaking vacuum diaphragm device. Reconnect the hose and pinch it firmly (or kink it) to trap vacuum. The valve in the air cleaner neck should close off with the vacuum applied. If the valve doesn't do this, or if the valve starts to open with the hose firmly pinched or kinked, a leaking diaphragm is likely. This test is excellent as a general check of the vacuum device, as it will spot a minor leak before it becomes major.

Checking the snorkel valve that responds only to vacuum changes is simple. With the engine idling, the snorkel should be closed off by the valve. Open the throttle (causing manifold vacuum to drop) and the valve should swing open. If you have an engine with a two-barrel carburetor and a double-snorkel air cleaner, one snorkel is strictly jazz. It's blocked off by a plate and that plate won't move.

There are all sorts of special thermometers and time-consuming techniques for checking thermostatic air cleaners to see if they are right within specifications. But the specifications are reasonably wide, and if the unit is out of specifications, the condition will probably show up with the engine dying immediately after starting, carburetor icing or poor gas mileage that can't be traced to something else.

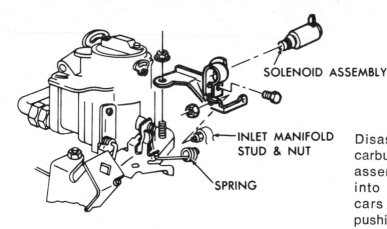

SOLENOID ASSEMBLY

INLET MANIFOLD
STUD & NUT

SPRING

Disassembled view of carburetor with solenoid assembly. Solenoid fits into bracket. On some cars it is adjusted by pushing through bracket; on others, solenoid rod is threaded for adjustment.

22

Carburetor Solenoid

THE CARBURETOR SOLENOID, designed to keep the engine from running on after you shut it off, was introduced on Ford and GM cars to deal with a condition that was occurring as a result of carburetion and ignition modifications made to reduce air pollution. Current engines in many cases are so sensitive they will "diesel" (run with the ignition shut off) if they are just a hair out of tune, or if they have been run a bit hard on a warm day.

The idea of the solenoid (called an anti-dieseling solenoid by GM and a throttle modulator by Ford) is to allow the throttle plate to close more completely. (It normally is held slightly open by the throttle stop screw.) The solenoid is mounted on the carburetor and has a plunger that extends and retracts.

When the engine is running at hot idle, the solenoid bears against the throttle linkage to hold the throttle plate open the amount necessary to maintain engine idle speed. When the engine is shut off, the plunger is retracted by a spring, and the throttle can close further. This further closing of the throttle shuts off the air supply to the cylinders, to prevent the engine from continuing to run.

The solenoid must be checked carefully and adjusted if necessary, as part of a carburetor idle speed and mixture adjustment. First check to see if the plunger moves forward when the engine is started and retracts completely when the engine is turned off. If it fails to do both, and the wire to the solenoid is electrically "hot," the solenoid is defective and must be replaced. To check

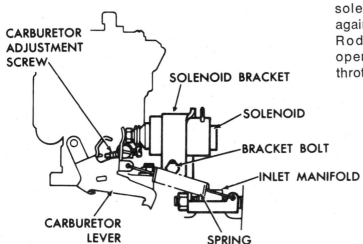

CARBURETOR ADJUSTMENT SCREW

SOLENOID BRACKET

SOLENOID

BRACKET BOLT

INLET MANIFOLD

CARBURETOR LEVER

SPRING

This view shows how solenoid rod bears up against throttle linkage. Rod can hold throttle open, but cannot open throttle by itself.

the wire, just disconnect it and with the ignition on, scratch the terminal against a carburetor nut. It should spark if it is electrically hot. If the wire is defective, run a new wire from the ignition switch to the solenoid terminal. If the wire is hot and the solenoid doesn't move, it is defective and must be replaced.

Now let's look at solenoid operation so we can see how to adjust the plunger. When the engine is cold-started, of course, it runs at fast idle, and the fast idle speed is determined by the position of the fast idle cam. Until the engine warms up, the fast idle cam and the adjustment of its stop screw will control engine idle speed and prevent stalling.

With the engine fully warmed up, the solenoid plunger should bear against the throttle linkage and the idle speed should be at specifications. If the solenoid wire is disconnected, the idle speed should drop markedly as the throttle closes, and the engine may even stall. These conditions indicate a correctly adjusted solenoid.

With this second test, the solenoid plunger will not reopen the throttle to the prescribed idle speed with the wire reconnected. Slowly open the throttle manually and then release it. The solenoid should hold the idle speed, even if it is unable to force the throttle linkage open by the force of the plunger movement.

If the solenoid must be replaced, or requires readjustment, here's how to do the job. On General Motors cars, to install a new solenoid, attach the solenoid bracket to the carburetor and close the throttle (choke should be off). Start the engine and set idle speed to specifications with the low speed throttle stop screw. Attach the wire to the solenoid and start it into its retaining bracket.

With the engine running, the solenoid plunger will be extended. Turn the plunger adjusting screw out two full turns from the bottomed position in the plunger. Slide the solenoid further into the bracket so that the plunger just lightly comes in contact with the carburetor lever. Tighten the bracket strap to hold the solenoid firmly. Back out the low speed throttle stop screw about one turn (counterclockwise). Then proceed with a normal idle adjustment to the specified speed.

On Ford products with one-barrel Autolite carburetor, slacken the locknut and turn the solenoid in or out of the bracket, with engine running, to obtain the specified idle speed. Disconnect the solenoid hot wire (retracting the plunger), then adjust the low-speed throttle stop screw to obtain specified idle speed. Reconnect the wire, open the throttle manually, and the plunger should hold the specified idle speed without stalling the engine.

On Ford products with one-barrel Carter carburetor, turn the plunger screw in or out to obtain specified engine idle speed. Disconnect the solenoid hot wire (retracting the plunger), then adjust the low speed throttle stop screw to obtain specified idle speed. Reconnect the solenoid wire and as with the Autolite carburetor, open the throttle slightly by hand and the plunger should maintain the idle speed to specifications. Unlike other carburetors, the solenoid hot wire is disconnected near the harness, not at the solenoid itself.

"A.I.R." SYSTEM

23

The Air Pump

IT MAKES GOOD sense, during routine tuneup and maintenance work on automobile engines, to service those components which may, if gone unchecked, contribute to inefficient engine operation and air pollution. One such component is the air injection system *(Fig 1.)*. This system forces clean air into the engine's exhaust ports where it combines with any unburned fuel that gets past the valves. The result is complete combustion in the exhaust system.

Engineers at Champion Spark Plug Company's Technical Services Department recommend that the air injec-

tion hoses and connections be checked for condition and proper fit whenever the crankcase oil is changed. A faulty injection system, if not corrected immediately, can cause backfiring, overheated spark plugs and excessive emissions into the atmosphere. Regular servicing prevents this and takes only minutes. However, to better understand complete servicing techniques, the accompanying illustrations describe the air injection system and how it works.

Fig 2. The pump itself is a belt-driven, rotary vane device which is located near the front of the engine. The pump

AIR PUMP AND FILTER

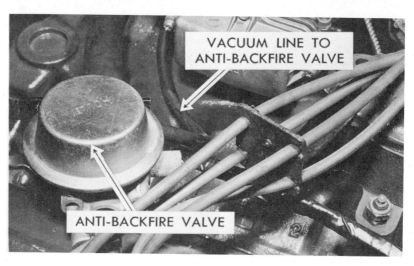

VACUUM LINE TO ANTI-BACKFIRE VALVE

ANTI-BACKFIRE VALVE

rarely gives trouble, unless some physical damage occurs such as a broken or bent housing caused by applying a pry bar during belt tightening. During high engine speeds, excess air pressure escapes through a relief valve fitted to the pump. The air filter which serves the pump may be a separate pleated paper element attached to a hose leading to the pump, or a plastic end paper insert within the pump housing behind the drive pulley. On some engines, air is drawn to the pump through the carburetor air cleaner itself.

Fig 3. The anti-backfire valve is installed near the carburetor. When the driver takes his foot from the accelera-

tor, causing intake manifold vacuum to rise suddenly, this valve diverts air from the pump to one of three locations, depending on the manufacturer. One sends the air into the intake system, another into the carburetor air cleaner, and the third directly into the atmosphere, rather than sending it to the exhaust. By temporarily "leaning-out" the excessively-rich mixtures encountered on "overrun," better combustion is encouraged in the cylinders. If the extra fuel were allowed to burn in the exhaust system, annoying backfires would result.

Fig 4. The check valve is installed in the hoses leading to the cylinder

CHECK VALVE

AIR DISTRIBUTION MANIFOLD

heads, or on the air distribution manifolds where these hoses attach, to prevent the backflow of exhaust gases into the anti-backfire valve and pump.

Fig 5. The air distribution manifolds. On some engines, passages are cast into the cylinder heads to affect the air delivery. On most engines there are separate steel tubes that conduct air to the individual air delivery tubes.

Before servicing the air injection system, the engine should be at normal operating temperature. The first step is to check the air output by removing the hose at the air distribution manifold. If air streams out of the hose at fast engine idle, the system, at least

up to the check valve, is probably in good condition.

Next, with the engine off, disconnect the air supply hose at the check valve and visually inspect the position of the valve plate inside the valve body. Normally, it should be lightly positioned against the valve seat away from the air manifold. Depress the valve plate with a probe. When released, it should return to the original position. Start the engine, and at fast idle, watch for exhaust gas leakage at the check valve. If a leak is present, the valve should be replaced.

A check should also be made of the anti-backfire valve or air bypass valve.

With the engine off, remove the hose connected at the bypass valve, between the bypass and the air manifold check valve. Then, with engine at normal idle, check to see that air is flowing from the air bypass valve hose connection. To duplicate the bypass circle, pinch off the vacuum hose for about five seconds. When released again, air flow through the air bypass valve should diminish or stop momentarily.

Reconnect the hose and remove the *vacuum* supply hose to the air bypass at the bypass valve connection. A vacuum gauge and a tee connection are required. With the engine at idle, the vacuum reading should be the same with the hose connected only to the gauge as it is when connected to the air bypass valve. If not, the valve should be replaced.

On systems equipped with a separate stationary filter, or on systems equipped with a rotating filter behind the drive pulley, replace the air filter at 24,000 miles or two-year intervals, whichever comes first. Some systems are fed through the carburetor air cleaner, and replacing that filter at the recommended periods will keep the air injection system operating satisfactorily.

On units with a plastic or paper element located at the end of a hose leading to the pump, just remove the wingnut and install a new filter element. On air injection systems employing the rotating filter, first remove the drive pulley, then pry out the plastic filter with a screwdriver. Precautions should be taken so that broken pieces of the filter do not fall into the air pump itself.

Once the rotating filter is removed, put the new filter assembly on the hub to start the installation. Then tighten the pulley bolts to drive the filter firmly into place. A slight squeaking sound may be evident for a short time while the engine is running but will disappear when the new filter wears in.

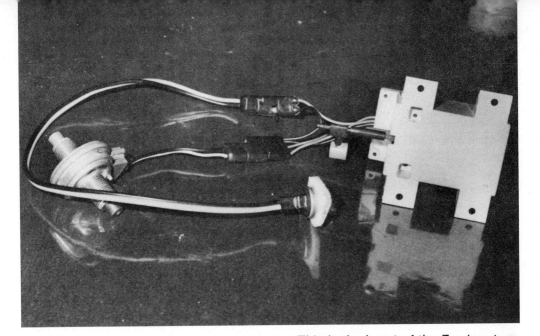

This is the heart of the Ford system, a speed sensor on the left, and an electronic-controller on the right. The electronic unit has vacuum ports and a solenoid.

24

Servicing the Vacuum Choppers

CAN A BROKEN speedometer cable cause an engine to run as if it has tired blood? On a Ford product, it may.

To meet Federal exhaust emission requirements, all the car manufacturers have been using special systems to chop off the ignition system's vacuum advance under certain operating conditions. The vacuum choppers were introduced in 1970.

The car makers found that by retarding the spark advance under many low-speed and idle conditions, they could reduce the amount of unburned gasoline spewed out by the exhaust system into the atmosphere.

Ford's system uses a speed sensor in series with the speedometer cable and a temperature sensor in the door jamb to regulate an electronic module that switches the vacuum advance on or off.

Ford's sensor actually is a tiny generator that produces a voltage directly proportional to road speed. Located under the dash, it is in series with a two-piece speedometer cable between the speedometer head and the transmission. On cars with automatic speed control, an adapter joins the speed control sensor and the vacuum advance sensor.

The system is so designed that it chops vacuum advance below 23 mph on deceleration and below 18 mph on acceleration, if ambient air temperature is above 58 degrees F. If it's below 58 degrees, a switch in the temperature sensor overrides and restores vacuum advance. (Otherwise the engine would buck on cold driveaway.)

If the speedometer cable snaps, the vacuum advance will always be off, and engine performance will drop noticeably. If the ambient temperature sensor switch fails, below 58 degrees there will be no vacuum advance under 18 mph on acceleration. Again, performance would be poor.

To check out the system, you need a vacuum gauge, which should be connected to the vacuum hose or tubing that attaches to the distributor vacuum advance.

The rear wheels of the car should be raised off the ground and the car should be supported on safety stands with the front against a wall. (Do not try this with a bumper jack on the rear.)

Start the engine and with the transmission in neutral, the vacuum reading should be zero. Shift into Drive and the reading should remain zero. Have

Schematic of Ford system shows how the parts are connected. The "PVS" valve is a thermostatic control valve in the water jacket.

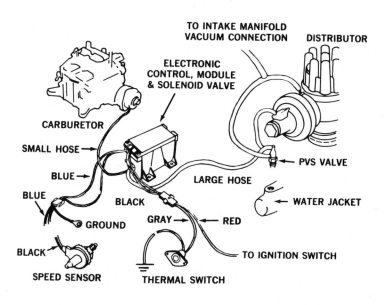

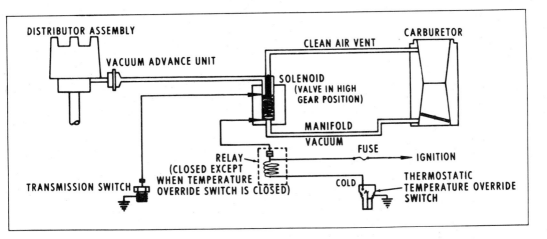

Schematic of GM transmission-controlled spark system (TCS).

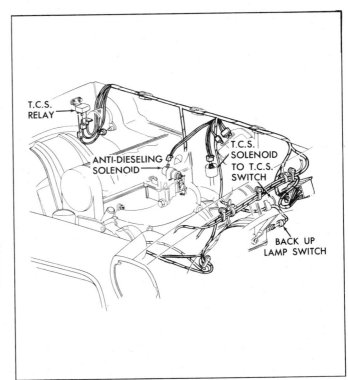

Engine compartment drawing shows typical layout of TCS relay and solenoid.

someone depress the gas pedal until the speedometer indicates a road speed in the mid-twenties. Vacuum readings should begin to occur at somewhere between 21 and 25 mph, and above 25 mph there should be at least six inches of vacuum. As your helper takes his foot off the gas pedal, vacuum should drop to zero by 15 mph on the speedometer.

This test is valid only when air temperature is above 58 degrees. When it is below 58 degrees, there should be vacuum advance at idle and low speed.

Lack of vacuum at 25 mph and above could be a bad electrical connection, loose hose, etc. But if the speedometer doesn't work, replacing the cable should also cure the problem with the vacuum advance.

If cable and wire connections and vacuum hoses are apparently good, the problem is probably a defective speed sensor in the cable. If the system fails to restore vacuum below 58 degrees at low speed and idle, the probable cause is a defective door jamb thermal switch.

GM cars use a system that chops the vacuum advance in first and second gears on all transmissions, including the manuals.

First and second gear are basically acceleration gears and emissions during low-speed acceleration are a significant part of the total.

The control of the vacuum advance is regulated by a solenoid switch that is energized by a switch in the valve body of the automatic transmission.

The system is designed so there is normally no vacuum to the distributor vacuum advance. When the transmission shifts into high gear, the hydraulic valve in the transmission valve body that moves to effect the shift also closes a switch.

This completes the circuit in the solenoid, which closes, permitting vacuum to reach the distributor.

On manual transmissions, the switch that completes the solenoid circuit is attached to the transmission linkage.

The GM system also incorporates a low-temperature override, so there is vacuum advance in all gears until the engine warms up. This is done by means of a relay between the solenoid and a water temperature sensor. When temperature is low, the sensor triggers the relay which energizes the solenoid, providing vacuum to the distributor.

The temperature sensor on some cars is also designed to actuate the relay when engine temperature is too high, generally 230 degrees F. Providing full vacuum at this temperature makes the engine idle faster, speeding up the fan and improving water pump operation.

The check for the GM system is basically the same as for the Ford. The rear wheels must be off the ground and the front of the car should be against a wall.

Someone must run the car at a simulated 30-35 mph, when the automatic transmission will shift into high gear. On manual transmission cars, the shift into third gear can be made when the speedometer indicates 10 miles per hour. Connect a vacuum gauge to the vacuum line attached to the distributor. There should be no vacuum advance on a warm engine until the transmission is in third gear.

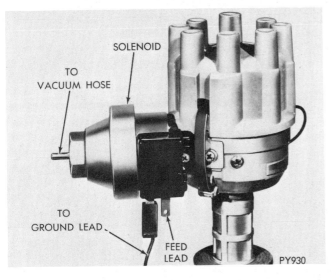

Chrysler distributor with solenoid control. Device with ground lead connected (and terminal for electrical feed lead) is the electronic module that controls the solenoid.

SOLENOID

TO VACUUM HOSE

TO GROUND LEAD

FEED LEAD

PY930

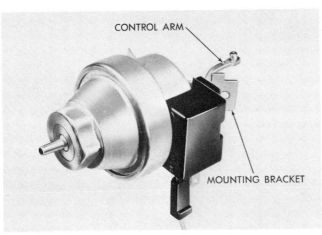

CONTROL ARM

MOUNTING BRACKET

Closeup of solenoid and electronic module assembly shows control arm (which connects to distributor breaker plate) and the mounting bracket.

On a cold engine, there should be vacuum in all gears.

Note: on a six-cylinder engine, there will be only a small amount of vacuum at idle speed and low temperature because of the location of the vacuum port. Open the throttle slightly and see if the vacuum reading increases.

Checking for specific defects requires the services of a professional mechanic, but you can at least check for a blown fuse, loose hose or wire.

The Chrysler system uses an electronic module with a solenoid attached to the distributor vacuum advance and a special switch on the carburetor linkage.

The system is designed to retard ignition timing when the throttle is fully closed and off the fast idle cam.

There are three connections to the Chrysler vacuum advance assembly: a vacuum hose, a wire that carries current from the alternator field circuit to

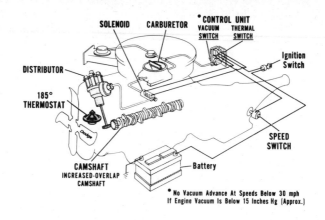

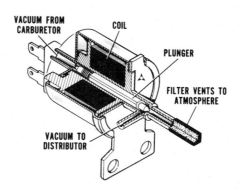

Top: Chrysler's speed-controlled vacuum chopper system is shown in this schematic. Above: Closeup of Chrysler speed-controlled chopper system valve assembly, which is solenoid controlled. Unit prevents distributor vacuum advance from working below 30 mph if engine vacuum is below 15 inches.

operate the electronic module, and a ground wire.

The ground wire is connected to the switch at the carburetor throttle stop screw.

To check the system, run the engine at idle and disconnect the ground wire connection at the carburetor. Ignition timing should advance at least five degrees; check this with a timing light. If you don't have a timing light, listen to the engine. Its speed should increase as the vacuum advance kicks on.

Chrysler products also are using a speed controlled vacuum chopper similar to Ford's. The Chrysler system eliminates vacuum advance at speeds below 30 mph if engine vacuum is below 15 inches.

As the car makers work to meet Federal emission regulations, they will be using more and more "gadgets" to more precisely tailor engine operation. You might as well start getting used to them now.

Checking anti-freeze concentration with a hydrometer.

25

ABC's of Flush and Fill

DRAINING THE COOLING system twice a year has been standard operating procedure for as long as most weekend mechanics can remember. Drain in the late spring and fill with water and rust inhibitor; drain in the fall and fill with anti-freeze.

However, that system is "down the drain." The anti-freeze and cooling system chemicals committee of the Automotive Division of the Chemical Specialties Manufacturers Association summed up modern practice in a detailed recommendation on cooling system care. The recommendation was distributed to the professionals, and now is here for weekend mechanics.

"The modern engine is designed to maintain efficient operating temperatures year-round with ethylene glycol (permanent anti-freeze) solutions. New cars have factory-installed ethylene glycol anti-freeze coolant which will afford freezing protection adequate for most areas of the country and which contains corrosion inhibitors to protect the cooling system. Under recommended service conditions, this anti-freeze coolant will function for at least one year." (Goodbye to the semi-annual drain.)

"The anti-freeze tester" (that's a hydrometer they're talking about— you can buy one for a dollar, although

"PRESTONE" FLUSH and FILL

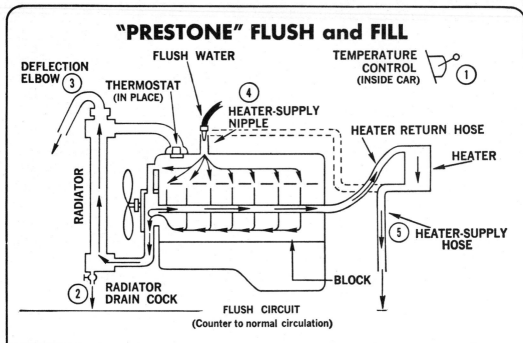

FLUSH CIRCUIT
(Counter to normal circulation)

DIRECTIONS *(Keyed to Schematic Diagram above:)*

A. Set heater temperature control (1) to high. (See Note #1 if car is equipped with a vacuum-operated heater valve.)

B. Open Radiator Drain Cock (2).

C. Remove radiator cap and install deflection elbow in the filler neck (3). This prevents excessive splash into the engine compartment. (Gates #CH-118 hose or equivalent fits the filler neck of most car radiators. A clear, flexible plastic tube attached to the elbow permits viewing the coolant as it drains from the system.)

D. Remove hose from heater supply nipple at the engine block (4). Point this hose downward for an auxiliary drain (5). (See Note #2 if heater supply nipple is inaccessible.)

E. Connect water supply to the heater supply nipple (4) at the engine block. CAUTION: DO NOT CONNECT WATER SUPPLY DIRECTLY TO HEATER—THIS COULD CAUSE DAMAGE. Cool flush water may be supplied through an ordinary hose or a flushing gun (cool water necessary to prevent opening of thermostat during flushing). If flushing gun has provision for air injection, air pressure should be controlled to prevent damage. (Radiator cap pressure rating may be used as a guide.)

F. Turn on water. Flush for 3-5 minutes. During the last minute of flushing, squeeze the upper radiator hose to remove any trapped liquid.

G. Turn off water (see Note #3 if anti-freeze is to be installed)—remove connection at heater supply nipple (4)—reconnect heater supply hose to nipple —remove deflection elbow from radiator—permit enough water to drain from radiator drain cock to accept anti-freeze—close radiator drain cock.

H. Install anti-freeze—replace radiator cap—start engine and warm to operating temperature—make final check of coolant level. Check for leaks.

NOTE 1:

If car is equipped with a vacuum-operated heater valve, start engine and run at 'idle' during the flushing procedure. CAUTION: SHUT OFF ENGINE BEFORE TURNING OFF WATER (primarily Chrysler products).

NOTE 2:

If heater supply nipple on the engine block is inaccessible, remove heater supply hose at heater and connect water supply to flow into engine block—not into heater. Attach a short piece of hose at heater and point downward. CAUTION: DO NOT CONNECT WATER SUPPLY DIRECTLY TO HEATER—COULD CAUSE DAMAGE.

NOTE 3:

If anti-freeze is to be installed, draining from the radiator drain cock should provide sufficient space for the addition of 50% anti-freeze (—34°F. protection). When greater freezing protection is required, or if it is not possible to install sufficient anti-freeze, AFTER FILLING THE SYSTEM the heater hose can be removed from the heater supply nipple (4) momentarily to allow additional water to escape from the system.

most of you probably have one already) "has now become a year-round service tool—check in warm weather months as well as winter for solution concentration and appearance. Maintain a minimum concentration providing minus 34 degrees F.—50 percent —for adequate corrosion resistance and temperature protection."

The temperature protection is not only for winter. Anti-freeze also raises the boiling point of the coolant and the entire cooling system is designed for this higher boiling point.

Most cars have temperature warning lights that go on at about 250 degrees F. In a system with pure water and a pressure cap holding to 14 psi, the water would boil at 244 degrees, meaning that you would have an overheated engine with no warning.

And that would be with a 100 percent sound pressure cap. If your cap were only holding 11 psi, the coolant would boil at 235 degrees with pure water, and 245 degrees even with minus 20 degrees F. anti-freeze protection.

All cooling systems leak to some degree. A perfectly good system will leak a pint in 1200 miles. If you just add water, the anti-freeze concentration will soon drop to the point where overheating protection is lost.

The new rules on cooling system service are:

1. Drain, flush and refill just once a year, but make sure the refill is at least 50 percent anti-freeze. (Never exceed two-thirds anti-freeze, as this is the highest percentage that will keep the freezing point down. As the anti-

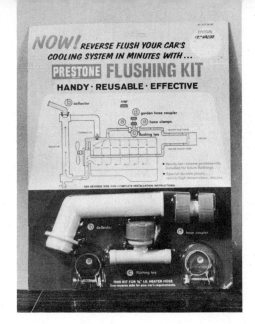

This is the easy-to-install flushing kit that eliminates need to remove engine coolant drain plugs.

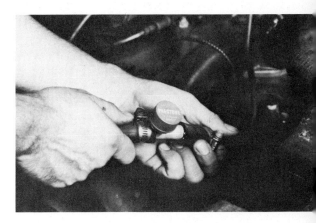

Above: Kit's tee-fitting is installed in heater hose and attached with hose clamps. Cap on tee stem is removed for attaching garden hose. Below: Cap is removed from tee and garden hose is threaded on.

Water deflector is installed in radiator neck.

freeze percentage is increased from two-thirds, the freezing point actually goes up. A 100 percent anti-freeze solution will freeze at only minus eight degrees F.)

2. When you top up the cooling system, do so with a 50-50 mixture of anti-freeze and water.

Cooling System Flushing. If the coolant is speckled with rust particles, you should add a can of flushing compound to the radiator and drive the car for about 100 miles to circulate it properly and give it a chance to work in.

The actual draining of the coolant can be done in either of two ways, but in any case should be preceded by a cooling system check, described in the chapter, "Cooling System Troubleshooting and Service."

1. You can open the drain cock on the radiator and remove the two drain plugs on a V-8 or open the drain cock on a six. Permit the coolant to drain

out, run some water through the system, refit the drain plugs, close the drain cock(s) or whatever, and fill the system with a 50-50 anti-freeze and water mixture.

This is a perfectly acceptable procedure and it will work nicely. The only problem is that the engine drain plugs on V-8s must be removed from underneath, and even the drain cocks on some sixes are not overly accessible.

You must have some way of safely jacking up the car. (After all, you will be getting underneath, and you don't really trust that bumper jack, do you?)

Even if you have a jacking setup, it is time-consuming to use. Most cooling system drainings are done in the soft earth backyard, not in the garage with its concrete floor. This can make the jacking somewhat difficult if not impossible.

2. You can use the Prestone Flush and Fill procedure illustrated in this chapter. Although designed for use with an air pressure flushing gun, it will work acceptably with a garden hose.

3. You can install a Prestone flushing kit, an inexpensive kit that includes the deflection elbow and a plastic tee that is installed in the heater hose. (The only tools necessary to install are a saw to cut the heater hose and a screwdriver for the hose clamps.)

The tee-fitting has a screw cap that is removed and a garden hose attached when you want to flush the system. Just turn on the water and the flushing procedure is essentially the same as with the illustrated procedure for the flushing gun.

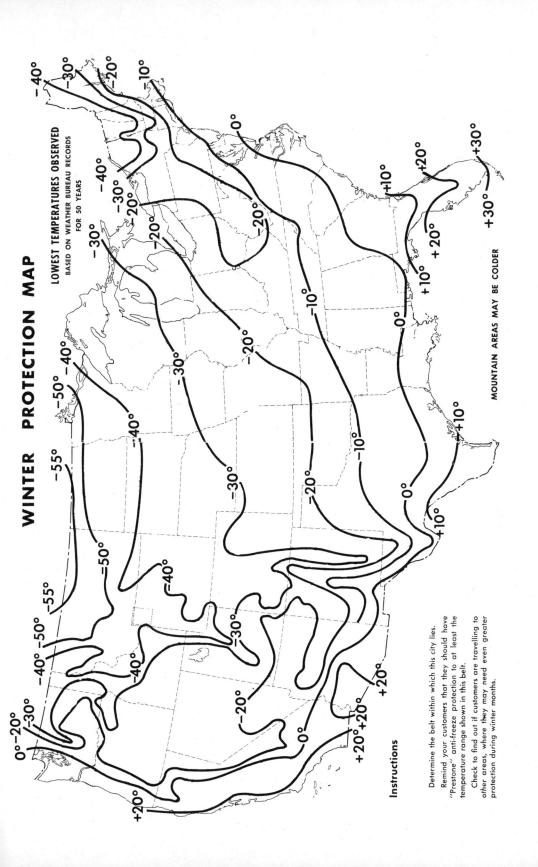

WINTER PROTECTION MAP

LOWEST TEMPERATURES OBSERVED

BASED ON WEATHER BUREAU RECORDS

FOR 50 YEARS

MOUNTAIN AREAS MAY BE COLDER

Instructions

Determine the belt within which this city lies.

Remind your customers that they should have "Prestone" anti-freeze protection to at least the temperature range shown in this belt.

Check to find out if customers are travelling to other areas, where they may need even greater protection during winter months.

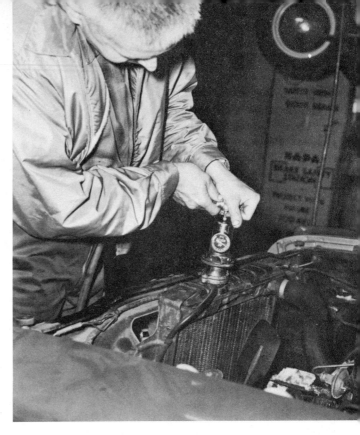

Modern cooling system is pressurized by radiator cap. The system and the cap must be checked to see they are holding pressure, using a special gauge.

26

Cooling System Troubleshooting and Service

THE COOLING SYSTEM is seemingly a very simple system. A pump driven by a belt draws water from the engine and pushes it through the upper radiator hose into the radiator, through which it flows, giving up heat to the air.

The coolant then flows through the lower radiator hose into the engine, where it picks up heat and the cycle starts all over again.

However, this apparently simple set-up is anything but simple.

First, there is a radiator cap with two valves—one, a spring-loaded valve that pressurizes the entire system to as much as 17 psi, which raises the boiling point of the coolant.

The other valve is actuated by vacuum. As the coolant cools, it contracts, creating a vacuum in the system. If the vacuum valve did not open, the vacuum in the system would cause collapse of weaker parts, such as radiator tubes and hoses. The opening of the valve permits air to rush in and eliminate the vacuum.

Second, there is the thermostat, a temperature-sensitive device between the pump and the upper radiator hose. This unit closes to prevent coolant from reaching the radiator when the engine is cold, speeding up coolant warmup.

As the engine warms up, the thermostat begins to open and some coolant can flow through the upper hose.

The thermostat then maintains a position that will send just the right amount of coolant through the radiator to hold overall coolant temperature at the desired level. Coolant that is kept from going through the upper radiator hose goes instead through a bypass passage or hose on the engine.

When the outside temperature is very high, the radiator cannot dissipate heat as well, and the thermostat is wide open.

The fan helps the radiator dissipate heat to the air at low road speed. Driven by a belt, it draws air through the radiator.

Many cars are equipped with thermostatic fans, another little complication. This type of fan is designed to free-wheel (thus requiring no real amount of power to turn) when the engine is running cool. When the engine is running hot, a thermostatic unit engages the fan.

In addition to all this, there are hoses to fail, hose clamps to come loose, gaskets to fail, and a water pump to go bad.

So our simple-seeming cooling system is really something you must pay attention to, and check and service

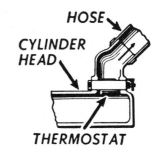

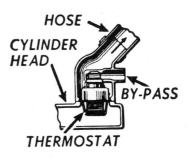

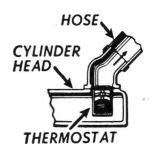

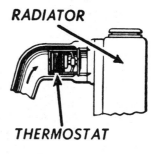

Four typical thermostat installations.

183

carefully. Just an annual drain, flush and fill is not enough.

In this chapter, we will cover the various parts of the system and what to check and repair.

Most engines use one thermostat. Some V-8s with two hoses from radiator to cylinders use two thermostats—one for each bank of cylinders. The thermostat may be mounted in any one of several spots: in the block, at the radiator hose elbow, in a secondary hose connection, or even in the radiator. Instead of playing "find-the-thermostat," check your owner's manual or a nearby garage. In most cars, the thermostat—wherever it is—can be removed by loosening two bolts.

If your engine refuses to heat quickly on cold mornings or to cool quickly on hot days, the thermostat may be at fault. If it is mis-aligned, or the valve inside it is stuck open, it will allow water to circulate freely through the radiator even when the engine temperature is below normal, and the engin may never heat. If the valve spring is worn or stuck closed, it will force the water in the cooling system to bypass the radiator—even when it's boiling—and the engine may never get a chance to cool. The remedy is a new thermostat.

Getting the Right One. All thermostats are not the same. Every auto manufacturer specifies the best type and the proper heat range for his car, and in some cases may even specify one thermostat for use with water and another for use with a permanent-type anti-freeze.

Be sure to buy the right thermostat for your car. If you bought the car second-hand, don't go by the one now

Left: Thermostat can be checked by placing in pan and bringing water to boil. Temperature at which thermostat opens is checked with radiator thermometer. Right: Check radiator hoses by feeling for excessive hardness or sponginess.

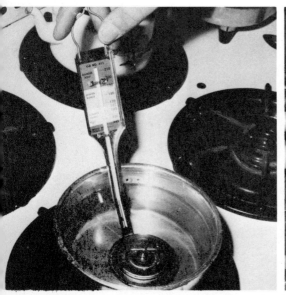

in the cooling system: it could be wrong. Check a thermostat catalog for the right model, heat range, and size.

Remove the Thermostat, if you think there may be something wrong with it, and check for corrosion. If you can't see anything wrong, test it before you decide whether to discard it or to put it back in.

Many thermostats have their temperature ranges stamped on the casing. The lower temperature is the one at which the thermostat is supposed to begin opening, and the higher temperature the point at which it should be fully open.

To test the thermostat, heat water on the stove to a temperature 10° below the point at which it should begin opening. Suspend the thermostat in the water for a couple of minutes. If it starts to open, discard it. If it remains closed, heat the water to a point 25° above the opening temperature, and suspend the thermostat in the water again. At this point, it should open fully; if it doesn't, discard it.

It may be necessary to remove one or more radiator hoses to remove the thermostat. Check the hoses for breaks and splits while they are off the car, and when you put them back on, be sure to clean the connections. Before you replace an engine-mounted thermostat, coat the elbow or housing with sealing compound. If the gasket is torn or chipped, replace it. Tighten the hose clamps, start the engine, and check for leaks.

Danger Signs. If your engine is running hot or using water, check the hoses in both the cooling system and the heater system. Since the system is pressurized, a poor hose in either sys-

An assortment of hose clamps. The big clamp surrounding the others is the two-wire type. Spring clamp is at upper left of circle formed by two-wire clamp. Cheap band clamp is at lower left. The best clamp, worm-drive type, is at right.

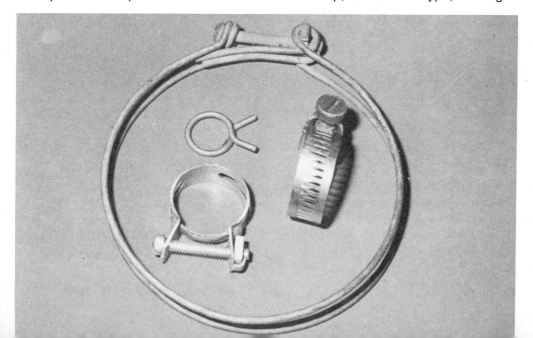

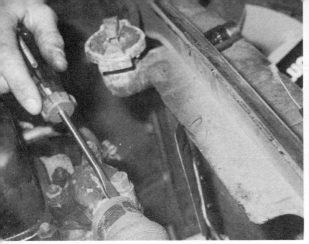

Replacing the hose is simple job. If hose sticks, pry with screwdriver. Clean necks onto which hose fits with a brush to remove rust and any cement residue.

Tighten hose clamp over neck after installation of new hose.

tem could mean trouble. A soft-walled hose may collapse inwardly, restricting the flow of water from radiator to engine. A worn hose, cracked or split, may leak water. A hardened hose may leak water around the connections. A leaky hose may also allow air to seep into the cooling system, and as the air bubbles form in the cooling system, they may promote rust. The rust, in time, can clog the radiator and the hoses.

In a recent survey, automotive engineers found that 15% of all cooling system complaints were caused by rotted or age-hardened hoses or by hoses with loose, leaking joints. The trouble may be in the age of the hose, but it can be in the quality of the hose itself.

Hoses are generally made with reinforcement, either an inner layer of fabric or an inner spiral of wire, or—in cases of extreme pressure—both. A hose without some kind of reinforcement can break without warning. In a recent test, Prestone engineers checked reinforced hoses against unreinforced types. Of all non-reinforced hoses, 54% failed during the test; only 15% of the reinforced types gave any sign of trouble.

To be safe, check the condition of hoses about every six months. Inspect them for cracks, splits and signs of leaks. Squeeze radiator hoses. Be sure they are springy and resilient, not spongy and lifeless. If any hose collapses under finger pressure and does not instantly spring back, it should be replaced. Hoses which are too hard may leak at the connections. Replace these. If the hoses seem in good condition and your engine still runs a fever, remove the hoses to see if they may be clogged with rust.

Replacing Hoses. When you replace a hose, use one with the recommended internal diameter. If there is any doubt about the hose clamps, replace them.

There are many types of clamps used on cars.

The best is the worm-drive type, in which a worm gear engages slots in the clamping band. This band clamp applies the closest thing to circular clamping pressure. (The pressure is actually tangental.)

As a band design, it also has the advantage of not digging deeply into the hose, as the wire-type clamps do. And the greater area under the clamp means that it holds its tightness longer.

You can glue the new hoses to their connections with a thin coating of sealing compound if you wish, but this is not necessary when you use the right clamp. But whether you glue the new hoses to the connections or rely on clamp pressure, be sure to clean the connections before you fit the new hoses.

To replace the upper radiator hose, drain the radiator by opening the petcock at the bottom. Drain only enough liquid from the radiator to lower the coolant below the level of the upper radiator pipe.

To replace the lower radiator hose, drain the entire cooling system. Open

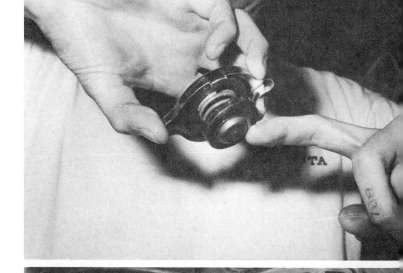

Check radiator cap vacuum valve by hanging fingernail on it and pulling. Release and it should spring back.

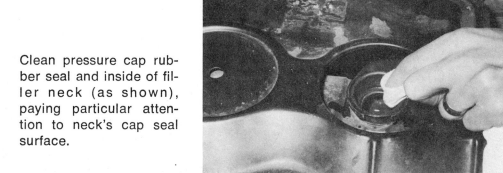

Clean pressure cap rubber seal and inside of filler neck (as shown), paying particular attention to neck's cap seal surface.

SERVICE DIAGNOSIS—COOLING SYSTEM

Condition	Possible Cause	Correction
EXTERNAL LEAKAGE	(a) Loose hose clamp.	(a) Replace the hose clamp.
	(b) Hose Leaking.	(b) Replace the hose.
	(c) Leaking radiator.	(c) Repair or replace the radiator as necessary.
	(d) Worn or damaged water pump seal.	(d) Replace the water pump seal and impeller.
	(e) Loose core hole plug.	(e) Install new core hole plug.
	(f) Damaged gasket, or dry gasket, if engine has been stored.	(f) Replace gaskets as necessary.
	(g) Cylinder head bolts loose, or tightened unevenly.	(g) Replace the cylinder head gasket and torque head in correct sequence.
	(h) Leak at heater connection.	(h) Clean the heater connections and replace the hoses and clamps if necessary.
	(i) Leak at water temperature sending unit.	(i) Tighten the water temperature sending unit.
	(j) Leak at water pump attaching bolt.	(j) Tighten the water pump attaching bolts to factory specifications.
	(k) Leak or exhaust manifold stud.	(k) Seal and re-drive the stud.
	(l) Cracked thermostat housing	(l) Replace the thermostat housing.
	(m) Dented radiator inlet or outlet tube.	(m) Straighten the radiator inlet or outlet tube as necessary.
	(n) Leaking heater core.	(n) Repair or replace the heater core.
	(o) Cracked or porous water pump housing.	(o) Replace the water pump assembly.
	(p) Warped or cracked cylinder head.	(p) Replace the cylinder head.
	(q) Cracked cylinder block.	(q) Replace the cylinder block.
	(r) Sand holes or porous condition in block or head.	(r) Replace the cylinder block or cylinder head as necessary.
	(s) Faulty pressure cap.	(s) Replace pressure cap.
	(t) Loose or stripped oil cooler fittings.	(t) Tighten or replace as necessary.
INTERNAL LEAKAGE	(a) Faulty head gasket.	(a) Install a new head gasket.
	(b) Refer to causes (f), (g), (p), (q), (r) and (t) listed under External Leakage.	(b) Refer to corrections (f), (g), (p), (q), (r) and (t) listed under External Leakage.
	(c) Crack in head into valve compartment.	(c) Pressure test cooling system, replace the cylinder head.
	(d) Cracked valve port.	(d) Pressure test cooling system, replace the cylinder head.
	(e) Crack in block into push rod compartment.	(e) Pressure test cooling system, replace the cylinder block.
	(f) Cracked cylinder wall.	(f) Pressure test cooling system, replace the cylinder block.
	(g) Leaking oil cooler.	(g) Repair or replace the oil cooler.

SERVICE DIAGNOSIS—COOLING SYSTEM *(Continued)*

Condition	Possible Cause	Correction
POOR CIRCULATION	(a) Low coolant level.	(a) Fill radiator to correct level.
	(b) Collapsed radiator hose. (A bottom hose with faulty spring may collapse only at medium or high engine speeds.)	(b) Check radiator cap vacuum valve. If good, replace hose.
	(c) Fan belt loose, glazed or oil soaked.	(c) Tighten or replace the fan belt as necessary.
	(d) Air leak through bottom hose.	(d) Reposition hose clamps or replace the hose. Check radiator outlets for dents or out-of-round.
	(e) Faulty thermostat.	(e) Replace the thermostat.
	(f) Water pump impeller broken or loose on shaft.	(f) Replace the water pump.
	(g) Restricted radiator core water passages.	(g) Flush the radiator thoroughly or rod out if necessary.
	(h) Restricted engine water jacket.	(h) Flush the engine cooling system thoroughly.
OVERHEATING (Refer to Causes and Corrections Listed Under "Poor Circulation")	(a) Low coolant level.	(a) Fill radiator to proper level.
	(b) Blocked radiator air passages.	(b) Blow out the radiator air passages.
	(c) Incorrect ignition timing.	(c) Time the engine ignition system.
	(d) Low engine oil level.	(d) Add engine oil to the correct level.
	(e) Incorrect valve timing.	(e) Correct the engine valve timing.
	(f) Inaccurate temperature gauge.	(f) Replace the temperature gauge.
	(g) Restricted overflow tube.	(g) Remove restriction from the overflow tube.
	(h) Faulty radiator pressure cap or seat.	(h) Replace the radiator cap. Clean or replace seat.
	(i) Frozen heat control valve.	(i) Free up the manifold heat control valve.
	(j) Dragging brakes.	(j) Adjust the brakes.
	(k) Excessive engine idling.	(k) Set at faster idle or stop engine.
	(l) Frozen coolant.	(l) Thaw out cooling system, add anti-freeze as required.
	(m) Faulty fan drive unit.	(m) Replace the fan drive unit.
	(n) Faulty temperature sending unit.	(n) Replace the sending unit.
OVERFLOW LOSS (Refer to causes listed under "Poor Circulation and Overheating.")	(a) Overfilling.	(a) Adjust coolant to the correct level.
	(b) Coolant foaming due to insufficient corrosion inhibitor.	(b) Flush the radiator and add anti-freeze or rust inhibitor as required.
	(c) Blown head gasket.	(c) Replace the head gasket.
	(d) Broken or shifted lower hose spring.	(d) Replace lower hose.

both the petcock on the radiator and the petcock on the engine.

To replace the heater hose, check the intake and exhaust levels of the hoses. If they take off and empty above the upper radiator pipe, you will have to drain only part of the coolant from the radiator. If they fit to connections below the upper radiator pipe, it may be necessary to drain the entire cooling system to replace them.

After you have drained the system to the safe level (or empty, depending upon the car and the hose to be re-replaced), loosen the hose clamps and remove the worn hose. If the hose to be replaced is a straight section, you can cut a new length to match. If the hose is premolded, buy one to match. Use the old hose as a pattern. If the hose is a flexible type, be sure you have the right replacement.

Place two clamps over the new hose. Clean the two connections and slip the hose onto the engine connection first. Attach the other end to the radiator connection, bending the hose near the center to fit over the radiator pipe. Tighten the clamp at the engine connection, then slide the hose upward on the radiator connection as far as it will go. Tighten the radiator clamp.

Refill the cooling system with water (or anti-freeze) and start the engine. Check the hose for leaks, then retighten the clamps after the engine has warmed.

Other Leaks: If there are traces of rust near any of the headbolts, remove the bolts (after the coolant has been drained) and wire-brush the threads clean. Then apply a film of nonhardening gasket cement to the threads and pull the bolts up to uniform tightness, using a torque wrench, if possible, to make sure the bolts are tightened uniformly. Refer to the engine or wrench manufacturer's specifications for the correct torque in foot-pounds, which may vary between 50 ft./lbs. and 120 ft./lbs., depending on the size of the headbolt.

If an expansion plug in the block is rusted, remove it by driving a sharp centerpunch through the plug about ¾ inch near its center and giving the punch a sharp tap sideways with a hammer. Scrape clean the recess in which plug fits, using a screwdriver blade. Then drive a new plug into place, after first applying a thin film of gasket cement to both the plug and the surface upon which it rests. Strike the domed side (which should always face *out*) a sharp blow with a machinist's hammer to cause plug to expand and form a tight fit in the block.

You will need a new cylinder head gasket if there is any sign of water in the crankcase oil. To check for leakage of exhaust gas into the coolant—and consequently the possibility of the leakage of coolant down into the engine—first remove the top hose from the engine and take out the thermostat. Then fill the engine with water and remove the fan belt. Carefully block all four wheels or set the emergency brake, then put the car into automatic drive. With a conventional transmission, shift into "high" and apply the load by slipping the clutch. Have an assistant start the engine and very quickly, before it has warmed up (which might create steam bubbles), accelerate it very briefly to rather high speed. If there is an exhaust gas leak into the coolant, you will see bubbles in the cooling system water in a matter of seconds. If bubbles appear, a new head gasket is in order. Before installing the gasket, be sure that head and block mating surfaces are clean.

Information on replacing a head gasket is in the chapter, "Tackling Valve and Ring Jobs."

The presence of a white deposit (lime) on the radiator core is a warning that water has leaked out and evaporated.

If you are using an anti-freeze with a sealer, the leak is apparently serious, for this type of anti-freeze will seal minor leaks. If you are not, try a can of sealer before going to the expense of having the radiator resoldered.

Water Pump. If there is any sign of leakage at the water pump joint, try tightening the bolts. If this does not cure the problem, the pump will have to be removed, checked for a defective gasket and replaced if the gasket is good. (The problem is in the pump shaft seal.)

Note: do not confuse minor seepage from the pump vent hole with a leaking pump. The vent hole is supposed to permit the small amount of coolant that gets past even a good pump seal to drop out.

Radiator Cap. The only sure way to test the radiator cap is with a pressure tester, a combination unit that also tests the ability of the cooling system to withstand the pressures built up by the cap.

If the cap holds specified pressure, it then can be physically inspected. The rubber seal should be in good condition. It and the inside of the radiator neck should be wiped clean of rust deposits. The vacuum valve should be checked by hanging a fingernail under it and tugging. It should open easily and spring back when released.

The System Itself. Even if a system shows no apparent leaks, it should be tested to see if it will hold at least the pressure of the cap. If the system fails to hold cap pressure, check for loose gaskets and poor hose connections.

A pressure test of cap and system should always be made before draining, flushing and refilling.

Very few weekend mechanics are likely to have a pressure gauge. You will have to pay a service station a service charge for this test.

Job of installing a replacement transmission filter starts with removal of oil pan bolts. Remove rear bolts and work criss-cross toward front, so pan will tilt down from back and drain into drain pan.

27

Servicing Automatic Transmission

THERE ARE THOUSANDS of automatic transmission specialty shops throughout the country, very busily rebuilding automatics at about $300 each. By giving your automatic some very simple care—a form of tuneup—you can greatly extend the life of your unit and hopefully avoid an overhaul for the life of the car.

Nearly 80 percent of the automatic transmissions on late-model cars have replaceable oil filters. More than 75 percent have vacuum devices—called modulators—that play a major part in the shift quality of the transmission. These two items, along with transmission oil, are the things that you can attend to, to keep your automatic in good condition.

The transmission tuneup should be performed at 24,000 miles, and once a year thereafter or 12,000 miles, whichever comes first.

The only tools you will need are ordinary hand tools, a good jack, a pair of safety stands and on Ford products, an inexpensive special wrench for the vacuum modulator.

You can buy a transmission oil filter from most parts houses, as independent filter manufacturers such as Purolator market them. The same is true for vacuum modulators.

All General Motors automatics have replaceable filters and vacuum modulators. All Ford products have replaceable vacuum modulators and one transmission has a replaceable filter (the C-4 unit). Others have cleanable screens. All Chrysler products have replaceable filters, but use mechanical linkage instead of vacuum modulators. American Motors cars have modulators and cleanable screens.

To Start. Start the job by dropping the transmission oil pan, which is held by screws. If the transmission has a replaceable filter, the filter container also will have a pan gasket. If the transmission merely has a cleanable screen, you should buy a replacement gasket before you start the job. (One cautionary note: because there is no drain plug in the oil pan, some care is necessary to avoid spilling oil all over the place when you drop the pan.)

Get the largest pan you can find and put it directly under the transmission oil pan. Undo the rear pan bolts first and then work evenly toward the front so the pan will tilt slightly down from the rear, allowing much of the oil to spill out from there, into your drain pan. (If the transmission oil pan gasket sticks to both pan and transmission, you'll have to free it.) About three quarts of oil will come out.

Remove Old Filter. With the pan off, the filter is readily accessible. On

Left: Pan will contain bits and pieces of gasket, sludge and metal shavings. Clean pan thoroughly with solvent. Scrape old gasket off. Right: Old filter sits just under transmission valve body. It will be held by screws (as shown) or perhaps by clips.

Once screws or clips are disengaged, pull old filter straight down. If there is a connecting pipe, it will come too. Make sure that if an O-ring is used on pipe, it comes out with it.

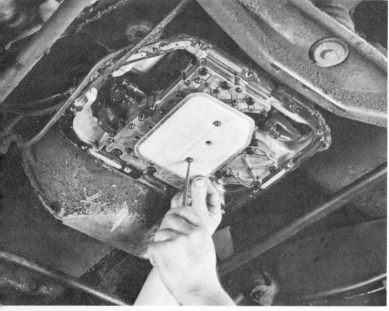

Install new filter. If there is a connecting pipe with O-ring, the new filter assembly will have it.

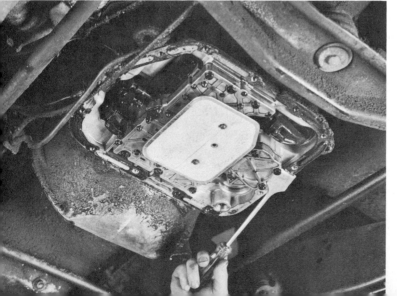

If any parts of old oil pan gasket stuck to transmission, scrape off with gasket scraper or putty knife. Do not use a screwdriver which could damage the gasket surface of transmission, which probably is aluminum.

most cars, it is retained by a few screws. Remove them and pull the filter straight down.

On a few cars, the filter is held by a clip, which either must be removed or twisted aside for filter removal.

Many filter assemblies have an O-ring on the neck that connects the filter to an oil tube or gallery. If the O-ring sticks when you pull the filter down, be sure to remove it. The replacement filter has a new O-ring already fitted to the neck.

If the old transmission pan gasket sticks to the bottom of the transmission, scrape it off. (Caution: many transmissions are made of aluminum and care should be exercised to avoid scoring the transmission's gasket surface.) A gasket scraper or putty knife should be used, not a screwdriver or chisel.

If there are grooves in the pan's gasket mating surface, they should be cleaned with a wire brush. Don't use a screwdriver or chisel, and don't use that wire brush to buff the transmission's mating surface.

Always clean the interior of the transmission oil pan with a general duty automotive solvent and wipe it dry before installing the new filter.

New Filter. Installing a new filter is a simple matter of slipping it into place, screwing it down and/or attaching the clip and making sure the O-ring is seated (no real problem).

If you have a 1967 GM car, you should be very careful to obtain and install the correct filter, as two different types were used that year, on the following models:

Buick (full-size) with Super Turbine 400

Top: Apply light coating of white grease to oil pan gasket surface to hold new gasket, which comes with filter. You may use a flexible sealant instead of grease. Never apply grease or sealant to the transmission gasket surface, only to the pan surface.

Above: Fit gasket onto oil pan surface. If gasket has dried out, it may have shrunk. The only way to save it is to soak it in warm water. Never try to stretch a dried-out gasket or it will probably break.

Chevrolet with Turbo Hydra-Matic
Cadillac except El Dorado
Oldsmobile (full-size) except Toronado
Pontiac (full-size) with Turbo Hydra-Matic
Pontiac GTO with Turbo Hydra-Matic

The early filter had a bypass valve and carries original equipment part No. 5579822. The late filter has no bypass valve and carries part No. 643-7741. (Note: the bypass valve was eliminated from the late-1967 filter to force replacement when it is completely clogged. If completely stopped up, the filter can be responsible for transmission growling, slipping and even a no-drive condition.)

The two filters are physically interchangeable, but the replacement must be the same type as the original or the filter may be crushed by the pan or cause transmission damage.

On cars with cleanable screens, dunk the screen in solvent, agitate for a few minutes, then remove, shake out excess solvent and allow to air-dry for half an hour.

Refit the transmission oil pan with a new gasket. To simplify installation, a flexible sealant can be sparingly applied to the oil pan's gasket surface (never to the transmission itself).

Modulator. Tighten the pan screws evenly in a criss-cross pattern.

Next, while the car still is up on safety stands, replace the vacuum modulator on cars so equipped. A new modulator will smoothen the shifting.

You can identify the modulator by ordering a new one for your car and

Left: Replacing a transmission modulator is easy, once you find it. You can identify it by vacuum hose on its neck and cylindrical shape. To replace, first take off vacuum hose. Check inside of hose with pipe cleaner and if you find oil, replace hose. Right: To remove old modulator or install new one, you need a thin wrench on most Ford products. On larger Ford products, a very thin wrench, bent slightly as shown, will get in on the nut.

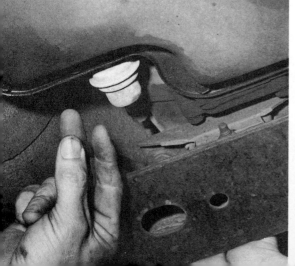
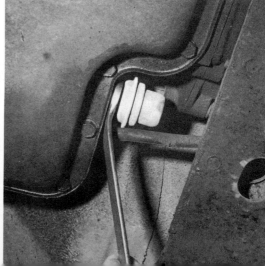

finding the equivalent on the transmission body somewhere underneath. It will have a vacuum hose attached to it.

To replace the modulator, simply pull off the hose and unscrew the unit. This is a simple and obvious job, but you can run into a wrench clearance problem on Ford products.

The modulator screws directly into the transmission, and on Ford products the hexagonal nut that permits removing and installing the modulator is flush with the transmission. An ordinary wrench is too thick to fit in.

The solution is to use a very thin wrench (the wrench size is ¾ inch) if you have one, or buy a special wrench made for the purpose. It is thin, C-shaped, and costs just a few dollars at auto parts stores.

Add Oil. Now you are through underneath. The job is finished by topping up the transmission with oil and adding a can of "sealer" through the dipstick hole.

Make sure you use the correct oil for your transmission. The wrong oil can severely damage a transmission. All Ford products should be topped up with a fluid that is labeled "F-M2C33-F, suffix 2P." All GM, Chrysler and American Motors cars should use fluid labeled "Dexron."

The topping up should be done on a level floor. The engine should be running and the shift lever should be in neutral on Chrysler and American Motors cars, and park on Ford and GM cars.

On smaller Fords, you may be able to get to modulator even with thin wrench. In this case, you can buy inexpensive crowfoot-style wrench designed specifically for the job.

Check Level. After the engine has been running for five minutes, cycle the transmission. That is, apply the brakes and move the shift lever into all positions, ending up in the position necessary to check fluid level. Then recheck the fluid level.

The "transmission sealer" is not really a sealer. It is a chemical designed to keep the seals supple, preventing them from shrinking and allowing oil to leak out.

When you reinsert a transmission dipstick to check level, be sure it is seated fully. Many dipsticks require twisting to seat, and will give false reading if not fully installed.

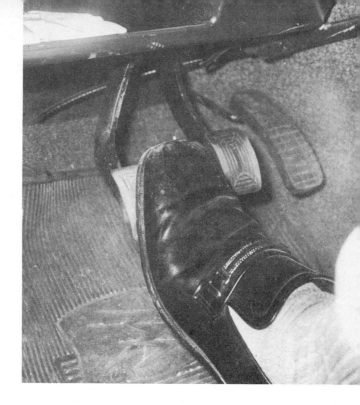

The manual clutch is anything but obsolete. Millions of motorists prefer it to the more expensive and less reliable automatic transmission.

28

Taking Care of Your Clutch

THE MAJORITY OF passenger cars being sold today have automatic transmissions driving through a torque converter, thus eliminating the need for a clutch, but manually operated friction clutches are still in millions of cars on the road, and sports cars and economy cars—both European and American—couple their engines to the transmissions with friction clutches. Fortunately, these precision mechanisms are built to stand up under an amazing amount of abuse before they fail.

First, let's understand why a clutch is necessary. Unlike a steam engine or an electric motor, a gas engine will not start from rest under load, since its power depends on the number of power strokes per unit time. In other words, it has to be turned up to cranking speed from an outside source (a starter motor) and reach a certain speed, free from load, before the load can be applied. Since the engine must be *kept* turning at an efficient speed—a speed higher than that at which the wheels should turn—the power must be applied to the wheels through a reduction gearing, the ratio of which is variable and under manual or automatic control. Also, suitable reverse gearing must be provided, since a conventional gasoline engine rotates in only one direction. These gear changes must be made while the engine is temporarily disconnected from the drive shaft or transmission. Further, as a matter of convenience, the engine must be enabled to keep running while the car is at rest (as at traffic lights or crossings). All of these functions are taken care of by the clutch.

Automotive engineers do everything they can to reduce friction in an auto's moving parts, yet a car would not budge an inch without it. For it is friction between the clutch parts, under spring pressure, that makes the drive shaft turn with the engine and propel the car.

The basic idea of driving a spring-loaded disc through friction, despite all the design changes over the years, remains unchanged. Notice, in particular, the effect caused when the driven disc is worn thin. The same thing happens in any conventional clutch, but it is self-compensating for normal wear. (The spring expands.) Also, the free play in the pedal can be adjusted. Of course, there may come a time when the friction disc facings are completely worn out and have to be replaced. If sensible operation methods are followed and excessive use avoided, however, there is no reason why the entire clutch should not last for the life of the car.

Almost all clutches are single plate designs, though they may vary from one another in small details. When pressure on the clutch pedal forces the release-fork rod back against the re-

Typical modern clutch assembly. Cover and plate assembly, shown disassembled, is supplied as a single part; so is release bearing and sleeve (also known as throwout bearing assembly).

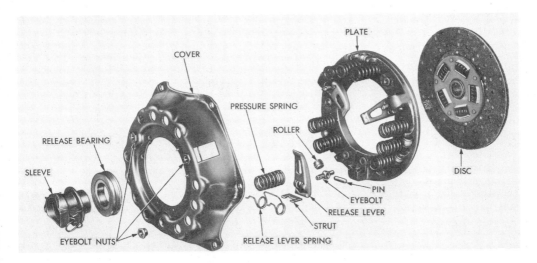

lease fork, it pivots on a ball-socket in the pressure-plate cover and moves the release (throw-out) bearing against the release levers. These levers pull the pressure plate back against spring pressure and allow the clutch-driven plate to rotate freely between the face of the flywheel and the pressure plate. Except for the release bearing and release yoke, the entire clutch assembly rotates with the flywheel and is, from a functional standpoint, actually a part of the flywheel. Powerful springs push the entire assembly together, squeezing the friction disc between the pressure plate and flywheel when the clutch is engaged. When disengaged, the pressure plate is pulled backward so that the friction plate floats free between, the flywheel and pressure plate. Thus, no power is transmitted to the main drive-gear shaft. The release levers are operated when the clutch release bearing is pushed against them by the forked release yoke. When pedal pressure is released, it lets the release bearing slide backward so that the springs in the pressure plate engage the clutch plate.

The release levers on some clutches are fitted with centrifugal weights to increase pressure at high engine speeds. One of the clutches illustrated has these weights. As they tend to fly out with increasing force at higher engine speeds, they force the levers to bear more strongly against the pressure plate, increasing the force holding the clutch disc. This arrangement, supplementing the springs when more pressure is needed, allows lighter springs to be used in the pressure plate, reducing the force necessary to operate the clutch

pedal at low engine speeds. To illustrate, the total spring pressure may be 1,000 pounds, while at high engine speed (say 4,000 rpm) the pressure is increased to nearly 2500 pounds. The spring pressure in this case is more than enough to start the car in motion, while the effort necessary to operate the pedal is reduced about 50%. Such an arrangement stands up better under the treatment of drivers who race the engine and let in the clutch violently.

Another method of reducing the pressure required to depress the clutch pedal is used on Dodge and Plymouth cars. Here, the pedal is suspended from above and is linked to the clutch release fork in such a manner that it moves part of the linkage to an "over-center" position where a spring assists in depressing the clutch. If you plan to do much work on your car, including clutch adjustments, write to the manufacturer for a price on a service manual. Cost is a few dollars, but it will tell you enough about your car to save hundreds. The Plymouth service manual, for example, will also tell you that if the clutch release-fork rod is adjusted so there is 3/16-inch play between the fork and the release bearing, the clutch pedal will automatically have the 1 inch required free play.

Friction discs in clutches are built with a spring-cushioned hub. These damper springs take up the shock of engagement and smooth out the torque impulses of the engine before they reach the splined hub and transmission shaft. Observe that the hub floats free in the assembly and is driven through the springs by the friction-faced discs. This type of construction is especially

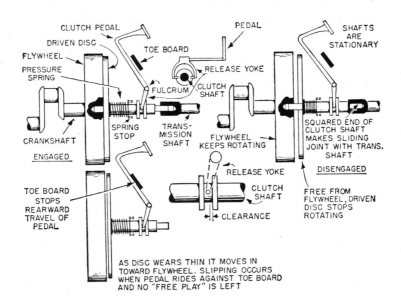

Principles of clutch operation are illustrated.

This is over-center spring design used to reduce pedal effort.

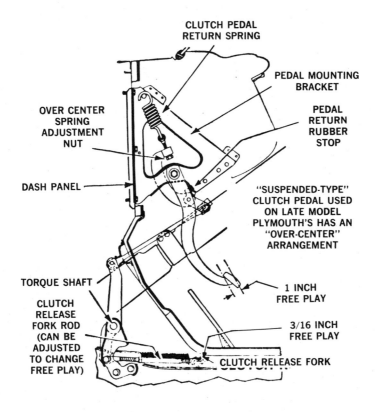

important because cars flexible engine mounts are designed to prevent engine vibration from being transmitted to the chassis of the car. What happens is that the engine bounces back and forth in its mounts when the clutch is engaged. Late-model cars often have torque rods, or a torque-absorbing thrust face on the rear motor mount, but in an older car with worn mounts, clutch chatter can be a problem. Before blaming your clutch for a chatter problem, however, check your motor mounts. They can be replaced a lot more easily, and for much less money, than can a clutch disc. When motor mounts are in good shape, the cushion springs in the friction disc eliminate chatter by permitting the friction facings to stay in contact during the fore-and-aft oscillations of the engine.

When a clutch is disengaged, it isn't necessary that the driven disc be separated from the driving members by any great distance. In fact, the distance that separates the parts in a disengaged clutch is almost microscopic—usually about .015 inch. You can see, therefore, why it is so important that the working parts be in correct alignment and free from warps or other defects. Any such faults will cause drag, chattering and other troubles. The pressure plate must travel about .090 inch (about 3/32 inch) backward to completely released position. After taking up about 1½ inch of free play, the pedal must be pushed downward about 4½ inch to produce this movement. The standard ratio for this action is 50 to 1.

As you ease back the pedal to let in the clutch, the pressure plate moves forward and pushes the friction disc toward the flywheel. The cushioned facings take up the load and start the car in motion even before the springs have exerted their full force. Thus, they are still under control of the driver and a smooth start is effected. To keep the release bearing out of contact with the release levers, a definite amount of play is provided in the clutch pedal. This play becomes less as the facings wear, since the inner ends of the levers move closer to the release bearing. If neglected, they would finally push against the bearing with sufficient force to let the clutch slip, for the effect is the same as if the bearing were pushed against the levers by the pedal. However, a simple adjustment, which takes only a few minutes, will restore the clearance, which is essential to efficient operation.

If the pedal shank hits the underside of the floor board (or the overhead bracket, in the case of suspended pedals) about the time the clutch is "engaged," it may not actually be fully engaged, and slipping will result, growing worse as the facings wear. The effect is the same as the notoriously bad habit of "riding the clutch." Just the weight of your foot on the pedal, especially if there is very little free play, exerts a powerful leverage and may reduce the effective spring pressure enough to cause slipping.

Slipping, by far the most common clutch trouble, not only wastes power and causes rapid wear, but also produces other bad effects. Anyone familiar with machinery knows that maladjustment, if neglected, leads to other trouble that aggravates the original condition. Nothing proves this point more than a slipping clutch. Beside the wear just mentioned, destructive heat is generated. This heat may warp or score the parts, burn the facings, or ruin the temper of the springs and weaken them, all of which combine to cause more slipping.

This can be further accelerated by heat cracks formed on the flywheel surface. These cracks expand as the clutch slips and present tiny but sharp edges that chew up the friction facing in short order. In this case, the flywheel must be replaced.

A simple turnbuckle arrangement is the usual provision for pedal adjustment. When checking for free play in a clutch pedal, don't mistake the pull of the pedal return spring for the pressure-plate spring tension. (To make

sure you do not, disconnect the spring while making this test.) If you listen carefully, you can hear the release bearing when it strikes the release levers. The exact amount of free play may be specified differently by various manufacturers, but a safe amount is 1 or 1½ inches of free travel before the levers and bearing make contact. Normal wear is so gradual that you may not notice it until actual slipping occurs. Warning is given, however, by the fact that complete engagement comes nearer and nearer to the upper limit of pedal travel.

In making adjustments, avoid the opposite extreme—too much free play —for then the pedal can't be pushed down far enough to free the clutch completely and it drags. Since there is then enough contact between the parts

What may seem to be clutch problems may be caused by weak engine mounts. Check mounts with pry bar by trying to rock engine side to side. Replacing mounts is not a difficult job, but it does require good jacking, as the engine must be jacked up off the mounts in order to pull them out and install new ones.

to keep the friction disc rotating, the gears clash—making shifting difficult and noisy—and doing the transmission gears no good. While the drag may not be enough to move the car when the transmission is in gear and the pedal is depressed, the friction disc, being held stationary under these conditions, will generate the same ruinous heat and disastrous results as it will when slipping.

If the adjusting nut is the self-locking type, it may give trouble by losing some of its self-locking quality. If the clutch adjustment refuses to "hold," you should try taking apart the adjusting mechanism, putting a second nut up against the original, and locking the two together in the correct position.

However rugged in construction, a clutch was never designed for continuous operation, it being assumed that it will stay engaged during most of the car's operating period. Neither the pilot bearing nor the release bearing will stand up under prolonged use, for no method is provided for positive lubrication of these parts in most clutches.

To illustrate, the release bearing turns only when you depress the pedal and push it against the rotating release levers to disengage the clutch. It may be either a plain thrust bearing of graphite, or a ball bearing or roller type. In any case, if the release levers are in constant contact with this bearing, it will spin all the time the engine is running. Finally, it becomes dried out and damaged and screeches a protest that can be heard for blocks. The same fate is in store for the pilot bearing in the end of the crankshaft when-

ever excessive use of the clutch is practiced. High temperatures prevail in this part of the clutch assembly and the bearing operates only when the speeds of the engine and clutch shaft are not synchronized, as when the engine is running with the clutch released and the transmission is in gear.

If the car is standing still, the bearing will turn around the stationary shaft. Or, if it is rolling very fast under the same conditions, as when coasting, the shaft will be turning faster than the engine, and, again, the bearing will be in operation. The final result of such treatment is that the bearing will become noisy or bind on the shaft end, causing the same effect as though the clutch were dragging.

The idea is to keep your foot off the clutch pedal at all times except when starting, changing gears or stopping. Even prolonged waits at traffic lights and crossings with the car in gear and pedal depressed should be avoided. In such instances, it is better to put the transmission in neutral while you are standing. This is a good safety precaution, too, against damage to the gears if you get a bad bump from the rear and your foot slips off the clutch pedal. Further, always make a practice of starting the engine with the gears in neutral.

Other troubles (see Table) that may cause rough or faulty operation include worn splines in the hub of the clutch disc, broken or weak damper springs, rough, glazed or broken facings, or grease or oil on the surfaces. These are all infrequent. A leaking rear main bearing in the engine sometimes will let oil leak through onto the clutch facings. The solution here is first to replace the bearing before repairing the clutch. Any of the faults mentioned will cause grabbing, drag or chattering. Rarely will a clutch stick or fail to disengage. Burned grease or gum will make the facings adhere to the flywheel and pressure plate. Also, there is the remote possibility of breakage in the release linkage or adjacent parts.

Many clutches will last for 100,000 miles or more in the hands of a careful driver, while continuous abuse may necessitate complete replacement after 5,000 miles. In other words, care pays off in long performance.

CLUTCH TROUBLESHOOTING CHART

POSSIBLE CAUSE	REMEDY
SLIPPING:	
1. Improper pedal adjustment	1. Adjust to provide free pedal travel to 1 to 1½ in.
2. Oil soaked clutch facings, badly worn or damaged facings	2. Replace driven plate
3. Sticking pressure plate	3. Check release levers for free action, also check fit between cover plate indentations and drive bosses on pressure plate
4. Weak pressure springs	4. Replace pressure springs
5. Sticking release sleeve, sticking cross shaft on which release yoke is mounted or retarded return travel of clutch pedal	5. Clean and lubricate bearing surfaces on release sleeve and cross shaft. Check clutch pedal movement and pedal return spring
6. Distorted pressure plate	6. Replace pressure plate
GRABBING:	
1. Defective, worn or glazed clutch facings	1. Replace driven plate
2. Sticking pressure plate	2. Check release levers for free action, also check fit between cover plate indentations and drive bosses on pressure plate
CHATTERING:	
1. Bent or badly worn driven plate	1. Replace driven plate
2. Oily clutch facings or facings which have become flaky from heat	2. Replace driven plate
DRAGGING:	
1. Bent driven plate or oily facings	1. Replace driven plate
2. Excessive free travel of clutch pedal	2. Adjust clutch pedal free travel to 1½ in.
3. Badly worn release levers or other release mechanism parts	3. Replace worn parts.
4. Defective or damaged splines in driven plate hub or on transmission clutch shaft	4. Clean and remove burrs or replace parts if defective

29

Brake Systems Hydraulics and the Single Master Cylinder

ALL PASSENGER CARS today use hydraulic systems to apply the brakes. Whether the brake shoe is a flat pad clamped against a disc or arc-shaped and pressed against a drum, a hydraulic system does the clamping or pressing. The pressure is supplied by your foot on a pedal, and the principles of hydraulics take it from there.

If you have an older car, it has a single master cylinder system. Even if you have a newer car with a dual master cylinder, a basic understanding of hydraulics and the single master cylinder will make the transition to the dual system easier.

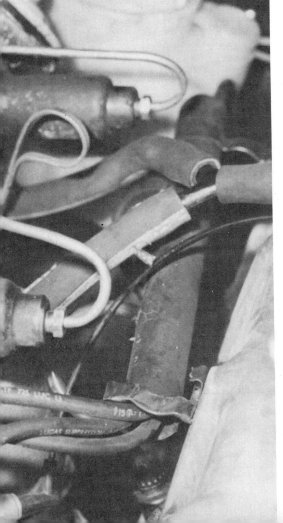

Hydraulic means fluid, and fluid cannot be compressed under pressure. Because it is incompressible, fluid makes an excellent transfer medium for the pressure applied by your foot (with possibly an assist from engine vacuum).

A basic principle of hydraulics is that pressure exerted at any point on a confined fluid will transmit this pressure equally in all directions. In a braking system, the fluid is confined to cylinders and tubing, using rubber seals to prevent leakage and loss of pressure.

Hydraulic Theory. A simple example of how hydraulic pressure works would be the following—a main cylinder and piston whose circular face has an area of one square inch connected through tubing to a cylinder and piston with a face area of one square inch and another with a face area of one-half square inch.

The system is filled with liquid, and 100 pounds force is applied to the main cylinder piston. Because hydraulic pressure is transmitted equally in all directions, the force against the one square inch piston will be 100 pounds; and against the one-half square inch piston, 50 pounds.

In actual practice, the cylinders for the front wheels are larger in diameter than the rear wheels (permitting the installation of pistons with greater face area in front).

The single master cylinder. No car uses just this unit anymore, and in fact, this particular one is from a foreign car that uses two single cylinders, one for front brakes, a second for rears.

This means that the front wheel cylinders will accept greater force, which is desirable. During braking, by the laws of physics, there is weight transfer to the front of the car, where, due to the engine, most of the weight is to start with.

The greater traction is therefore on the front wheels, and the maximum braking effort should also be on the front wheels. If you have owned a car for any amount of time, you know from experience that the front wheel brake linings wear out before the rear linings.

Hydraulic Cylinders. The main or master cylinder, to which the brake pedal is directly connected by linkage,

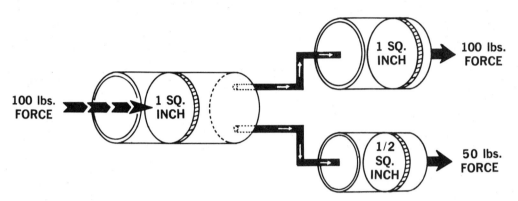

Above: Principle of hydraulics is illustrated. 100 lbs. of force in a main cylinder is applied, such as your foot on the brake pedal connected to the master cylinder by linkage. Pressure is exerted equally in all directions, so there is 50 pounds of force against a cylinder with a 0.5 square inch bore, 100 pounds against a cylinder with a one-square-inch bore.

Below: Cutaway of a typical single master cylinder, shown in the applied position and covering the compensating port "A." Other parts are: breather port "B"; piston "C," pushrod "D"; dust cover "E"; fluid reservoir "F," and tubing to the wheel cylinders "G."

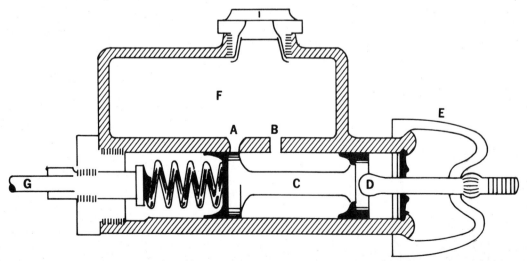

is composed of a fluid reservoir, a piston assembly with seals, and a valve assembly. The valve maintains a slight pressure in the brake lines so that the system will respond quickly when you press on the pedal. The slight pressure also tends to keep the wheel cylinder seals partly flexed for best sealing.

NOTE: this residual pressure in the brake lines is not designed into disc brake systems. The article on disc brakes in this section explains why, and how the shoes are retracted. Cars with front discs and rear drums have the check valve, plus a bypass for fluid to the discs.

The master cylinder reservoir has two passages to the cylinder itself, the compensating and breather ports. As you get ready to hit the brakes, there is no pressure on the master cylinder piston. Fluid from the reservoir flows through the compensating port to the part of the cylinder ahead of the piston, and through the breather port to behind the piston.

As the piston moves forward by force transmitted by the brake pedal, the rubber cup seal—called the pressure cup, in front of the piston—covers the compensating port, trapping the fluid ahead of it in the cylinder. The breather port remains uncovered and allows fluid to flow into the space behind the piston, keeping the space between piston head and the secondary sealing cup filled with fluid. The piston's forward motion forces fluid through a check valve at the front of the master cylinder to actuate the little cylinders at the wheels. These little wheel cylinders spread the brake shoes against the spinning drum to stop it, and the wheel attached to it.

When the brakes are released, the piston starts to retract, but the check valve at the front of the cylinder limits the flow rate back into the master cylinder on the pressure side of the piston. To prevent the possibility of air entering the cylinder, there are drilled holes in the piston head, which permit fluid to flow from behind the piston, through it.

The release of pressure permits the seal, which had flexed to hold pressure, to relax, and the fluid that flows through the piston continues around the lip of the primary cup.

This design has another feature: it permits *pumping* the brake pedal to apply the drum brakes if the shoe-to-drum clearance is excessive. This occurs because it allows more fluid to get into the lines, and the incompressible fluid just pushes the wheel cylinder pistons out further.

When the brakes are released, the brake shoe return springs pull the shoes back, and put a return force on the wheel cylinder pistons. The force is transmitted through the hydraulic fluid, and lifts the master cylinder check valve off its seat. The inrushing fluid pushes the piston and primary cup back, uncovering the compensating port and allowing the extra fluid that entered the system to return to the reservoir.

Wheel Cylinders. Now let's look more closely at the wheel cylinders. There are three types of drum brake cylinders and several in the disc system.

The drum types are single piston and two dual piston designs, one with equal bores, another with different size bores. The cylinder contains a sealing

Fluid from master cylinder exerts equal pressure in all directions. Pressure transmitted to each wheel cylinder operates on pistons, pushing them out. Pistons push out actuating links which spread the brake shoes against the drum.

cup for each piston, a positioning spring or springs, rubber dust covers for each cylinder opening, and an operating rod from the piston to the brake shoe.

The disc types also contain a piston, a dust seal, sometimes a spring behind the piston, and a seal that fits in a recess in the cylinder bore. The disc cylinder is discussed in more detail in the chapter on disc brakes.

To test the hydraulic system, brace your foot on the brake pedal and hold it there for a minute or more. If the pedal holds firm, your hydraulics are in good shape. If it gradually sinks to the floor under continued pressure, then fluid is leaking somewhere. Cor-

rect this by inspecting flexible hoses and other brake pipes for leaks. Replace faulty hoses or tighten leaky connections. If moderate tightening does not cure the leak, replace the fitting. Leaks at the master cylinder or in the wheel cylinders should be fixed promptly because loss of hydraulic fluid can cause complete brake failure even when the power assist system is working perfectly.

Note: on cars with power brakes, the test can be made with the engine running, and as a double-check, with the engine off. After turning off the engine, release vacuum by applying the brakes several times. Then hold firm pressure on the pedal.

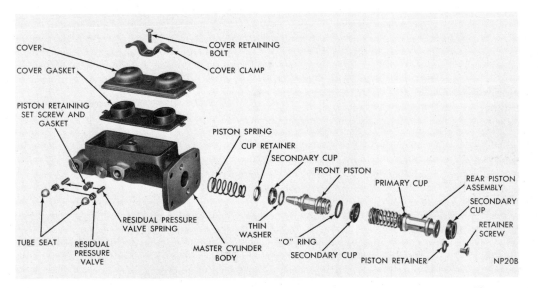

Exploded view of typical dual master cylinder.

30

Dual Master Cylinders

THE SINGLE MASTER cylinder is gone completely, and conventional drum brakes may soon join it. It's all dual master cylinders now, and they actuate disc braking systems in a growing number of cases. If the old stuff was the last you worked on, here is the information you will need to work on the new systems.

First, let's look at the dual master cylinder, see how it works, and what the service differences are. The basic design is one cylinder with two pistons, one behind the other, with a seal on one piston that effectively divides the cylinder into two parts. Above the cylinder are two separate reservoirs, each with its own breather and compensating ports. When you step on the brakes, each piston forces fluid to a separate outlet port, and there is separate tubing for front and rear brakes.

The larger of the two reservoirs feeds the front brakes, for two-thirds of the braking is done on the front wheels. The operation of the unit is as follows: the primary piston is moved by the pushrod. (On manual brakes, the pushrod is connected by linkage to the brake pedal; on power brakes, the pushrod is connected to the vacuum unit.)

When the primary piston moves forward, it creates hydraulic pressure in front of it. This hydraulic pressure applies one pair of brakes and at the same time moves the secondary piston (also called a "floater") to apply the other set of brakes.

If the brakes applied by the primary piston fail, the pushrod moves the primary piston into the back of the floater piston, pushing it forward, and the floater applies one set of brakes. To make physical contact with the floater, the primary must move forward a bit more than normal. If the brakes applied by the floater piston fail, the piston hits the end of the bore, or a stop screw threaded into the bore, and

Below: When tubing seat is a press fit, it is removed as shown. Sheet metal screw is threaded into seat with washer underneath, and you pry up on washer to pull seat. Bottom: When tubing seat is threaded in, it can be removed most easily with a special tool called an "easy-out." Seat will not be damaged, and residual pressure valve can be removed. This particular master cylinder has disc brakes up front, so the residual pressure valve is only for the rear brakes.

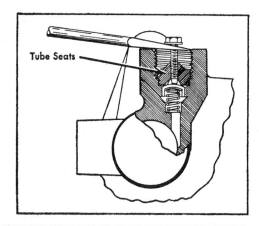

Tube Seats

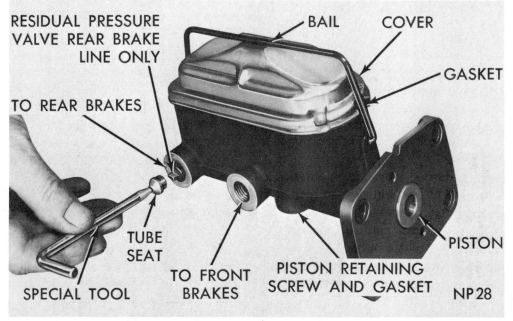

RESIDUAL PRESSURE VALVE REAR BRAKE LINE ONLY

BAIL COVER

GASKET

TO REAR BRAKES

TUBE SEAT

SPECIAL TOOL

TO FRONT BRAKES

PISTON RETAINING SCREW AND GASKET

PISTON

NP 28

it stops. The primary piston again must move forward a bit more, this time to build up hydraulic pressure (because the movement of the floater piston has created more space in front of the primary piston).

The additional forward movement necessary to apply the brakes in either case means that the pedal will have to be pressed down further, which provides a fairly positive indication of failure in half the system. There is another tipoff: a switch in the system lights a bulb on the dashboard, if that bulb happens to work.

It is important not to become overconfident. Even if the rear brakes have gone, leaving the system with approximately two-thirds of its effectiveness, you should take care of the problem right away. The extra load thrown on the front brakes will shorten their life, and certainly make them prone to fade.

Rebuilding a dual master cylinder is not difficult, particularly if you are a typical weekend mechanic who has rebuilt the old single master cylinder. Just work slowly, and keep the parts in order as you take them out, and you will be able to put the unit back together without difficulty.

The floater piston stop screw is a part you may not have seen before. It must be loosened or taken out to remove the inner parts of the master cylinder. Most dual master cylinders have the outlet bosses at 90-degree angles to the cylinder bore, and it is these outlet bosses that hold the residual pressure check valves and springs on drum brakes and possibly a special check valve on the disc brakes.

You must remove the tubing seats from the outlet bosses in order to get the check valves. You could reuse the old check valves, but the typical master cylinder rebuilding kit has brand new ones, and should have new tubing seats too. There is no sense in taking chances on reusing old parts when the new ones are so inexpensive, or even included in the rebuilding kit.

To pull the seats, you can use any one of several methods. The two most popular are: 1) insert an "easy-out," an inexpensive tool designed for removing broken screws and bolts, or 2) thread a self-tapping screw, with a flat washer under it, into the tubing seat. Then pry up on the washer with screwdrivers.

On a car with disc brakes all around, it might seem that effort could be saved. A residual pressure check valve is not used, because the system does not maintain residual pressure in the lines. But some disc setups do have a special valve in the outlet boss to control the rate of return of the fluid when the brakes are released. It is different from the residual pressure check valve of drum brakes, so on a car with discs up front and drums in the rear, don't get the two valves switched.

Also, on discs-in-front, drums-in-rear cars, without this special return flow valve, make sure you put the drum brake's residual pressure check valve in the right outlet boss, or the discs will never release fully once applied.

The dual master cylinder tends to trap air bubbles somewhat more easily than the old single master cylinder, so

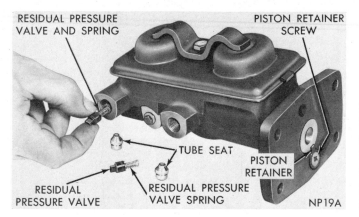

RESIDUAL PRESSURE VALVE AND SPRING

PISTON RETAINER SCREW

TUBE SEAT

PISTON RETAINER

RESIDUAL PRESSURE VALVE

RESIDUAL PRESSURE VALVE SPRING

NP19A

Once tube seats are out, residual pressure valve comes right out. This master cylinder feeds drum brakes front and rear, so there are two residual pressure valves.

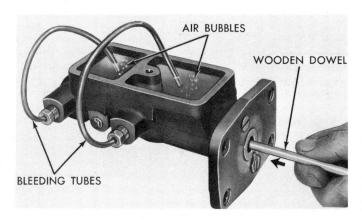

AIR BUBBLES

WOODEN DOWEL

BLEEDING TUBES

Bleeding dual master cylinder can be done on the bench, using wooden dowel and bleeding tubes you can make.

bleeding will be a bit more time-consuming. One effective way is to bleed the master cylinder on the bench, as follows. Clamp it into a vise. Make up bleeding tubes out of fittings and tubing. It is a good idea to attach a fitting and residual pressure check valve (an old spare) to the end of the fitting that goes into the large reservoir if the front wheels are fitted with disc brakes. This prevents fluid from being siphoned out of the reservoir during bleeding. The bleeding tubes should be long enough to go from the outlet bosses into the reservoirs, and can be used over and over.

Fill both reservoirs with fluid, and using a wooden dowel on power brake-equipped cars as a pushrod, press in (noting the air bubbles). Allow the pistons to return under the pressure of the springs inside the cylinder. Repeat until the bubbles stop. Remove the bleeding tubes and install a plug in the rear outlet. (As the tubes are removed, the fluid remaining in them will siphon out.) Put the cover and gasket over the reservoirs and pull over the retainer.

Another technique is to install the master cylinder, reconnect the tubing and have someone pump the brake pedal and hold it. Loosen the tube fitting at the cylinder outlet boss and allow fluid containing bubbles to escape. (Have rags handy to absorb the fluid, or you will have a mess). The wheel cylinders must also be bled in any case.

The job is finished by checking the compensating ports. To identify the compensating from the breather port, note which way the brake pushrod moves. If it goes from front to rear, the compensating port is the rearward of the two ports in each reservoir. If the pushrod moves from rear to front, the compensating port is the forward of the two ports.

To check for an open compensating port, insert a piece of thin wire down the reservoir into the port, with the brakes off. An alternate method is the old fluid geyser check, which indicates that the port was open when the brakes were off. Have someone hit the brakes (engine idling with power brakes) and look for a geyser of fluid in each reservoir. If the geyser only occurs in one reservoir, have the helper pump the brakes, hold the pedal and slowly release it. There should be either a geyser or at the least a fluttering of the fluid in the reservoir.

If the port isn't open, adjust brake pedal free play (on the threaded pushrod of the master cylinder or an adjusting rod or nut at the pedal, whichever setup is used). The adjustment is for one-quarter inch free play with manual brakes, and for maximum pedal height on power brakes.

31

Drum Brake Service

THERE'S NO DEEP, dark mystery about how a car's brakes are supposed to operate. And it doesn't take a master mechanic to spot the most common brake ailments or to actually make the necessary repairs and adjustments.

Working carefully, you can do a safe, sure job of brake repairing, and count on an $8-$10 savings for each hour you work.

To determine whether your brakes need servicing, first check out their performance with this simple road test, performed on a deserted parking lot if possible. While driving in a straight line at 15-20 mph, try a quick stop.

See if any of the tire marks in the gravel are heavier than others or if the rear wheels have swerved out of line. Try the same test again, but ease up on the steering wheel as you stop. If the wheel spins to one side, you know the brakes are not equalized and are dangerous on slippery roads. Now let the car coast and listen to the brakes while they are applied and released slowly. Carefully note any noise or faulty operation and then check the symptoms on the table for possible causes. We will locate the defect exactly by eliminating the most easily checked and repaired causes first.

Next, perform the hydraulic system test described at the end of the chapter "Brake Systems Hydraulics and the Single Master Cylinder."

Pedal Clearance. Let the car set a few minutes after the road test and then push the brake pedal down hard and hold it there. Then see how much clearance or *reserve* you have between the brake pedal and the floorboards. If this clearance is less than 3 in., check the fluid reservoir at the master cylinder to make sure the fluid is within ⅜ in. of the threads on the filler neck. This reservoir is usually part of the master cylinder, or else it is a small tank connected to it by a line. If the fluid level is low, refill with a heavy-duty, nationally-available brand that is guaranteed to mix with all other brake fluids. Then repeat the pedal reserve test.

Free Play Test, Next, test the brake pedal for *free play.* Apply just enough pressure on the pedal with your fingers to move it. The pedal should move about ½ in. before you feel the resistance of the master cylinder piston. If there is less, the piston is not returning

to its normal "brakes-off" position and is blocking the compensating port. Consequently some of the fluid pressure may be retained, preventing the brakes from releasing completely. Adjustment for free play is usually made by loosening the lock nut on the push rod linkage between the brake pedal and the master cylinder. Then adjust the travel of the rod by turning it un-

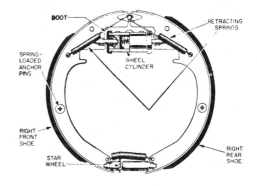

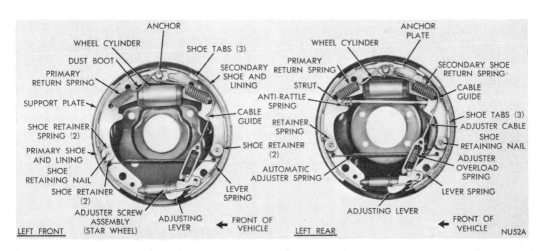

Modern self-adjusting drum brake is shown, with all components labeled, in upper two illustrations. Note self-adjusting assembly, which includes cable, guide flange on secondary shoe and lever assembly to actuate star wheel. Compare with manual adjusting setup in lower illustration, in which there is the simple star wheel and a tensioning spring over it.

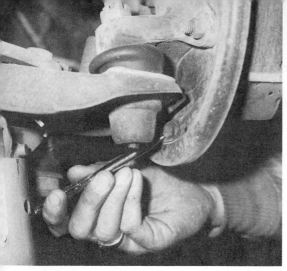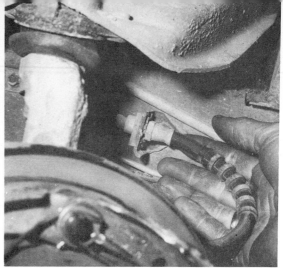

Left: Pen points to access hole in brake backing plate. When rubber plug is removed, you can adjust manual adjusting brakes, or manually back off self-adjusting brakes that have overadjusted and prevent drum from coming off. In this case, however, awl and adjusting spoon must both be inserted into hole, (awl to push away adjusting lever, spoon to turn star wheel). Right: Check brake hydraulic hoses for leaks, cracks and other signs of weakness.

til the correct amount of free play is obtained. On some older Ford cars, the free play is adjusted by turning an eccentric bolt.

Adjusting the Brakes. Virtually all American cars for some years have had self-adjusting drum brakes.

With this system, a cable is attached to the anchor pin, run around a flange on one of the brake shoes and attached to a lever which bears up against the familiar star wheel adjuster, described later.

When the car is operating in reverse and the brakes are applied, the outward movement of the shoe tugs on the cable and this actuates the lever, which moves the star wheel adjuster. No manual adjustment is normally necessary.

If, however, the system becomes corroded and freezes, it must be disassembled and penetrating solvent applied or the parts replaced.

Older cars and some high-performance cars of recent years have manual adjusting brakes, and they are described here.

The most common system, to which the self-adjusting mechanism has been added, is the star wheel.

To adjust this type of brake, raise the wheel, remove the oblong rubber rust plug from the back plate and insert a screwdriver or brake adjusting tool. By working the tool in a prying motion, you will be able to turn the star wheel inside the drum until the shoes are expanded to their limit and the wheel is locked tight. Then, by prying in the opposite direction, back off the star wheel just enough to let the wheel turn freely. Apply and release the brakes several times, and check again for shoe drag by rotating the wheel. If there is any drag, readjust until the wheel turns freely. Be sure to replace the rubber plug.

The second type of adjustment is an *eccentric cam*. The cam adjustment may be made at the back plate with a wrench or through a hole in the front of the drum using a screwdriver. The adjustment is the same regardless of the method used to turn the cam. Working on one shoe at a time, rotate the cam until the brake shoe is tight against the drum and the wheel is locked. Now back off the cam just enough to allow the wheel to turn without the shoe dragging. Repeat the operation on the other cam and brake shoe and then check as with the star wheel system.

Hydraulic Line Inspection. Now with the car indoors, continue your inspection by getting under it with a flashlight to inspect the hydraulic lines. These lines should be firm and dry. Replace a line if there is the slightest

trace of brake fluid or oil on the covering or if it shows signs of gumminess and softening.

Although they are less subject to damage or deterioration, the metal lines that connect the master cylinder with the flexible lines should also be checked carefully. Check for leaking connections, dents, loose fastenings at the frame, and for signs of abrasion or wear on the guards where the line bends around the frame. While you are under the car, check the parking brake cables for wear and the inside of the wheels for bearing grease leaks. Such a leak can affect the operation of your brakes due to grease entering the brake drum and soaking the linings.

Now inspect the master cylinder closely for leakage. Leaks at the brake line connection can often be corrected by tightening, but if the fluid is coming from around the piston rod, the master cylinder is in need of overhauling and must be removed. To remove it, disconnect the brake line, remove

When you check a master cylinder for leaks, begin by cleaning it off thoroughly first, so you don't confuse road splash and engine oil with brake fluid.

Top: Leaking wheel cylinder can be checked by pushing away dust cover at each side with a screwdriver and looking for signs of brake fluid seepage.

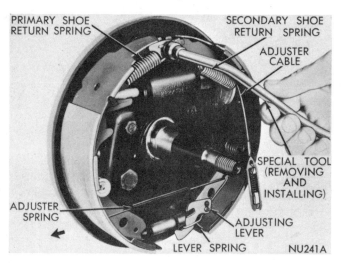

PRIMARY SHOE RETURN SPRING

SECONDARY SHOE RETURN SPRING

ADJUSTER CABLE

SPECIAL TOOL (REMOVING AND INSTALLING)

ADJUSTER SPRING

ADJUSTING LEVER

LEVER SPRING

NU241A

Left: Disassembly of drum brake can begin with disconnection of self-adjusting cable on cars so equipped, and removal of brake shoe return springs. Taking off and refitting springs is easier with the special tool shown, but you can also use a screwdriver.

the wires from the stoplight switch and unfasten the push rod from the pedal. Then remove the mounting bolts and lift out the cylinder for rebuilding as described later.

Continue your brake check by removing a front and a rear brake drum to inspect the linings and shoe mechanisms. Don't decide whether relining is necessary on the basis of a front or rear wheel alone. It is true that the front linings wear faster, but a poorly adjusted, dragging parking brake can put wear on the rear shoes in a hurry.

In the classified section of your phone book, locate an auto parts dealer who advertises pick up and delivery machine shop service. Go to see him to make certain he has all the parts you may need to complete the brake overhaul and get an estimate of their cost. Also, while you are there, for some cars you may have to borrow or rent a universal wheel puller to remove your rear brake drums. There is occasionally no charge for the use of this tool when accompanied by a parts order.

Now block up the car and place a piece of wood under the brake pedal to prevent it from accidentally being pushed while the drums are removed. Remove the hubcap and dust cap from a front wheel and then, without removing the wheel, pull the cotter pin and remove the nut from the spindle. Get a good grip on the two sides of the tire, wiggle it a bit, and pull straight back. The tire, wheel, brake drum and wheel bearing should slide off easily as a unit.

See the chapter, "Set Your Bearings Straight," for illustrated information on pulling the front wheels.

To remove a rear brake drum, you may need the universal wheel puller. After removing dust cap, cotter pin and castle nut, fasten the three arms of the wheel puller under three lug nuts of the wheel and then turn the screw until it is against the axle shaft. Rap on the striking anvil with a hammer until the drum comes free.

Lining Inspection. As soon as the drum is removed, brush the dust off of all parts and make a close visual inspection of the linings, brake drums and wheel cylinders. If the shoes are to be removed, label each one to show its location. Don't mark on the linings; when they are replaced, the marks will be lost. It may help you to remember the location of the springs and pins if you make a sketch of the assembly for a front and rear wheel.

If the linings are worn down to within 1/16-inch of the rivets or shoe steel back, they must be replaced. For safety's sake, also change linings if they have become coated with brake fluid or grease.

To remove the brake shoes, first unhook the retractor spring. This spring is most easily removed with a special pliers that can be purchased for about $2. You can use an ordinary pliers, but it takes a powerful grip and extra care not to let the spring slip.

Tie a cord around the wheel cylinder or use the special clamp to keep the pistons from popping out of the cylinder when the shoes are removed. Then, if the shoes are held to the back plate by a spring-loaded pin, compress the spring, turn it 90° and release it to free the brake shoes.

When disassembling the rear brakes, remove both shoes, the parking lever, the shoe adjusting screw and its lock spring as a unit. Then disconnect the parking brake lever from the shoes and just let it hang from the cable.

Drum Inspection. If the linings have worn down to the rivets and the drum is scored deeply enough to have made lengthwise marks on the shoes, have the drum reground at a brake shop. Brake drums should be replaced if there are any signs of cracking, warping or heat discoloration. The number of times a drum can be reground depends on the amount of metal removed during grinding. Since .060 in. is the maximum amount that can be safely removed, drums can seldom be reground a second time.

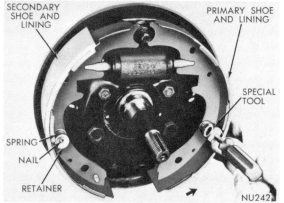

SECONDARY SHOE AND LINING

PRIMARY SHOE AND LINING

SPECIAL TOOL

SPRING

NAIL

RETAINER

NU242

Top: With return springs removed, anchor plate can be taken out.

Above: Retainer spring assembly is shown being removed with special tool. Job also can be done with screwdriver. Just press down spring with screwdriver and twist the retaining nail with fingers to free the assembly.

Check to see if there is a sharp shoulder at the back edge of the braking surface in the drum. This means the drum has been reground at least once and that if it is deeply scored now it is likely the drum must be exchanged. In either case, wire the la-

beled brake shoes and their drum together so they can be sent to the brake shop as a unit and the shoes fitted to that drum or its replacement.

Now turn up the edge of each of the rubber boots on the wheel cylinders to see if fluid has been leaking by the piston. Also check along the back plate for signs of leaking. If there is the slightest amount of leakage, all of the cylinders probably need service.

If your car is in need of a complete brake overhaul order a rebuilding kit for each wheel cylinder and one for the master cylinder, along with a hone for the cylinder bores. Also ask to have the brake shoes relined and, if necessary, have the drums reground. With this, purchase a quart each of heavy-duty brake fluid and a brake line flushing compound. If all of these materials are necessary, you will have spent between $30 and $50 as the total expense for your brake overhaul; a small fraction of the cost of having it done.

Since the replacement parts for rebuilding the cylinders may differ slightly in appearance from the original, check to see that there are instructions for assembling them in each kit. Also see that the brake shoes are still with the correct drums by checking the markings you have made during disassembly.

Then remove the boot and brake shoe push rod from each wheel cylinder and gently press against one of the pistons until the opposite piston and its rubber cup are forced out of the other end of the cylinder. Remove the piston spring and push the remaining piston and cup out from the other side. If the brake system has two wheel cylin-

Shoes are pulled away from the anchor pin and lifted away from the backing plate.

ders, one end of each cylinder will be closed and the piston must be forced out by applying a light pressure on the brake pedal. On some models there is also an expander located between the end of the piston spring and the cup which should also be replaced.

Note: wheel cylinders can only be rebuilt if the cylinder bores are in good condition. Very light scratches and corrosion can be cleaned with crocus cloth. If there is any question in your mind, replace the wheel cylinder.

The practice of honing out wheel cylinders that are moderately scored is of questionable value. A replacement cylinder is little more expensive than one that is professionally honed and rebuilt by you. Your safety is worth the small extra expense.

If the cylinder bore looks bright and free from scratches, wipe it thoroughly with a soft clean cloth dampened with brake line cleaner. Then insert one of the new pistons and check the clearance between the piston and the cylinder wall with a feeler gauge. This

clearance must not be more than .004 in. If it's over .004, which is very unlikely, you'll have to replace the cylinder housings.

Master Cylinder Overhaul. Then mount your master cylinder in a vise and clean the outside of it thoroughly before beginning disassembly. Position the cylinder so the push rod from the pedal is toward you and you will see either a retaining wire or a metal collar held with a pair of capscrews. Remove this retainer first so you can take out the piston, piston cups, spring and valve from the cylinder. Lay these parts out in order for reference when assembling the new parts, but do not under any circumstances use them when reassembling the cylinder. The exact number and style of the parts will differ with each make and year of car.

Some Buick cars in the late 1950's had a unique master cylinder in which the piston did not fit against the cylinder walls. This cylinder is serviced by separating the cast housings and removing the retaining wire to expose the long, rod-like piston.

Check the bore and the valve seat at the end of the bore for rust or corrosion and clean, if necessary, with crocus cloth or a commercial rust remover. Follow the same procedure for the master cylinder as was used on the wheel cylinders if the bore is pitted or scratched. Then reassemble the cylinder with the new parts from the kit, following the enclosed instructions.

Install the master cylinder in the car, connecting the lines and the stoplight switch and checking to be sure that the push rod is lined up to work freely before tightening the mounting

Star wheel should be inspected carefully. It must thread in and out easily, or threads should be dunked in solvent to remove rust and then coated with silicone lubricant. Teeth of star wheel should not be damaged. This is particularly important on self-adjusting brakes, which have 24 small teeth per star wheel, compared with 12 larger ones for the manual adjusting brakes.

bolts. Adjust the freeplay as described. If it is necessary to replace any of the hydraulic lines, do so now. No sealer of any kind is necessary or desirable here as the brass fittings will make a very tight seal under moderate pressure.

Brake Line Flushing. Pack each wheel cylinder with a clean cloth and fill the master cylinder with the brake line cleaning fluid. Then remove the cloth from one cylinder at a time and flush the brake line by pumping the fluid through it with the brake pedal. Refill the reservoir and continue this until the distinct color of the cleaner can be seen when it is forced out at the wheel cylinders.

Pump the cylinder until the system is empty and then reassemble the wheel cylinders according to the instructions in the kits. Lubricate all the new parts

with brake fluid before assembly and insert them from the end of the cylinder in which they will operate. Don't try to push the cups through from one end as the rubber parts may snag on the bleeder or inlet hole and be damaged. If trapped air forces one piston out when you insert the other, open the bleeder valve to relieve the pressure.

If any of the parts become dirty while they are being assembled, rinse them in the brake line cleaning fluid, allow them to dry and then dip them into fresh brake fluid again. *Caution:* do not use the brake fluid that has been used for lubricating these parts or the hone to refill the master cylinder as it will contain grit and air bubbles. Also, do not allow any oil or grease to come into contact with the cylinder assembly as it will deteriorate the rubber parts. When the wheel cylinders have been

Brake drum surface that comes in contact with brake shoes should be smooth. If you can hang a fingernail on a score, drum must be resurfaced or replaced. Minor scratches can be removed with crocus cloth.

completely assembled, snap on the boots and push rods and secure them temporarily by tying or using clamps.

Brake Shoe Assembly. Before installing the brake shoe assembly, coat the threads and contact surfaces of the adjusting screw with a high temperature fiber or silicone grease. Also coat the raised shoe guides on the back plate with this grease.

Then mount each brake shoe on the anchor pin and set it in the cylinder push rod slots. On Bendix type brakes, screw the adjusting screw all the way in, that is, make it as short as possible and fit it between the lower ends of the shoes. Assemble the hold-down pins by placing the plates over the spring and pin, compressing the spring and turning the assembly 90°. On other type brakes, turn the eccentric cam adjustment so its low point will be against

the shoe. Finally, secure the entire assembly with the retracting springs and attach the self-adjusting mechanism.

Be sure to replace the parking brake lever on the rear wheel by connecting it to the shoe with the pin and then crimping the horseshoe washer over the pin end. Repack the front wheels and replace the grease seals in the hubs if necessary. Then fit the drum over the shoe assembly. On brake assemblies where both ends of the shoes fit in slots, it may be necessary to center the shoes somewhat to install the drum. Do this by moving each shoe in the right direction by hitting it with a soft mallet or the heel of your hand.

Be sure to replace the key and lock washer on the rear drum and then draw all of the hubs up tight. Back off the front axle nut to the next cotter pin slot, insert a new pin and replace the dust cover. If the rear brake drum is fastened to the hub with sheet metal nuts, use new ones when reassembling.

Bleeding. Before replacing the wheels, bleed the entire brake system of air. The principle of operation in a hydraulic system is built around the fact that fluids are not compressible. The presence of even a small quantity of air, which is easily compressible, will seriously affect its efficiency. Your car is equipped with bleeder valves which allow this air to escape when they are opened, but it is up to you to see that air is not drawn back into the system.

You can bleed your brakes by having a helper operate the brake pedal while you control the flow of fluid through the bleeder valves. First close all the valves and then fill the master cylinder. Replace the cap and have

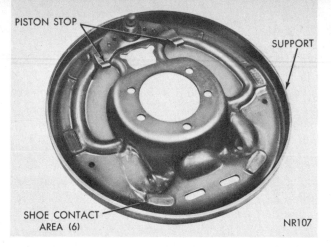

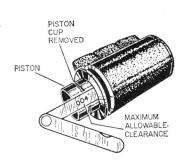

Right: To check wheel cylinder bore, take piston with sealing cup removed and insert in bore. Try to insert an .005-inch feeler gauge. If it can fit in, the bore is too large and the wheel cylinder should be replaced. A clearance of .004-inch between piston and bore, measured with a feeler gauge, is maximum permitted. Left: With everything off the backing plate, it should be cleaned and the raised shoe contact areas (six on the backing plate illustrated) should be coated lightly with silicone grease.

your helper pump the brake pedal a few times. Then check the level of the fluid again and add more if necessary. Now have him hold a steady pressure on the pedal while you open the bleeder valve with a small wrench.

Check the color of the fluid that escapes to be sure the cleaner is completely expelled. The fluid will squirt through the valve with a sputtering sound until there is no more air in the line. This may take two or three pumps of the pedal. Your helper should let you know each time the pedal is just about to the floorboard so you can close the valve while there is still pressure in the line. Check the master cylinder reservoir after each wheel is bled and keep it filled to the proper level.

Bleeding attachments are available which will allow you to do this job by yourself. These will usually have three fittings to adapt to all cars and will

have a ball-check valve to prevent air from being drawn into the system when the pedal is released.

When all points have been bled, the pedal action should be firm and should maintain the correct reserve clearance under continued pressure. On the second pump of the pedal the reserve should be no greater than on the first pump. If this is not the case, repeat the bleeding operation. If the second bleeding still does not provide the proper pedal action, check for leaks that may have been overlooked during assembly.

The next step is to adjust the brakes. On the typical late-model car, all that is necessary is to drive in reverse at low speed and apply the brakes, and they will adjust automatically.

Brake shoes, like most equipment on your car, should be broken in carefully for long, trouble-free use. Allow the shoes about 100 miles of moderate use before attempting mountainous roads or frequent fast stops. After 100 miles make another service adjustment as before and recheck the lines for leaks.

Then, with these service adjustments and inspections at 5,000-mile intervals, the brake system overhaul as described will provide safe, carefree service for 30,000 miles.

WHAT'S THE MATTER WITH YOUR BRAKES?

Here Are the Possible Causes...   **And Solutions...**

IF BRAKES PULL CAR TO ONE SIDE:

1. Tires unevenly inflated or worn unevenly — Replace with matched tires on each side and inflate evenly
2. Shoes need adjustment — Adjust brakes
3. Back plate or wheel bearings loose — Tighten plate; replace and/or adjust bearings
4. Grease or fluid soaked lining on one wheel, lining charred — Replace linings and repair grease or fluid leak
5. Moisture or mud on shoes — Clean out brake assembly with water if muddy. Drive slowly and maintain light pressure on brakes until friction dries lining. Replace rubber plug in back plate if necessary
6. Drum scored or out of round — Regrind or replace drums
7. Dissimilar linings on one side of car — Replace with matched linings
8. Weak or loose chassis spring — Tighten or replace worn part
9. Worn king pins — Replace worn parts

IF ONE BRAKE DRAGS:

1. Shoe clearance insufficient — Readjust dragging brake
2. Hydraulic line clogged or crimped — Flush system or replace line
3. Loose wheel bearings — Tighten or replace bearings
4. Weak or broken shoe return spring — Replace spring
5. Shoe sticking on anchor pins — Lube anchor pins and other contact points
6. Wheel cylinder pistons sticking — Hone cylinder and replace piston

IF BRAKES ARE HARSH OR GRAB:

1. Linings are wet or damp — Drive car slowly while maintaining light pressure on brake pedal until friction dries linings
2. Back plate loose — Tighten back plate screws
3. Charred, grease soaked or improper linings — Replace linings
4. Drums scored — Regrind or replace drums

IF BRAKES SQUEAK:

1. Loose wheel bearings — Replace and/or adjust bearings
2. Metallic particles or dust imbedded in lining, worn lining — Replace lining
3. Bent back plate — Repair or replace backplate
4. Bent shoes — Check installation and replace shoes

IF BRAKES KNOCK:

1. Roughly finished or warped drum — Replace or regrind drum
2. Adjusting slot in shoe is not square — Repair or replace shoe

IF THERE'S INADEQUATE RESERVE CLEARANCE AT BRAKE PEDAL:

1. Low fluid level in master cylinder — Add fluid
2. Pedal and/or shoes need adjustment — Adjust pedal and shoes
3. Air or fluid vapor trapped in system — Bleed system
4. Fluid leak in system — Repair or replace defective lines or cylinders
5. Worn lining — Replace lining

IF ALL BRAKES DRAG AFTER ADJUSTMENT:

1. Vent in filler cap is clogged — Clean vent
2. Inadequate freeplay at pedal — Adjust master cylinder push rod or brake pedal eccentric bolt
3. Brake lines clogged or crimped — Replace line and/or flush system
4. Rubber pistons swollen — Check and replace brake fluid

This is a typical floating caliper disc brake. Caliper floats along rods attached to brace. In this type, only one side of caliper has piston.

32

Disc Brakes

DISC BRAKES ARE standard or optional equipment on the front wheels of virtually all cars, and some cars even offer discs front and rear.

Instead of pumping fluid into wheel cylinders, the master cylinder pumps the fluid into a hydraulic piston device called a caliper. The caliper is much like a clamp. Pistons are pushed out by fluid pressure and squeeze a pair of friction pads against the sides of a disc. The disc is bolted to the wheel, just like a brake drum, and when the pads are clamped against it, the car is brought to a stop.

The disc is exposed to the air, so it keeps cool. As a result, the disc braking system is virtually immune to fade caused by heat, the brake system's No. 1 enemy. The disc also spins off water, so driving through a deep puddle does not cause extended loss of braking efficiency.

The front wheels do two-thirds of the brake work on a typical car, so the discs are usually installed on the front wheels. The old drum brake is better as an emergency brake, so many companies still fit drums to the rear wheels. The reason the drum does better as an emergency brake is the self-energizing effect, which is the wedging action of the shoes into the drum. This wedging action reduces the pedal pressure necessary for braking effort, and also the pulling action on the hand brake (or pushing action on the foot-actuated emergency brake). Because it has no self-energizing effect, the disc brake usually requires a power assist, particularly on larger cars.

In the drum braking system, return springs retract the shoes, so for fast response when you hit the pedal, a small amount of residual pressure is maintained in the hydraulic lines by that residual pressure check valve in the master cylinder. The disc system has no return springs, so it has no residual pressure check valve. It gets its fast response by keeping the friction pad lightly touching the disc or just a few thousandths of an inch away.

Because it doesn't retract the shoes, the disc braking system is self-adjusting. As the friction material on the pad wears, the piston pushes out further to press the friction pad against the disc. Because there is no spring to retract the piston, it keeps its new position each time.

The absence of residual pressure in the lines keeps the brakes from really dragging when you take your foot off the pedal. Some disc systems retract the piston mechanically (often with nothing more than a flexing seal around the piston) a few thousandths of an inch to eliminate drag of any sort. Others actually use a spring behind the piston to keep the friction pad and disc in light contact.

Two disc braking systems have been used. The first was the fixed caliper type. The caliper is bolted in position around the disc, and has one or two

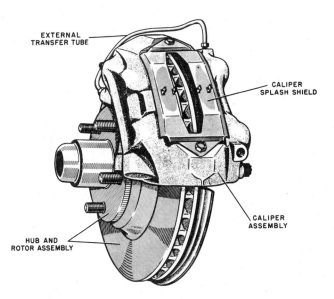

EXTERNAL
TRANSFER TUBE

CALIPER
SPLASH SHIELD

CALIPER
ASSEMBLY

HUB AND
ROTOR ASSEMBLY

Typical disc brake setup of the fixed caliper type. Notice cover plate (called caliper splash shield) over end of caliper.

pistons on each side to push the friction pads against the disc. Most new American cars use a floating caliper design. It has just one large piston.

The caliper floats a few thousandths of an inch along a bracket that is fixed over the disc. The single piston comes out, pushes the pad in front of it against the disc, and the caliper floats, opposite to the direction of the piston. This movement pulls the other side of

the caliper into the other side of the disc. The friction pad on this side then is pressed against the disc. The caliper moves very little in its float, so there is really no obvious movement.

The basic repair on a disc system is replacement of the friction pads, equivalent to fitting new brake shoes on a drum system. It's a job the weekend mechanic can easily do. The first step is to see if the pads need replacing. On

Right: This type of floating caliper disc brake has been used by Ford. Fingers point to bolts along which the caliper floats.

Below: Disassembled fixed caliper. Notice four-piston design. Grooves in brake shoes are wear indicators used in those designs. When groove was worn away, it was time to replace shoe.

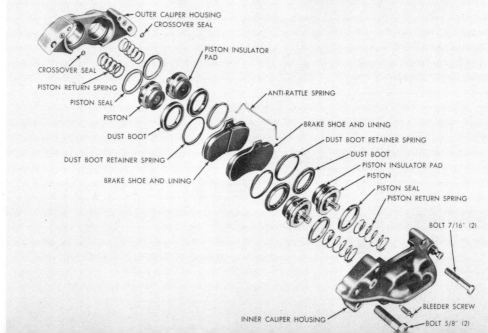

most disc systems, you can see the condition of the pads simply by looking in through the end of the caliper. You may not even have to pull a wheel.

On most American fixed caliper systems, there are slots to a certain depth in the friction material, and when these slots are worn away, the pads must be replaced. The pads should wear evenly, and about the same on both sides, so if you can see what one pad looks like, you can safely assume the condition of the other. Pads on some floating caliper systems wear to a slight taper (normally a maximum of ⅛ inch). In either system, the pad should be at least 1/32 inch thick at its thinnest point.

Begin pad replacement by siphoning out a few ounces of fluid from the reservoir, if it is full. Otherwise, when new pads are installed, and the pistons are forced further back into the caliper, they will displace fluid, pushing it up through the lines into the master cylinder, causing it to overflow. Discard the siphoned-out brake fluid. If the master cylinder was not topped up as the pads wore and the pistons projected out, there will be no need to drain out fluid.

The fixed caliper design is the easiest in which to replace pads. In virtually all cases, there is a cover plate (held by pins or screws) on the edge of the caliper. Take off the cover plate and pull out the old friction pads. You may have to work the pad back and forth a bit to gain the clearance to pull it out easily. Now push the pistons back in. (If they won't go back in, the caliper must be overhauled.) To gain the proper leverage, insert a small piece

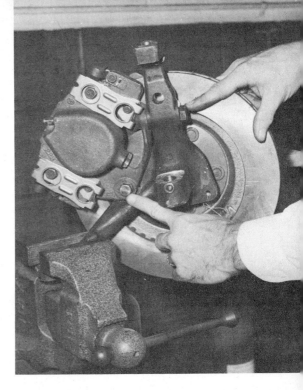

Fingers point to bolts which must be removed on aforementioned Ford floating caliper discs to pull away caliper and bracing plate for access to friction pads (brake shoes).

of steel and exert force against the steel with a large screwdriver (which will protect the aluminum pistons against scoring). Once the pistons are back, you can push the new pads into place. Refit the cover plate and the job is done.

The floating caliper design takes more time. One type has a caliper bracing plate (to and from which the caliper floats) attached to the spindle. Two bolts hold the brace, and once you remove these, the caliper and brace drop as a unit. If you are careful, you will lower the caliper onto a box and work at the wheel. Otherwise, you will

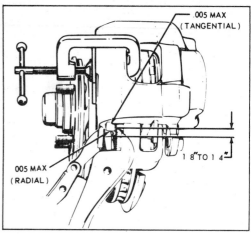

Left: Pads on that Ford system are easily removed once caliper is lowered. (It is shown on bench for illustrative purposes only.) Piston can be pushed back with thumb pressure. Right: Outboard friction pad had to be aligned by clinching on early GM floating caliper disc brakes. Clinching was done by holding assembly onto disc with C-clamp and bending ears of the friction pad (brake shoe) with vise-type pliers.

have to disconnect a brake line and bleed afterwards. The friction pads may be held by guide pins or slots in the caliper. When you refit the brace, tighten the top bolt first. Each bolt should be tightened to factory specifications, normally 90-100 ft./lbs. using a torque wrench.

The other popular design has a bracket bolted to the spindle and the caliper mounts to the bracket on two bolts, along which it floats. To change friction pads, undo the bolts and remove them. This allows you to lower the caliper from the disc. With the caliper lowered, the new pads can be fitted into place. (There may be a spring between the caliper piston and the inboard shoe; if there is, be sure to reinstall it.)

The sleeves and bushings through which the float bolts pass should be re-placed when installing new pads, to be sure the caliper will continue to float properly. Lubricate the sleeves and bushings and the small ends of the bolts with a silicone grease.

Once the pads are in position, on some early models the outboard pad must have its ears properly lined up, a process called "clinching." This is done by starting the caliper with new pads back onto the bracket, so that the bottom edge of the outer pad is just resting on the outer edge of the disc. Clamp the outboard pad to the caliper with moderate pressure, using a C-clamp. (The caliper is cut out at the outer end, so you'll need a metal plate, such as an old brake pad, to span the opening.

With vise-type pliers, clinch the out-board shoe ears as illustrated. Locate the pliers $\frac{1}{8}$ to $\frac{1}{4}$ inch from the outer

This current design of floating caliper disc brakes is simple to service. Clips are removed from end of float rod, then rod is pulled with pliers, permitting removal of caliper. Once caliper is off, float rod guides are slid out, freeing friction pads.

edge of the ear. The clearance of the ear from each edge of the caliper should be no more than .005 inch, as illustrated.

Floating caliper discs were changed in 1970 to eliminate the need for clinching pads.

The condition of the disc itself is important, of course. But scratches .015-inch deep, which would certainly require refinishing of a drum, do not require attention on a disc. A few years ago, a badly scored disc had to be replaced. But the manufacturers of brake drum lathes now have attachments that permit perfectly acceptable refinishing of discs.

As you can see, there is nothing complex about disc brakes. In fact, when you compare them to today's self-adjusting brakes, with that mess of links and springs for self-adjustment, they almost look simple.

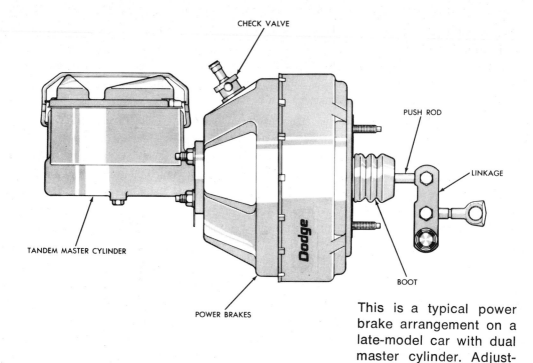

CHECK VALVE

PUSH ROD

LINKAGE

TANDEM MASTER CYLINDER

Dodge

BOOT

POWER BRAKES

This is a typical power brake arrangement on a late-model car with dual master cylinder. Adjustment of pedal height is on the link at the extreme right, which is threaded.

33

Power Brakes

SO-CALLED POWER brakes are not really power brakes at all. Power assist from engine vacuum helps you push down the brake pedal of an otherwise ordinary hydraulic brake system. All makes of power brakes, or more exactly power boosters used on American cars, are similar in operation, maintenance and troubleshooting.

Basically the power booster is a vacuum operated cylinder added between the brake pedal and the hydraulic master cylinder. When you even touch the brake pedal lightly, vacuum sucks a piston forward to push hydraulic fluid from the master cylinder into the brake lines and out to each wheel cylinder. Without power assist, your foot pedal linkage pushes directly on the piston in the master cylinder. (This is what gives non-power brakes much better feel and controlability than power brakes even though it takes more leg power to operate them.)

Most vacuum brake booster units have three major parts: vacuum cylinder, vacuum piston with built-in control valve, and end plate with bracket and lever assembly. Vacuum to power the unit comes from a tube attached to the intake manifold of the engine.

When your foot is off the brake pedal, the vacuum unit is in the released position. The vacuum port to the engine remains closed, but the atmospheric port is open. Air can pass freely from one side of the piston to the other. With equal pressure on both sides, the return spring holds the piston in the off position. Another port, the compensating port, between the vacuum cylinder and the hydraulic master cylinder is also open. This lets hydraulic fluid from the brake lines return to the master cylinder.

When you touch the brake pedal, the atmospheric port closes and the vacuum port opens. Vacuum from the intake manifold then sucks the piston forward against the pressure of the return spring. This motion pushes the operating rod in the hydraulic master cylinder to apply the brakes.

Should the power booster fail, then the operating rod for the power system would move forward to push directly on the operating rod for the master cylinder hydraulic piston. Thus, when you stepped on the brake pedal, you would notice slightly longer pedal travel and increased braking effort, but you could still stop the car.

Troubleshooting power brakes calls for some simple tests you can make yourself. As with power steering systems, you can repair leaks in connections and hoses, or replace the whole vacuum unit with a rebuilt; but very possibly, repairs to this unit may require special tools and skills as well.

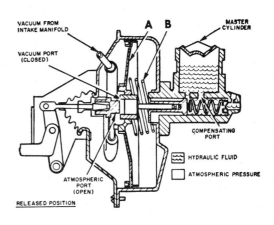

Upper drawing shows vacuum power cylinder in released position with air pressure equal on both sides of power piston (A), located by return spring (B). Lower drawing shows power cylinder with brakes fully applied. Piston (A) has been sucked forward by engine vacuum, through vacuum valve, compressing spring (B) and forcing piston in brake master cylinder to apply the brakes.

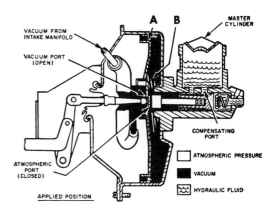

Start by testing booster operation. Shut off the engine and pump the brake pedal several times to exhaust all vacuum in the system. Older model power brake systems often incorporate a vacuum reservoir tank, so these may take a few more pumps on the pedal to clear them of vacuum.

Now step on the brake pedal and hold it down firmly while you restart the engine. If the vacuum system is working right, the brake pedal will move forward slightly when the engine starts. No movement and a pedal that feels hard mean the vacuum unit is not working.

The fault may lie in the unit, or it may not be getting any vacuum. Check by removing the vacuum hose from the power cylinder. Hold your thumb over the open end of the hose; you should be able to feel the suction.

No vacuum at the hose means there is a leak in the system, or the engine is not in good shape. Check the hose for kinks, collapsed areas, or tears. Replace the hose if defective.

If the hose is OK, but you still get no suction, check for vacuum at the intake manifold. A vacuum gauge should show 17 to 21 in. with the engine idling. If it does not, check first for manifold leaks. A quick way is to idle the engine after putting oil on the joints at carburetor flange to intake manifold and intake manifold to cylinder block. If there is a leak, vacuum will suck in the oil to seal it temporarily. With proper vacuum, the engine will speed up. Fix the leaky joint by tightening the attachment bolts, or if this does not work, by replacing the gasket.

If you find no leaks, lack of manifold vacuum points to the need for an engine tune-up or possibly even an overhaul.

If there is vacuum at the hose, but the booster unit does not work, the vacuum booster itself is at fault. Before removing the unit from the car, test the vacuum check valve, a common cause of trouble.

The vacuum check valve is a one-way affair which lets air be sucked out of the vacuum booster into the intake manifold but doesn't let the vacuum out of the unit when the engine is shut off. To remove it from the cylinder, disconnect the vacuum hose and simply unscrew the valve. In most systems you can do this without removing the vacuum cylinder from the car.

Check the valve by blowing through it first one way and then the other. No air should come out the end to which the vacuum hose is attached, but you should be able to blow through other end. If the valve is faulty, replace it.

If the valve is in good condition but the unit still does not operate, you must remove the vacuum unit from the car. Further disassembly and inspection should be performed by a serviceman experienced in vacuum unit repair who has the proper tools for the job. He can repair the unit for you, or you can exchange it for a new or rebuilt unit.

You can, however, test your vacuum unit to see if it is causing the brakes to drag. This can wear out one set of linings after another in addition to cutting deeply into your fuel mileage.

First make sure brake shoes are properly adjusted and that wheels turn freely. Raise the front end of the car

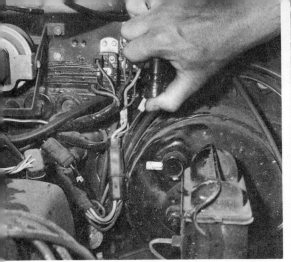

Left: Vacuum hose to power brake unit is disconnected and with engine running, you should feel vacuum at end of hose. Right: If vacuum valve is defective, it can simply be pulled out of the rubber grommet in which it sits in the power brake unit.

and start both front wheels spinning. Immediately start the engine and let it idle. Keep your foot off the brake pedal. Each front wheel should coast to a stop and still turn freely. If one or both stops more quickly than it should, or if you can feel a noticeable drag, there is trouble in the vacuum unit. You may have to have it repaired or even replaced.

Power booster units all have a filter to clean the air drawn into the system. On some boosters this filter is external and can be removed for cleaning. Check the workshop manual for your car to see if it has this type of filter and how often it should be serviced. Many makes have an internal filter which only needs servicing when the booster cylinder is removed from the car.

To clean either type of filter, wash it in alcohol or some other non-oil base solvent. Gasoline or similar solvents should be avoided because they can damage rubber parts in the braking system.

One last check completes the work you can do on your power brake system. Make sure no brake fluid is being sucked through the vacuum line into the intake manifold. To do this, remove the vacuum hose from the intake manifold and run a screwdriver or pencil around the inside of the open end. If if comes out wet with brake fluid, there is a serious leak past the vacuum cylinder piston. The whole unit will have to be rebuilt or replaced to cure this leakage. If it continues, the engine will idle roughly, perform poorly, and hydraulic fluid can form gums which cause sticking valves and may create a variety of other problems.

These simple checks will enable you to tell when your power brake booster is working properly. When it is not, they will help you pinpoint the trouble, and in many cases you can cure it yourself.

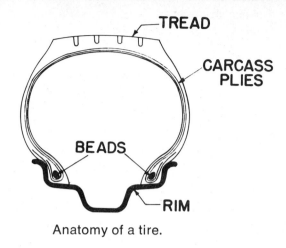

Anatomy of a tire.

34

How to Buy and Care for Tires

How CAN YOU keep your tires safe and make them last longer? And when you buy new ones, what kind should you get?

Not so many decades ago motorists were not faced with these bewildering questions. Only one kind of tire was available—a solid rubber doughnut—and it required no maintenance to speak of. You just waited for the tire to tear itself to shreds (which it did in quick order) and then replaced it. Of course the road-holding and ride qualities of those primitive old tires were nothing to brag about.

Today's tires are much better, and much more complex. They are made from a variety of materials, in many designs, sizes, proportions, and tread patterns. Prices also vary widely, with so-called premium tires costing up to three times more than the same size low-line models. Each kind, even the cheapie, has advantages as well as drawbacks, and the tire that is best for your next door neighbor may not be best for you.

All modern tires consist of four basic components:

- The carcass, or casing.
- The bead—the steel-wire-reinforced edge that keeps the tire on the wheel rim.
- The tread—the flat, grooved "footprint" that contacts the road.
- The compressed air inside the carcass that supports the weight of the car.

Some tires use a tube inside the carcass to contain the air, others do not. More on that later.

Today's passenger car tires are expected to provide reasonable traction for accelerating and braking; sufficient lateral adhesion for safe cornering; fairly comfortable ride; low noise level; adequate tread life; good resistance to damage from impact, heat, flexing, and weather. The result is a compromise. You can't improve on one function of a tire without hurting one or more other functions.

Racing tires, for example, give the ultimate in traction and cornering power, but would be unthinkable on a passenger car. Their extremely stiff sidewalls give a very harsh ride; also, the sidewalls, unprotected by the extra layer of rubber found on passenger car tires, could be damaged seriously the first time you scraped a curb or hit a pothole. And the soft tread rubber, compounded for maximum adhesion, would wear bald within a few thousand miles. Conversely, engineers could build a tire that would last the life of your car—but you would want no part of its deadly handling characteristics.

The way the carcass is constructed determines to a great extent a tire's "personality." In the conventional bias-ply tire (virtually the only kind sold in this country until a few years ago), the carcass is made up of several fabric plies, or layers, bonded in rubber for protection. Each ply consists of rayon or nylon cords, which run at an angle to the cords in the next ply.

The angle at which the plies intersect is important. A wide angle, such as is found in most tires, gives a comfortable ride. Special high-performance tires usually have a narrower cord angle; this gives a stiffer sidewall and

In conventional bias-ply (above), cords cross at an angle. In a radial-ply tire (center), the cords run straight across with an additional layered belt of fabric or steel cord between plies and tread. Belted bias-ply tire combines both, with cords crossing at an angle and belts between plies and tread.

U.S. Department of Transportation requires much information on tire sidewall, including size, maximum inflation pressure, and type of construction. In fact, everything you see on the sidewall is required except the brand name.

239

improved cornering at the cost of a harder ride. All-out racing tires have a very small angle, one of the reasons they are unacceptable for street use.

Until recently, the only important choices a tire buyer had to make were between tubeless and tube-type tires and between rayon and nylon cords. The tubeless tires, when punctured, tend to lose air more gradually than do tube-type tires; they usually "slow-out" rather than blow out. However, the wheel rim must be in perfect condition; even a slight dent can allow air to escape. Also, during hard cornering it's possible to pull the bead away from the rim and lose air pressure abruptly —which is why tubeless tires are unpopular on race tracks.

As for materials used in the cords, rayon is considerably cheaper and provides a softer ride, especially when first starting out. When a car has been parked a few hours, a nylon tire has a habit of flat-spotting—that is, temporarily losing its round shape at the point where the tire rests on the ground. It takes a few mildly bumpy miles of driving before this flat spot is worked out.

However, most experts agree that nylon tires are better for hard driving; at high speeds they are more rupture-resistant and the plies are less likely to separate. That's why police pursuit cars and competition machines generally run on nylon. And yet, generalizations are dangerous; the Italian-made Pirelli Cinturato, a special-construction rayon-cord tire, is rated safe at a sustained speed of 130 m.p.h.

The Detroit auto makers know that demonstration rides often influence new car sales, and they won't put up

Left: Comparison of two wide tread tires. The one on the left is the 70 series, which is six inches wide. The 60 series is 7.5 inches wide. Right: Studded tires markedly improve traction on ice, but they don't do any good for the dry highway, so many states restrict their use.

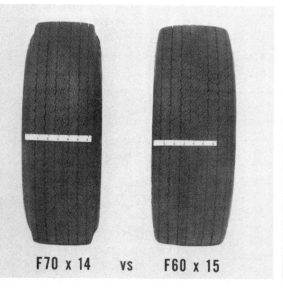

F70 x 14   vs   F60 x 15

with nylon's flat-spotting. Almost all original-equipment tires are rayon. When it comes time to replace, however, 75 percent of all motorists specify nylon.

Until a few years ago, almost all passenger car tires had four plies. (A few, intended for heavy-duty use, had eight.) Then the tire makers began pushing two-ply tires. The public was suspicious, figuring that the manufacturers simply were out to reduce their costs. The manufacturers insisted, however, that the two-plies are at least as safe as the old four-plies. In fact, the two-plies usually were advertised as having a "four-ply rating," meaning that they could carry the same load as an earlier four-ply tire.

According to the manufacturers, the tread shoulders of a two-ply tire run cooler during normal turnpike driving,

Regular tire pressure checks and adjustments when necessary are the best maintenance you can give your tires.

Chart shows many causes of tire wear and how to correct them.

	RAPID WEAR AT SHOULDERS	RAPID WEAR AT CENTER	CRACKED TREADS	WEAR ON ONE SIDE	FEATHERED EDGE	BALD SPOTS
CONDITION						
CAUSE	UNDER INFLATION	OVER INFLATION	UNDER-INFLATION OR EXCESSIVE SPEED	EXCESSIVE CAMBER	INCORRECT TOE	WHEEL UNBALANCED
CORRECTION	ADJUST PRESSURE TO SPECIFICATIONS WHEN TIRES ARE COOL			ADJUST CAMBER TO SPECIFICATIONS	ADJUST FOR TOE-IN 1/8 INCH	DYNAMIC OR STATIC BALANCE WHEELS

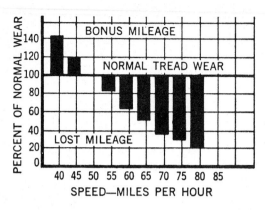

Moderate speeds provide a big bonus in tire wear, as chart shows.

Periodically check your tires for tread wear. Tire makers simplify job by providing tread wear indicators. When tire is worn down to $\frac{1}{16}$-inch tread, tire shows bald bands across tread.

making the tire more durable. Also, they say, two-plies give a better ride. One manufacturer, Uniroyal, claimed that extensive field tests and tabulations of warranty claims showed the two-plies to be more resistant to fabric breaks, tread separation, impact ruptures, and road-hazard damage. Also, the tread lasted longer. However, for rough roads or extra-high-speed driving, especially when tires are loaded to capacity, independent experts still recommend four-plies.

Another decision you must make is how much to spend—and the deciding factor needn't necessarily be the fatness of your wallet. The most expensive tire may actually give you the worst service!

What does a high-priced, premium tire offer? Mainly, just an extra-deep tread. That extra tread rubber means longer tire life under moderate-speed, around-town driving conditions. It also

means hotter running temperatures at sustained turnpike speeds, and more chance of failure. For hard, high-speed driving, avoid premium tires.

Generally, first-line (original-equipment-quality) tires are more than adequate for any driving needs. Second-line tires are somewhat cheaper, and third-line are the cheapest. But this doesn't mean they are less safe; just that they probably have less tread rubber and will need to be replaced sooner. In fact, a tire with a thin tread tends to run cooler, and actually may be safer at high speeds.

Far more important is a tire's maximum load rating, which now must be marked on the sidewalls of all new cars according to federal law. Total up your car's curb (ready-to-run) weight plus the maximum weight of cargo and passengers you expect to carry, and divide by four. If the tire you are considering doesn't give you at least a 100-pound safety margin, buy the next larger size (if your wheel rim is wide enough) or a tire with more plies.

Now don't go away, you have still more decisions to make. For example, consider the radial-ply tire, a design developed in Europe (but now being made by many U. S. manufacturers).

As mentioned earlier, in a bias-ply tire the cords of one ply form an angle with the cords of the next ply. In a radial-ply tire the cords run at a right angle to the tread, like the stripes around a zebra's body. Additionally, a fabric or wire-reinforced belt is added around the circumference of the tire, parallel to the tread, to add support.

Unlike the tread in ordinary bias-ply tires, which squirms and distorts at speed, the tread in a radial-ply is stiffened by the circumferential belt so it stays flat to the ground. This means less rolling resistance, noticeably greater fuel economy, and up to twice normal tread life. Also, the radial runs much cooler, thus is safe at higher speeds. What is more, the soft, flexible sidewalls allow the tread to stay flat on the ground even when the car is leaning hard into a turn, thus giving far greater adhesion.

But there are drawbacks. Since a radial has more components, it costs considerably more. Its low-speed ride —say under 40 m.p.h.—is noticeably harsher. Also, radials can have subtle —and sometimes not-so-subtle—effects on a car's handling. With some types of suspension, radials give less warning of impending breakaway, or skidding. Many foreign cars have suspensions designed especially for radi-

als. Most American cars don't—which explains why so few radials are sold here.

Incidentally, radials should never be mixed with bias-ply tires; such a combination could make a car uncontrollable.

The drawbacks of radials led to the development of the bias-belt tire—basically a conventional bias-ply tire but with fiberglass cords and a radial-ply-type circumferential belt. This tire's cost, tread life, cornering ability, high-speed capability, and ride all are compromises between those of the conventional bias-ply and the radial-ply tire. Since suspension design is less critical with this new tire, it may become widely used as original equipment on new cars—particularly since fierglass doesn't flat-spot.

Still another development is the extra-wide-tread, or 70-series, tire, now available in radial-ply as well as bias-ply designs. The 70-series tire provides greater adhesion under all conditions except on wet roads. The newest size is the 60-series, which is wider still.

The numbers 60 and 70 refer to aspect ratio, which is height versus width.

The height of a 60 series tire is 60 percent of the width.

Original equipment tires are 78 percent high as wide, so you can see that optional wider-tread tires take a long lead over original equipment lines in reducing aspect ratio.

How about winter tires? Here again you have to sacrifice one characteristic to improve another. The aggressive tread pattern greatly improves traction on packed snow, slightly improves trac-

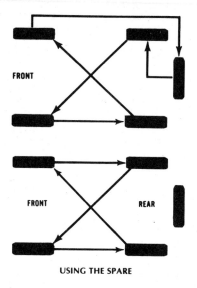

Wisdom of tire rotation is being questioned by some engineers. If you do decide to rotate, here are two typical patterns — one for four wheels (above), the other including spare. Whichever pattern you pick, stick to it.

USING THE SPARE

What's Inside a Tire

Bias Ply Tire	Belted-Bias	Radial

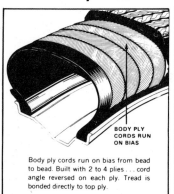

BODY PLY CORDS RUN ON BIAS

Body ply cords run on bias from bead to bead. Built with 2 to 4 plies . . . cord angle reversed on each ply. Tread is bonded directly to top ply.

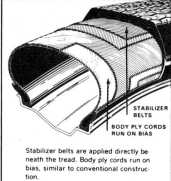

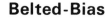

STABILIZER BELTS

BODY PLY CORDS RUN ON BIAS

Stabilizer belts are applied directly beneath the tread. Body ply cords run on bias, similar to conventional construction.

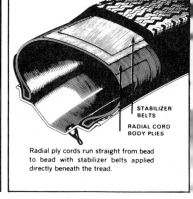

STABILIZER BELTS

RADIAL CORD BODY PLIES

Radial ply cords run straight from bead to bead with stabilizer belts applied directly beneath the tread.

tion on ice. But on dry roads, adhesion, ride comfort, and noise level all are worse. And with all that extra tread rubber, the snow tire is poorly suited to sustained high-speed driving.

Tire studs (mounted in a conventional or snow tire) are effective on ice, particularly when used on front as well as rear tires. But the studs wear down quickly and sometimes are thrown from the tread. Within a few thousand miles they lose much of their effectiveness. On dry roads, studded tires show slightly poorer adhesion and noticeably higher noise level. Check your state ordinances before buying. Studs are illegal in a few states, and restricted to winter months in some others. Chains? They're the most effective for traction on ice and hard-

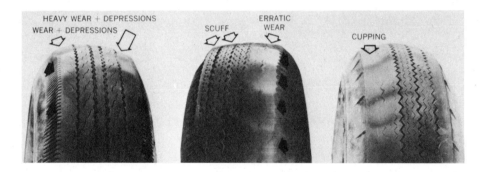

packed snow, but they're rough on tires. Save them for emergencies.

What about retreaded tires—used carcasses to which new tread rubber has been bonded? Their cost, roughly half that of a new tire, makes them a tempting buy; but they are only as good as the shop that turns them out. A reputable retreader uses only sound, undamaged carcasses—and he is will-

ing to give you a new-tire guarantee. Just in case, check the tire inside and out for signs of damage before having it mounted.

One final shopping tip: different brands of tires may be of different sizes even if their numerical designations are the same. Add to this the differences in tread pattern from one brand to another, plus differences in tread wear, and you'll see that one tire can handle very differently from another. If possible, buy an entire set of four tires at a time—or at least a matched pair for both front or both rear wheels.

Whether a pair of new tires should go on the front or rear wheels is practically a toss-up. Some experts prefer new tires in front for extra blowout protection. (Generally a front blowout is more dangerous.) On the other hand, rear tires wear faster (unless your car has front-wheel drive), and mounting new tires in the rear will help equalize wear.

Here are some easy hints on how to make your tires last longer. Most important check inflation pressures of all tires, including the spare, once a week. Owning a good pressure gauge is a must; service station air pumps are notoriously inaccurate. Remember that even a healthy tire leaks air slowly. Also, each 10-degree drop in temperature causes tire pressure to drop about one pound. Neglect your tires during seasonal temperature changes and you could be running several pounds low.

Underinflation causes increased tread wear along the edges. Also, the tire flexes more and runs hotter, increasing the chances of a failure. Overinflation causes faster tread wear along the center, and makes the tire more vulnerable to high-speed impact damage. Of the two, underinflation is worse.

Since 1966, U. S. car owners' manuals generally have given reliable advice on tire pressures. Before 1966, manufacturers generally recommended overly-low pressures for the sake of riding comfort; better add four extra pounds.

Also add three or four pounds for sustained high-speed driving or when carrying a heavy load.

The Rubber Manufacturers Association, or RMA, a tire manufacturer's trade organization, recommends a *maximum* of 32 pounds pressure for four-ply-rating tires and up to 40 pounds for eight-ply-rating tires. A few cars require different pressures in front and back tires because of unusual weight distribution or suspension design; failure to observe this differential could cause extremely dangerous and unpredictable handling characteristics. Don't bleed air from tires after a long, hard run. Such pressure buildup is normal—which is why tires should be checked when cold.

Your driving habits also affect tire life. High speeds, jackrabbit starts, panic braking, and hard cornering scrape away rubber fast. Tires wear five times faster at 80 m.p.h. than at 50 m.p.h. High speeds are especially hard on brand new tires. To give the plies a chance to seat, limit your speed to 50 m.p.h. for the first 500 miles.

Avoid driving on rough shoulders or the edge of the pavement. Bumping a curb during diagonal parking is a good way to damage the tire carcass and knock your front end out of line. Tire damage may not show up immediately; but it may grow worse as you drive and eventually, perhaps months later, result in a failure. When you park, stop a few inches short of the curb.

The front end should be realigned every 10,000 to 15,000 miles or, if you drive on bad roads, even oftener. At the same time have your front wheels balanced statically (while stationary) and dynamically (while spinning). What's the difference? Imagine a perfectly symmetrical, perfectly balanced wheel to which two identical weights are added, one at the front, the other exactly half-way around but in back. The wheel would still be balanced statically; while spinning, however, it would develop a side-to-side, wobbling motion.

An out-of-balance wheel can cause uneven tire wear and, if it's in front, front-end shimmy and steering wheel vibration. A misaligned front end causes excessive tire scrubbing and, again, uneven and accelerated wear. Other mechanical causes of uneven tire wear include faulty shock absorbers, grabbing brakes, and sagging or broken springs. A word of caution: don't fall for those mail-order ads for do-it-yourself wheel-balancing gadgets. Proper balancing requires expensive, sophisticated equipment and special training, and is not a job for amateurs.

The best preventive medicine is to check the condition of your tires often. If you spot uneven tread wear, have your car's running gear checked immediately. Knots, bulges, or cuts also should be checked by an expert. If any grease or oil gets on your tires, wipe it off; petroleum-base materials cause rubber to deteriorate.

When your car is raised on a lift for servicing, carefuly pry out any pebbles, nails, or other foreign matter imbedded in the tread, using needle-nose pliers.

Does it pay to rotate tires? Engineers disagree. Most still recommend switching tires every 5,000 miles or so to equalize wear and allow the spare to see some use. Some say switching is okay providing you don't rotate diagonally, from left to right or vice-versa. Treads develop a directional pattern, they say, and reversing the direction of rotation will increase wear. A spokesman for Pirelli, an Italian tire maker, says tires shouldn't be switched at all. Not only is it not worth the cost, he says; it also masks uneven tread wear caused by mechanical defects. What should you do? Here your guess is as good as anyone's.

No matter how well you take care of your tires, they may occasionally go flat. When this happens while you're driving, stop immediately (but don't hit your brakes until your car has slowed considerably, or you may lose control). Driving on a flat tire is the quickest way to ruin it.

If you have tubeless tires, use externally applied plugs or aerosol sealers only in an emergency. Such repairs are temporary, and are not safe at speeds above 50 m.p.h. Have the tire removed from the rim, inspected, and repaired from the inside as soon as possible. Also have it rebalanced.

Remember, your tires represent the only contact your car has with the road. Give them the care they deserve.

Typical replacement shock absorbers. The three at the left are conventional heavy-duty units. The two at the right are fitted with auxiliary springs. The narrower unit is for front wheels, the wider one for the rears.

Typical replacement shock absorbers. The three at the left are conventional heavy-duty units. The two at the right are fitted with auxiliary springs. The narrower unit is for front wheels, the wider one for the rears.

35

Testing and Replacing Shock Absorbers

TESTING YOUR CAR'S springs and shock absorbers is not difficult. With your car ready for the road but unladen with extra passengers and luggage, it should sit level on flat ground. If it does, your car's springs are okay. There should be no sagging at any of the four corners, the front end should not be lower than the rear end, and vice-versa. All of this presupposes that you have never modified your car's stance with lowering blocks or oversize tires in the rear.

If you wish to make sure that your car's springs retain their factory height control specification, measure vertically from the bottom of the lower control arm, and at the extreme outer end, to the ground at each side of the front. If this measurement differs more than ¼ inch, the installation of spring spacers is recommended. No more than two spacers should be used on any spring; to exceed two spacers would allow the front coils to close up on rough roads. The rear springs, too, can be checked for height in a similar manner—by measuring vertically from the left and right ends of lowest point of the rear axle to the ground. If there is more than ¼ inch difference noted, spring spacers should again be employed. We suggest, if you should find the need of spacers, that you take your car to a reliable spring shop where the correct spacers are available. There is the additional possibility that your springs have lost their flexibility, or some of it, and in this case either new springs are indicated or, in the case of leaf springs, redishing.

There are several ways to test shock absorbers. But the only ways that mean anything are a severe road test, and as a double-check, the tap-the-brakes method illustrated.

If the car drifts on hard cornering; shakes, rattles and rolls on washboard roads; and the shocks have about 20,000 miles on them; you can bet the cookie-jar savings account they are gone. Most original equipment shocks are ready for the scrap heap by 12,000 to 15,000 miles.

What about the "hopping on the bumper" test? Though it is good exercise, it really doesn't tell you much about your shocks.

Very few modern shocks will give you a definitive answer with that test. They are designed for ride control when the car is moving down a road, and all you could simulate with the hopping-on-the-bumper test is very, very low-speed operation. Most shocks are designed for medium-to-high-speed ride control, and are virtually inactive at two mph.

Modern telescopic shocks cannot be refilled. Some British sports cars have lever shocks that are refillable, but you probably do not have one of those.

Whether you replace worn-out shocks with the equivalent of original equipment or get something better depends on how heavily you load your car and the type of driving you do.

And, hard as it may seem to believe, there are cheapie shocks that are worse

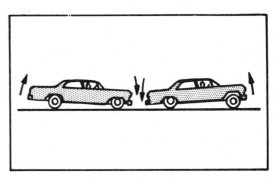

To double-check apparently bad shocks, drive car on smooth pavement at about 10 mph. Tap the brakes repeatedly, and if this sets up a rocking motion (front end down, rear end up; then rear end down and front end up), the shocks are bad.

than original equipment. Avoid these altogether.

In fact, you should always replace with a premium shock. Even if your springs look good, they have lost a bit of their zest, and a premium shock will compensate for this.

If you carry heavy loads, you should install shocks with an auxiliary coil spring in the rear. These shocks are the best for the average weekend mechanic who may carry a few hundred pounds of tools and parts in his trunk.

In fact, the coil spring shock can cure a minor spring sag problem and eliminate the use of spring spacers, which have limits to their use, as explained earlier. If your car has relatively low mileage, you should consider an adjustable shock. This type is expensive but it will normally last twice as long as a conventional design. The shock permits adjustment of the compression stroke to compensate for wear

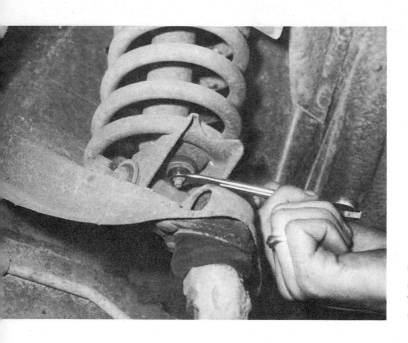

On most cars, shocks can be replaced easily. Wrench is shown on bottom shock nut.

within the shock. The adjustment feature is not the only reason this type of shock lasts longer. It is a super-premium design in every respect, with a nicely finished piston rod, better sealing, more sophisticated valving, etc. The adjustable shock is available with the auxiliary coil spring too. There are several brands of adjustables sold in the United States, among them Gabriel, Koni and AC. (The latter offers a take-apart type primarily for performance buffs.)

Probably the most important thing is to make certain that you purchase the correct size for your make and model. I've known do-it-yourselfers who, upon removing the old shocks, found that the replacements they had just purchased were either too long or too short and they had to call for help in taxiing back to the supplier for the right size of shocks for their car.

The most important thing about changing shock absorbers is to securely block your car so that it cannot possibly roll in either direction. Hide the ignition key and block the end that stays on the ground. You would do well, if there are children around, to roll all the windows up on your car and then to lock all the doors to prevent any tampering with the clutch or brakes. You don't want to find yourself pinned beneath two tons of steel for want of foresight, so also use safety stands under the A-frames after you jack up the car.

Some front shock absorbers are inside of the coil springs, other are angularly displaced outboard of the front coils. Removal is simple and consists mainly of removing the top nut and lifting off the washers and rubber bushings from the top lug. The latter is either attached to the car's frame or it extends vertically through a web-like plate that is attached to the top of the

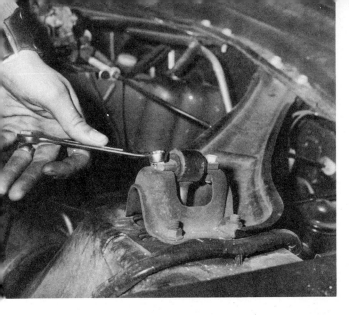

Upper mounting of shock normally is conveniently located in engine compartment up front. In rear, top mounting may be in trunk compartment, but you probably will have to get underneath and reach way up for it.

coil spring. The bolt that secures the bottom of the shock absorber through the mounting plate on the lower A-frame arm is then removed. Some bottom mounting plates must themselves be removed from the lower A-frame in order to allow removal of the shock absorber. Some makes use a saucer-shaper washer of generous size to hold the bottom end of the shock absorber to the A-frame or the bottom of the coil spring.

Take note of the order in which washers, rubber grommets or bushings, and various small parts are removed so that the same order can be retained when you install the new units. Make a rough diagram of the order to aid your memory.

To install the new shocks, first fit them in place loosely securing top ends first. In some cases the top of the shock has an integral steel ring inside of which there are rubber bushings. You should always receive new bushings with a new set of shocks. Before replacing the new shocks, squirt a bit of brake fluid on the rubber bushings to

make them seat more easily. Now on the bottom end of the new shock install the mounting plate (if that web-like piece comes free upon removal or has to be removed), the bushing, the washer, the lock washer if any, and the locking nut—in that order—and tighten securely.

In some cases, especially where the shock absorber is mounted inside of the coil spring, it will be necessary then to replace the bolts which hold the bottom end mounting plate against the lower A-frame arm. Once the bottom end is secured, the washers and nut are replaced on the top mounting bracket. With a torque wrench preferably, tighten the bolts. (See the chapter, "How Tight is Tight?")

Rear shock absorbers, generally, install much as do the front units. There are some variations depending, again, on whether the rear shocks attach on the bottom ends to a web plate mounted to the side of the leaf springs, to a bracket on the top or bottom of the leaf springs, or to a bracket on the ends of the axle housing. In a few cases the shock absorbers mount inside of the coil on rear coil spring suspensions of older cars; this is rarely found, however.

Generally, the rear shock absorbers are canted outward in order to achieve greater stability and, therefore, lugs or brackets are employed to secure the bottom ends. Most rear shock absorbers mount, at the top ends, through the steel floor of the car—the mounting bolts extend through and into the trunk compartment or, in the case of many station wagons, into the spare wheel bin beneath the rear floor. Washers, lock washers, and nuts secure the top ends and the removal of these is generally easier than to loosen the top ends of the front shocks due to more space.

The removal of any shock absorber, front or rear, is made easier if you take a few moments to inspect the means by which those used on your car are mounted. Sometimes, in order to reach the upper mountings in front, it is necessary to remove the front wheels. The same is true of the rear shock absorbers.

Try the car out over the same course on which you discovered the old shocks to be faulty. Make some quick stops and note how the new units stop the vertical jounce and rebound.

The tools you will need for replacing shocks are the open-end or box-end wrenches generally found in the kit of the average do-it-yourselfer. A large screwdriver is sometimes handy for prying loose a stubborn lug bolt once the nut is removed, and a torque wrench is desirable, but I'll bet a buck that more shock absorbers have been installed with a simple wrench than with the torque type.

Quick check for front wheel bearings is to grasp wheel at top and bottom and try to rock in and out. If you can feel play, wheel bearings should be inspected.

36

Set Your Bearings Straight

WHEN YOUR CAR begins to roll as if it was going uphill through a bucket of glue, wanders back and forth across the highway, and eats gasoline like it was going out of style, it's time to have a look at those hard-working bearings whose job it is to keep your ton-and-a-half car rolling effortlessly along in a straight line at 90 mph or more.

These periodic inspections and adjustments are your best safeguard against bearing failure when you can least afford it. Only the front wheels need to be inspected because only they are adjustable. Rear wheel bearings are usually not disturbed unless there is some specific reason for removing them, and, once removed, they are replaced.

To Inspect your front wheel bearings, first block the car so it will not roll, and then jack up a front wheel, supporting it so the wheel can be re-

Start by prying off metal dust cover.

Above: Pull out cotter pin. (Make sure you have a replacement; cotter pins should never be reused.)

Below: Remove nut lock and then unthread castellated nut.

moved. Take off the wheel cover, dust cover, cotter pin, adjusting nut (be careful, it might be a left-hand thread), and flat washer. Then carefully remove the wheel, hub and bearings at one time.

Next, lift out the small bearings at the outer end of the hub and turn the wheel over to remove the rest of the bearing assembly. First pry out the oil seal and lift out the large bearing; then remove the bearing cups.

When the bearing is removed, note the color and odor of the grease. If it looks burned—almost black—or has an acrid odor, it is a dead giveaway that the bearing has been running hot. If the grease looks and smells normal, clean each part of the bearing assembly in solvent and allow to dry. Do not dry the bearings by *spinning* them with a blast from an air hose as it will drive grit into the bearings.

When the bearings and cups are clean and dry, check them for signs of *brinnelling* or *spalling*. These are just two of the several ways in which wheel bearings are damaged or worn. Brinnelling is a series of indentations where the rollers have slammed into the surface of the cup (caused by severe impact, such as when a wheel goes into a rut in the road). Spalling appears as chipping or crumbling on the small ends of roller bearings (caused by excessive clearance).

Fractures will appear as fine hairline cracks across the surface of the cup or cone. These are usually a result of forcing bearings onto oversize spindles, forcing cups into warped hubs, or improperly seating the cups.

Corrosion results in pits or pock-marks and appears similar to spalling, but is located at random along the bearings and cups. It is usually an indication that moisture or road chemicals have entered the bearing through a defective seal and have contaminated the bearing grease. It is also possible for corrosion to be caused by handling a bearing when all of the oil has been washed from its surface. Ordinary perspiration is often highly corrosive, so it is good practice to handle clean bearings with a dry, lint-free cloth.

End wear is also similar to spalling, but appears on the large ends of roller bearings. It is generally caused by too-tight bearing adjustments, resulting in insufficient clearance.

Dangerous Dirt: If you find any of these defects, replace the entire bearing assembly. Never replace just one or two parts as the reason for failure in one part was very likely working on the entire assembly. Also, keep the workbench, tools, lubricant, and your hands free of dirt and grime when working with bearings. Grit is the mortal enemy of free-rolling, long-lasting bearings.

When installing replacement bearings, no on-the-spot lubrication is necessary. All new bearings are prelubricated to be used just as they come from the box. Old bearings that are in good condition should be repacked with special wheel-bearing grease.

Before refitting the bearings, clean out the bearing cavity with solvent. Make sure you have a tube of wheel-bearing grease to coat the bearing cavity. Coat the cavity, then install the bearings.

Pull out on wheel and outer wheel bearing will pop out as shown.

Reassembly: Check the replacement races and bearings against the old parts to be sure you have the right ones. Install the races and large bearing. Then dab the seal with clean oil and start it into the hub by hand, with lip positioned. The oil will make the seal slide on the spindle easily, preventing damage during reassembly, and will also make it soft and effective as a seal immediately. Never install a seal with just a hammer or use a steel punch which could damage the casing and cause leakage. Under no circumstances ever attempt to reuse a seal. Mount the wheel carefully to avoid tearing the seal on the spindle and install the outer bearing, washer, and adjusting nut.

Adjustment: The most common forms of adjustment are illustrated in this chapter. In all of these, the amount of tension applied on the thrust washer by an adjusting nut is set to the manu-

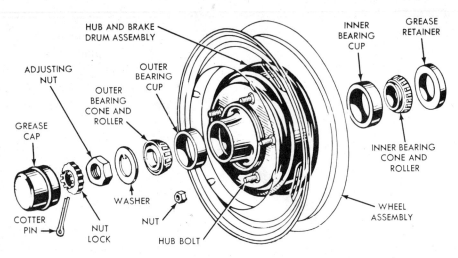

With wheel off, turn it over and pry out grease seal to gain access to inner wheel bearing. Parts in typical assembly are as shown.

facturer's specifications, or according to feel for lack of free play and smooth rotation of the wheel. Adjustment by feel, although reasonably accurate and practical, should be done only if a torque wrench is not available.

Note: cars with tapered roller bearings should only be set with a torque wrench if the car maker specifies a torque setting to seat the bearings.

Tapered roller bearings can be damaged by improper installation very easily.

To adjust a bearing by feel, first seat the bearing assembly by tightening the nut with a long wrench until you feel a definite resistance while rotating the wheel. Then loosen the nut and run it up again finger-tight. Continue tightening it with the pliers, rotating the wheel and checking for free play constantly with your other hand. Stop tightening at the point where free play

has just been eliminated. Be careful not to overtighten the bearing, mistaking looseness at the ball joint for free play.

Now spin the wheel, stopping at several points to check for free play, and, if necessary, tighten the nut to eliminate it. Never back off more than one slot on the nut to get to the point where free play is eliminated. If the bearing becomes too tight, back the nut off to finger-tight and start over.

Torque Wrench Adjustment. The exact procedure for torque wrench adjustment varies according to make of car. Here are the procedures for popular late-model cars:

Ford products: With wheel rotating, tighten adjusting nut to 17 to 25 ft./lbs. Back adjusting nut off ½ turn. Tighten adjusting nut to just one ft./lb. Install the nut lock and a new cotter pin.

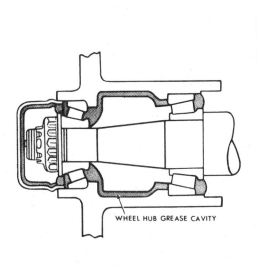

WHEEL HUB GREASE CAVITY

Left: This illustration shows wheel hub grease cavity, which should be cleaned out with solvent and repacked. Best method of repacking is with special tool with bearings back in place, but if you do not have the tool, just coat cavity surfaces generously. Right: Wheel bearings should be cleaned in solvent, and allowed to air dry; then coat with wheel bearing grease as shown. Below: Torque wrench in position for adjustment of wheel bearings.

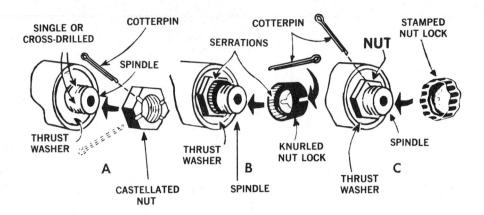

Different methods of retaining wheel and bearings are illustrated.

Chrysler products: Tighten bearing nut to seven ft./lbs. while rotating wheel. Position nut lock so that a pair of slots lines up with the cotter pin hole. Back off the nut lock (with the nut inside it) one slot, then install the cotter pin.

Chevrolet: Tighten bearing nut to 12 ft./lbs. while rotating wheel. Back off adjusting nut one flat and attempt to insert cotter pin. If the slot and pin hole do not line up, back off the nut until they do (an additional ½ flat turn or less should do it).

Not all car makers specify a torque wrench setting, and in some cases, the nut is never to be torqued.

Cars equipped with disc brakes on the front wheels pose a special problem insofar as wheel bearing service is concerned: the caliper and disc must come off.

This means that you must remove the wheel first by unbolting it from the wheel hub.

On older cars with fixed caliper disc brakes, removing the caliper may be a chore. If possible, hang the caliper with wire from the front suspension, so you do not have to disconnect a brake line (which would force you to bleed the brakes).

Under no circumstances should you let the caliper dangle by a brake hose. This is a sure-fire way to cause a premature brake hose failure.

If you find shims under the heads of the bolts that attach the caliper to the front suspension, you must refit them as they were, for they center the caliper over the disc.

Once the caliper is off, pull the dust cap from the disc and proceed as with drum brakes.

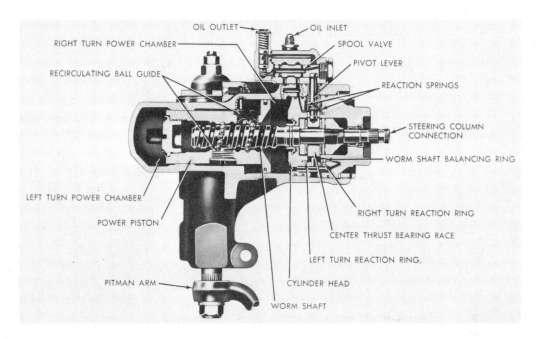

OIL OUTLET · OIL INLET · RIGHT TURN POWER CHAMBER · SPOOL VALVE · PIVOT LEVER · RECIRCULATING BALL GUIDE · REACTION SPRINGS · STEERING COLUMN CONNECTION · WORM SHAFT BALANCING RING · LEFT TURN POWER CHAMBER · POWER PISTON · RIGHT TURN REACTION RING · CENTER THRUST BEARING RACE · LEFT TURN REACTION RING · PITMAN ARM · CYLINDER HEAD · WORM SHAFT

Shown is a sectional view of a Dodge power steering gear, which consists of a gear housing containing a gear shaft with a sector gear, a power piston with gear teeth milled into the side of the piston (which is in constant mesh with the sector gear), and a worm-shaft connecting the steering wheel to the power piston (through a U-joint). The worm shaft is "geared" to the piston by recirculating balls. The steering valve, a spool type, is mounted on top of the steering gear and directs the flow of fluid into the system.

37

Power Steering

UNDERSTANDING YOUR POWER steering is easy and important when pinpointing trouble. Fixing it, though, may be another matter. You can easily make some repairs, but if the trouble is in the power steering unit itself, most repairs are best left to an expert who knows what he is doing and has the special tools and gauges. However, if you watch the repair being done and know your power steering, you should get a more careful and less expensive job.

All power steering systems have these three components: 1) a pump which supplies oil under pressure to provide the power and 2) a control valve assembly to meter the amount of fluid delivered to 3) the cylinder and piston assembly that does the work.

Systems differ in design and location of control valves and cylinder and piston assemblies. The two basic categories are those where the power is applied to the steering gear and those where it is applied to the linkage. Gear-type units are built into the steering gear box with opposed power pistons working on a crank attached to the pitman arm shaft. Some use a single power piston working on the pitman arm shaft through a power rack. Both of these gear-type units have the shaft from the steering wheel passing through the control valve assembly.

Linkage-type power steering mounts the cylinder and piston assembly between one of the steering rods and the vehicle chassis or frame.

Here is what happens when you turn the wheel on a power steering equipped car. The pump, belt driven by the engine, draws hydraulic fluid from a reservoir and sends it out under pressure. Inside the pump, flow-control and pressure relief valves govern the amount of pressure in the system. The harder you turn the steering wheel, the more hydraulic pressure is applied to help you turn it.

Two hydraulic lines connect the pump to the control valve. One is a

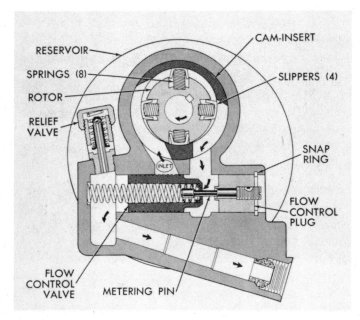

RESERVOIR
SPRINGS (8)
ROTOR
RELIEF VALVE
INLET
CAM-INSERT
SLIPPERS (4)
SNAP RING
FLOW CONTROL PLUG
FLOW CONTROL VALVE
METERING PIN

This is a typical power steering pump, designed to deliver most of its pressure at low speeds for easier parking. At low speeds, the flow control valve is so positioned that additional oil flows through the valve orifice to the power steering gear. At higher pump speeds, the increased oil flow moves the flow control valve against the spring pressure, diverting much of it back into the pump inlet. At the same time, the metering pin reduces oil flow to the power steering gear.

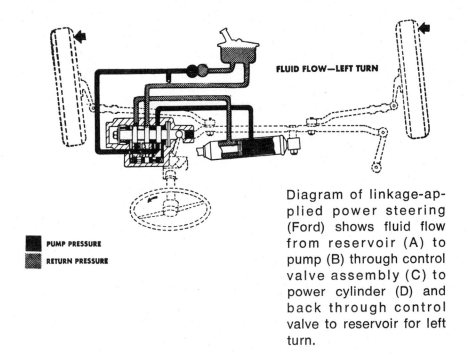

FLUID FLOW—LEFT TURN

PUMP PRESSURE

RETURN PRESSURE

Diagram of linkage-applied power steering (Ford) shows fluid flow from reservoir (A) to pump (B) through control valve assembly (C) to power cylinder (D) and back through control valve to reservoir for left turn.

flow line, the other a return line, or both may be flow lines depending on front wheel position. The control valve, like a traffic cop, directs fluid under pressure to the power cylinder.

With the wheels straight ahead, a centering spring holds the control valve spool in the neutral position. Fluid from the pump bypasses the valve, enters the power cylinder and returns to the reservoir. Pressure is equal on both sides of the piston.

When you turn left, twisting the steering wheel makes the valve spool move to the right, overcoming the control valve centering spring. Hydraulic fluid, under pressure from the pump, flows through the line to the right side of the power cylinder. Fluid on the left side of the cylinder is forced back through the return line as the piston moves to the left to assist your turn. On a right turn the process is reversed.

Spotting Power Steering Troubles. Leaking fluid, hard steering, binding or poor recovery, excessive free play, noise, steering chatter, rattles and complete loss of power assist are all trouble symptoms. Fluid loss and hard steering are the most common.

When you notice one of these symptoms, there is usually no need to replace any of the complete power steering assemblies, let alone the entire system. Never let yourself be talked into such replacement until you are absolutely certain you need it.

Fluid leaks show up as a few drops or even a puddle on the garage floor. Ignore this warning and you're in for hard steering and the expense of replacing fluid.

To find the leak, get under the car. If you can get it up on a hoist, it is much easier. Clean off the pump, control valve, power cylinder, and all the flexible lines and fittings. Drain the pump reservoir, catching the fluid in a clean container. Add ½-teaspoon of premixed red oil-soluble analine dye to each pint of fluid. J. C. Whitney Co. and an occasional auto supply store carry this dye. Then refill the pump reservoir with dyed fluid. Start the engine and turn the steering wheel from one side stop to the other at least ten times to circulate the dye through the system. Get an assistant to turn the wheel from one stop to the other and hold it at each stop for 10-15 seconds while you look for leaks in the system.

If a tubing fitting leaks, try tightening it. Use special tubing fitting wrench in preference to an open end wrench. (If you don't have a tubing wrench, go ahead and use an open-end. Just be careful.) If this does not help, replace it with a new fitting of the same size and type. If the leak is in one of the fluid lines, replace the line.

Leaks can occur at six places on the power steering pump and reservoir unit: cover joint, cover center stud, reservoir body to pump housing joint, between pump body valves, carrier shaft, and relief valve retainer. Fix any of these leaks by removing the pump and reservoir units from the car and replacing the leaking gasket or seal. Individual gaskets and rebuild kits are available from auto supply stores and mail order houses.

Bleed air out of the system whenever a line has been disconnected, a component replaced, or the reservoir has been emptied to change the fluid. Make sure the reservoir is full. Jack up the car so the front wheels clear the ground. With the transmission in neutral, the rear wheels blocked, and the engine running, depress the accelerator until the engine races at a speed equal to about 35 mph. Slowly turn the steering wheel all the way left, then all the

Above: Dipstick permits easy checking of power steering pump reservoir. Below left: Although tubing wrench is best, open end can be used on power steering hoses.

Two bolts hold pump. Slacken both for pump belt adjustment. (Finger points to bolt on elongated hole adjusting brace; arrow points to other bolt.)

way right. Lower the car to the ground and again turn the wheels slowly all the way left, then right. Recheck the reservoir, add fluid if needed and the job is done.

Hard steering can be caused by a slipping power steering drive belt. All belts squeal to some extent when you have the steering wheel cranked all the way during a parking maneuver, but the belt should not squeal during normal low-speed or high-speed driving. If it does, adjustment or replacement is indicated.

Two bolts hold the typical power steering pump. Slacken both and tension the pump with a pry bar.

Any further service on power steering requires special test gauges and should be left to the professional mechanic.

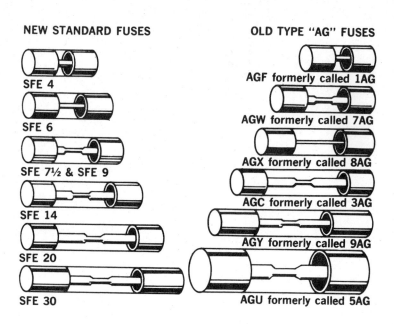

NEW STANDARD FUSES

SFE 4

SFE 6

SFE 7½ & SFE 9

SFE 14

SFE 20

SFE 30

OLD TYPE "AG" FUSES

AGF formerly called 1AG

AGW formerly called 7AG

AGX formerly called 8AG

AGC formerly called 3AG

AGY formerly called 9AG

AGU formerly called 5AG

38

Servicing Electrical Controls

MOST CAR OWNERS have experienced blown fuses in their homes and know how and where to remove the damaged fuse and replace it with a good one. Your car's light and electrical-accessory wiring system is not very different from your home's, and if you carry several new fuses—and know where the fuses are located—the job of handling a blown fuse is simple.

Correcting the trouble that was responsible for the fuse blowing is not always so easy, however. Besides, an electrical system, such as wipers or clock, may be protected with a "circuit breaker," which, unlike a fuse, does not "blow," but intermittently opens the circuit to reduce the current and serve as a warning that a "short" exists and something must be done about it.

The small fuses used on cars are of the cartridge type and slip into fuse clips or in-line retainers. Do not attempt to remove fuses with a screwdriver; you may touch one clip with the screwdriver's blade and at the same time ground the blade on nearby metal. The resulting sparks may not only startle you badly, but on a 12-v system could instantly burn out every wire under the instrument panel, since the overload factor inherent in the older 6-v systems is missing. Use a small wooden stick to remove fuses. Better still, purchase a small, inexpensive plastic or hard-rubber fuse puller that not only permits you to get a good grip on a cartridge fuse, but also is completely insulated. Such pullers are available at auto-supply stores.

Now let us suppose, for example, that the electric clock in your new car does not work. You go about troubleshooting it as you would if the lights in your home go out—you look for a blown fuse. (A chart that tells you the specified size, type, and location of car fuses for all makes and models of cars for the last 15 model years is available free from the Bussman Mfg. Division of McGraw Edison Co., University at Jefferson, St. Louis 7, Mo.) Once the fuse is located, you can tell by looking at it that the link inside the glass casing has melted to interrupt the circuit. Occasionally, clock fuses are in the line and you have to undo the bayonet lock on the fuse housing to drop out the fuse. If the fuse is blown, replace it with one of correct type and size. Correct fuse amperage is important. Installing a fuse of greater capacity than specified may damage the unit it is intended to protect.

The single-wire system, wherein the metal parts of the car serve as a return wire or ground, is universally used on cars. With the switch on a car lamp closed, the circuit to and from it is complete and, consequently, the lamp lights. If a connection to the lamp loosens, or becomes corroded, or bebegins to chafe, resistance is set up in the circuit, heating occurs, the lamp burns dimly and—if the wiring grounds—the battery will discharge. Heavy discharge reading on an ammeter would warn of this, but if a light is used instead of an ammeter (as is common with later model cars) a very heavy short would be required to cause the lamp to glow.

If such a simple circuit is protected with a fuse, however, any of the conditions mentioned above will melt the fuse link, breaking the circuit, thus protecting the units and wiring and preventing danger from fire.

To locate the cause of a blown fuse, always check wiring terminals for tightness first. Look for spots where a wire is rubbing against a sharp metallic surface. And if you do put in a new wire, don't let it hang loosely. Tape it wherever possible to a bracket, or insert it in the regular clips made to hold it.

If any of the car lamps fail to light and the bulb is known to be okay, then it can be due to a blown fuse and replacement often restores the circuit. If a second fuse blows, the trouble lies elsewhere in the circuit. A vibrating circuit breaker always means a short which you must find and correct. To do this, disconnect the switch wires one at a time until the relay stops vibrating; that is the line or wire in which the trouble will be found. If you get no

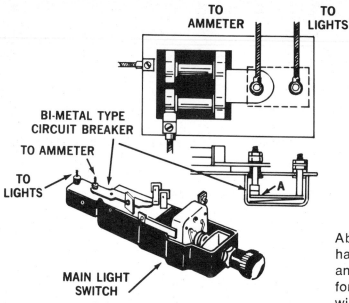

TO
AMMETER

TO
LIGHTS

BI-METAL TYPE
CIRCUIT BREAKER

TO AMMETER

TO
LIGHTS

A

MAIN LIGHT
SWITCH

Above: Circuit breaker has been used for lights, and is now primarily used for accessories, such as windshield wipers. Cutaway and schematic show how it works. Circuit breaker is usually built into a switch, as illustrated.

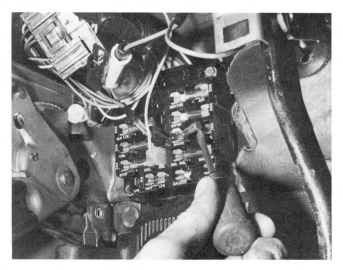

Left: Removing a fuse with a screwdriver is risky, as screwdriver might touch another fuse's clip or an electrical ground and cremate some car wiring. A wooden stick, such as from an ice cream pop, is the best choice.

light and the lamps are okay, the circuit breaker contacts could be disengaged. Replace an open circuit breaker. You will find, too, that electrical circuits will work better if you occasionally take out the fuses and clean the fuse clips and the ends of the fuses to remove corrosion.

The lighting system is the largest and most involved as to wiring and the like-

lihood of shorts or grounds. The circuit basically includes head lamps, parking lamps, taillights, stoplights, directional lights and interior lamps. It often is supplemented by spotlights, back-up lights and fog light, all of these circuits usually being fused. Fuses also are used in the accessory circuits such as heaters, radio, underhood lights, hand brake lights, cigarette lighters, overdrives, trunk lights, air conditioners and many other units.

Fuses seldom have been used for headlamps except in very old cars and trucks. Protection for headlamps, tail lamp, parking lamps and instrument lamp circuits on most older cars is through a thermostatically-controlled limit relay or a bi-metal type circuit breaker, usually attached to the main light switch. On most cars built in the last few years, all circuits but the headlamps have been removed from the circuit-breaker line and are fitted with separate fuses. The reason for this is that the headlamps and tail lamps are used the most and are the most important in operation of the car.

Headlamps, generator—in fact, the entire battery system on today's cars—is protected by "fusible links." A fusible link is nothing more than a piece of wire that is spliced into a circuit in which the wiring is one or two standard thicknesses larger. For example, a piece of 14-gauge wire is spliced in, to protect a 10-gauge wire circuit.

This piece of wire is often covered by a plastic sheath of special shape for easy identification.

If the circuit is overloaded, the higher-number (thinner) wire burns out and separates, just like a fuse.

The location of these links varies according to the make of car. On late-model Chevrolets (except Corvette), for example, there is a 16-gauge black fusible link to protect all unfused wiring of 12 gauge or thicker. This link is at the horn relay.

The generator warning light and generator field circuit, which is 16 gauge, is protected by a 20-gauge fusible link also at the horn relay.

If a fusible link breaks, the repair (after correcting the cause) is to splice in a new piece of the appropriate gauge wire, solder or crimp-connect the terminals and tape over with plastic electrical tape.

Remember that the wiring circuits in your car are like those in your home. If you have too many lights and appliances on one circuit, a blown fuse will result. The same thing is true in a car. Using a larger capacity fuse will prevent a blown fuse, but trouble is built in. The best method is to run a new circuit, with its own proper capacity fuse, to protect the new spotlight or other accessory. In some cases there is a junction block wired to the ignition switch that has spare connections that can be used. This heavy-duty circuit will handle the added electrical load, and has the added advantage of shutting off the current when the ignition key is turned off.

Although sophisticated electrical troubleshooting is for the professional, most problems are not all that sophisticated.

If a bulb circuit fails to operate, there are five possible causes:
1. bad bulb
2. poor connection at the socket or bulb terminal.
3. defective wiring.
4. defective switch.
5. blown fuse (if the circuit is fused).

Clearly, a wiring problem is only 20 percent of the possibilities, and in actual practice, occurs perhaps five percent of the time.

Checking a bulb is simple. Attach a jumper wire to one terminal of the battery. Sit the bulb on the other bat-

Left: Headlamp is checked by connecting two of three terminals to battery posts, using jumper wires. By trying all three possible combinations, you should get low and high beams to work. Right: Corrosion and rust are usual causes of socket failure. Clean with a wire brush.

tery post, holding it so that its bottom terminal is in contact. With the jumper, touch the metal side of the bulb. If it is good, the bulb will light.

To check a headlamp, which has three terminals, the procedure is similar. Connect any two terminals to the battery posts in the three different combinations possible and you should get a low beam and high beam.

A socket can be checked with a test lamp. With the appropriate switch on, one lead goes to the metal tab contact in the center, the other to the cylindrical metal side. If the lamp lights, the socket is good.

Corrosion and rust are the usual causes of a socket failure, and if you see any, clean with a wire brush.

Corrosion not only affects sockets, but fuse contacts as well. If you see a white corrosive coating on the fuse contacts, also clean with a wire brush.

Wire and switch terminals are still

another area corrosion can affect, causing a poor electrical connection. You are probably familiar with the effect of corrosion on the battery cable connections, and how this can interfere with engine starting by restricting the flow of current.

Plainly, if current cannot get to a light or accessory, it will not work. Even if a connection is physically tight, it may be electrically weak if corrosion is present.

Poor connections also can be caused by loose terminals which you can physically feel, particularly on a switch.

A switch may also have an internal break. This can be checked, but like the defective wiring problem, is best left to an expert. If you can get a replacement switch on a "return it if I don't need it" basis, you can check the old switch by substitution with a new one.

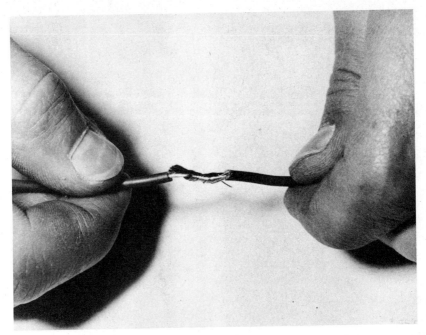

Twist the wires together for solder connection.

39

Making Connections

To do electrical work on cars, it frequently is necessary to repair damaged connections and make new ones. There are two popular techniques for making permanent connections: solder and solderless.

To make a solder connection, bare some wire from each end and twist together as illustrated. Hold the soldering iron at the twist and a piece of solder, also as illustrated. When the solder melts and flows into the twist, filling it, the job is done. Insulate the connection with plastic electrical tape, start-

ing one inch from the bared wire and continuing across the twist and onto the insulation of the other piece of wire, also for an inch.

To make a solderless connection, you need a kit, which consists of solderless connectors and terminals, and a crimping tool. There are kits for conventional terminals and others for those insulated with plastic sheaths.

Strip some insulation (about ½-inch from each wire), twist the strands of each wire, but do not join the two wires. Insert one end into the connec-

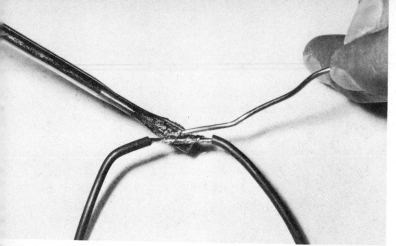

Hold solder and iron so that the twist fills properly.

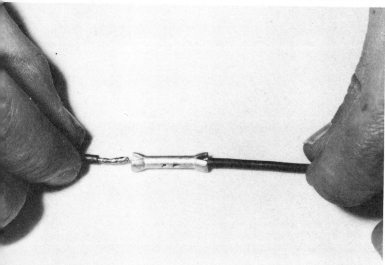

Typical crimp connector. Notice that strands of each wire are twisted before insertion into connector.

Below left: Crimp the ends of the solderless connector. After this, insulating tape is applied, unless connector or terminals are already insulated by a plastic sheath.

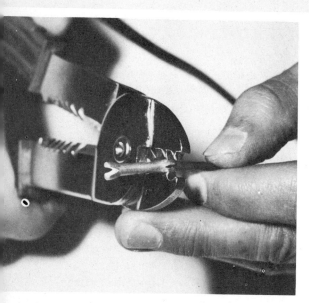

tor and squeeze the end together with the crimping tool. Repeat for the other end and cover with insulating tape if necessary.

Installing terminals, for screws and spade connections, also can be done with solder or solderless terminals, in a similar manner.

Professional mechanics prefer the solderless terminals and connectors because of the speed and simplicity; you should too. The solderless kit and terminals are no more than the price of a good soldering iron and solder terminals.

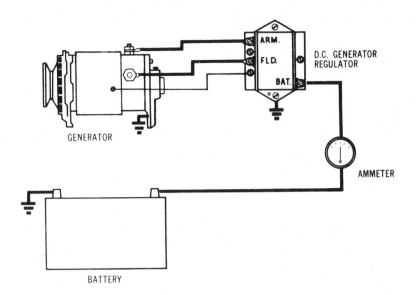

Typical DC generator charging circuit.

40

DC Generator
Troubleshooting and Service

YOU MAY SAVE yourself a long walk to the "nearest service station" some day with an on-the-spot repair if you know what to look for when your generator gives out.

But if you inspect the generator-voltage regulator system every 10,000 miles or so, you may forestall more serious trouble by making bench repairs before they become emergencies. At any rate, you can do most of the work yourself.

These electrical powerhouses for your car are of three types. The generator field in some Delco-Remy and Auto-Lite systems is externally grounded through the mounting bolts. In types used in cars made by Ford, and some others (Ford, Bosch systems), the generator field is internally grounded. Beginning with 1958 models, many General Motors cars had a third type controlled by Delco-Remy dual contact regulators that was used until GM went to alternators in the 1960's.

All systems with an internal ground

271

can be identified by the presence of a ground terminal (marked "G" or "GND") on both the generator and regulator. All dual contact regulators are plainly marked with a red tag and also bear the warning *"do not ground"* plainly stenciled in white ink (but the tag and markings are gone by now). This warning cannot be overemphasized. A momentary grounding of this new system will burn the second set of points in the dual contact regulator and may easily burn out the whole generator system.

What Can Go Wrong? Basically, only three things: no charge (complete failure of the output), insufficient charge, or too much charge.

When there is no charge—the usual fault—the generator is not taking over for the battery the job of supplying electrical power to run your car. In a late model car, you can tell this by your charge indicator bulb (irreverently dubbed "idiot light," as any idiot supposedly can tell when his generator isn't charging). It will light when you switch on the ignition and refuse to dim no matter how fast you run the engine. If you have an ammeter, the needle will stay on the negative side through these operations.

Before running any tests, open the hood and check that the generator drive belt has not broken or slipped off its pulley. If in place, but loose, tighten the drive belt adjustment.

Basic No-Charge Tests. You need only a length of insulated wire, preferably with an alligator clip at each end, to check all generators except those using dual contact regulators.

Normal generator disassembly begins with removal of two long through screws.

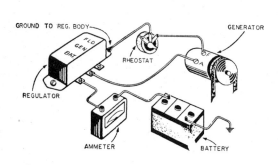

Connect one end of this jumper wire to the generator field terminal (marked with a big fat "F"). If generator field is externally grounded, connect the other end to a good ground as in Fig. 1; if internally grounded, connect it to generator armature (marked "A" or "ARM").

Now start the engine and run it at a fast idle. If the idiot light goes out or ammeter needle swings to the plus side, the generator is OK and the trouble is in the wiring or regulator.

If you have a Delco-Remy system with a double contact regulator—once again—*don't ground anything.* This must be checked at the regulator, requires some equipment and is somewhat involved. If you want to try it, here is what to do.

Secure a voltmeter-ammeter and connect it in series between the battery terminal ("B" or "BAT") on the regulator and the *nongrounded terminal* of the battery. Disconnect field wire from "F" terminal on the regulator and connect it to one lead of a 25-ohm, 25-watt variable resistance rheostat. (An old "clamp-under-the-dash" heater control will work.) Ground the other rheostat lead to the regulator body and set rheostat to wide open position.

Turn on all car accessories (lights, radio, heater, etc.). Start engine, run about one-third throttle and slowly turn off the rheostat until voltmeter reads slightly under 15 volts. A charge on the ammeter indicates regulator trouble. If no charge shows, make one more check.

Drop engine speed to a fast idle, remove the previous set-up and turn off the accessories. Connect jumper be-

Above: Generator end plate is gently pried up with screwdriver. If end plate is really stuck on, a paint scraper may be used to start it off.

Below: In the center of the generator is the armature. Rectangular segments form the commutator.

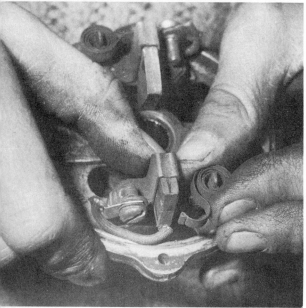

Top: If commutator segments are rough, they can be smoothed with 00 sandpaper. While one person holds sandpaper, another should rotate pulley at front (turning armature). This procedure insures uniform sanding.

Above: Generator brushes may be in field pole body or on end plate (as illustrated). Replacement is simple: push back spring (at right) and push out brush from guide. Brush's wire lead is retained by screw, left.

tween the battery terminal on the regulator and the regulator armature terminal ("A" or "ARM"). If you get a charge now, the trouble is in the circuit breaker or current regulator. If not, the regulator is OK and the generator is at fault, or possibly the wiring.

Dirty Commutators, probably responsible for most generator failures, are one of the easiest ailments to cure. Sand commutator surface gently. *Never use emery cloth* since particles will imbed in the commutator surface to cause hot spots and burning. Do not use your fingers to hold the sandpaper. If you are stuck on the road somewhere, you can do an emergency cleaning job with an ordinary lead pencil eraser.

Where commutator appears worn or rough, you will be wise to have it turned down and the mica undercut at a garage. The cost is slight ($5 at most) when compared to that of a new or rebuilt unit.

Midnight Burr. While burring may not be so common, it has been known to happen, as I can personally testify. Apparently something got caught under a brush and dug a small groove in the commutator—just deep enough to form little burrs that shorted all commutator segments into each other. This was one of those "middle of the night and 90 miles from nowhere" emergencies, but by scraping along the mica separators with a pocket knife, I managed to cut away enough burr to restore charging capacity. In fact, it worked so well, I never did have it turned down. In any event, it saved me a long walk on a cold night.

Assuming we have pinned down the problem to the generator, but have not yet located it, remove the unit from the engine for the following tests and repairs.

Take off the cover band and clean the commutator thoroughly. Remove all grease, using a rag dampened with carbon tetrachloride and follow with the wood block-sandpaper technique for a good polish job.

Sticking or Worn Brushes. If brushes do not move freely in their holders, slip the holder retaining springs and lift out the brushes. Clean both brushes and holders thoroughly with a toothbrush and some carbon tet. If brushes are worn to half original length, install new ones. Seat new brushes against the commutator with sandpaper.

The common practice of wrapping sandpaper around the commutator and rotating it back and forth is not recommended. Since brushes usually face different directions, such procedure will not seat one of the brushes properly, which will lead to arcing in the generator.

If brush connecting wires or tension springs are broken, replace them. The same goes for any spring with tension so weak it will not hold a partly worn brush firmly against the commutator.

Commutator Out of Round; High Mica. This usually accompanies severe commutator wear caused by a lot of generator mileage. In a case of severe wear, the remedy is to turn the commutator on a lathe and undercut the mica 1/32 in. below the surface of the segments. You can do the latter job alone (and often get many more miles of generator service before having the commutator turned) with a section of hacksaw blade stoned down to proper thickness.

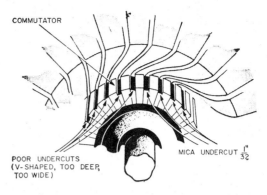

COMMUTATOR

POOR UNDERCUTS
(V-SHAPED, TOO DEEP,
TOO WIDE)

MICA UNDERCUT $\frac{1}{32}''$

Mica insulates commutator segments from each other. Mica should be recessed $\frac{1}{32}$ inch (by undercutting, which can be done with hacksaw blade). Undercutting prevents a dirt coating from shorting segments.

Thrown Solder on Cover Band. If little dabs of solder are splattered on inner surface of the cover band, something caused your generator to overheat, melting solder that holds the armature windings to commutator segments. In this case, some winding ends are probably loose and not contacting the commutator. If the separation is not too severe, you may be able to save the armature by a resoldering and re-insulating job.

Bench Tests. Where trouble is still not located, lift the grounded brush and insulate it from the commutator with cardboard. Hook one clip of the test set-up to the "A" terminal and ground the other to the generator frame. If the generator is inoperative, has passed all other tests and shows negative (no short) on this one, you had better replace it. Further tests would require an investment in specialized knowledge and equipment to detect the trouble and repair it.

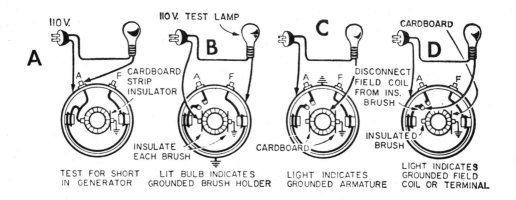

A — 110 V. — CARDBOARD STRIP INSULATOR — INSULATE EACH BRUSH — TEST FOR SHORT IN GENERATOR

B — 110 V. TEST LAMP — LIT BULB INDICATES GROUNDED BRUSH HOLDER

C — DISCONNECT FIELD COIL FROM INS. BRUSH — CARDBOARD — LIGHT INDICATES GROUNDED ARMATURE

D — CARDBOARD — INSULATED BRUSH — LIGHT INDICATES GROUNDED FIELD COIL OR TERMINAL

If the test bulb lights up, however, the short is in the brush holder, armature or field coils. Determine the source by close visual inspection, if possible; otherwise make the remainder of the illustrated tests. Once the short has been pin-pointed, the chances are you can correct it by taping the bared wire or replacing the faulty terminal insulator.

For low or irregular generator output, any of the conditions previously discussed may be the answer, except the loose drive belt. The cure is also the same.

For the cause of an overly high output in an externally grounded generator, make the test illustrated for grounded field coil or terminal. Trouble in the internally grounded type is probably a short between the field and insulated main circuits. Correct this by taping up the exposed leads and eliminating the short.

What Kind of Replacement? If you decide to install another unit, let your pocketbook be your guide. Prices for new current model generators exchanged for your old unit are approximately $30 to $40; rebuilt units completely overhauled, turned, undercut and with new brushes installed average $20. You can get a junkyard unit taken from a wreck (no guarantee, but they usually work) for $10, or less if you bring your own tools and take it off yourself.

Regulator Checks. A typical voltage regulator consists of three distinct magnetic switch units which automatically control the rate of charge within the battery-generator circuit. One switch— a cut-out or circuit breaker—automatically connects the generator circuit to the battery wherever engine speed is above an idle, and disconnects when engine is idling or stopped.

The other switches regulate voltage and current, cutting resistances into or out of the generator field circuit. When battery charge is low, resistances cut out, allowing the generator to deliver maximum power to the battery and

If a jumper wire from regulator base to ground cures a no-charge problem, try tightening regulator mounting screws, which provide the electrical ground. If tightening doesn't help, check screw threads for rust.

Polarizing generator regulators. Regulators for "A" circuit generators can have terminals in different sequences, so be sure to identify armature and battery terminals on regulator before making jumper wire connections.

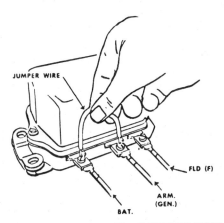

DELCO-REMY — AUTOLITE — PRESTOLITE TYPES
("A" CIRCUIT)
GENERATOR REGULATOR

After making all connections but **BEFORE** starting engine:

1. **Momentarily touch** a jumper wire between "Arm" or "Gen" and "Bat" terminals of regulator. (The occurrence of a spark is normal.)

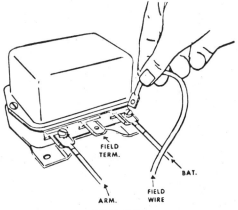

FORD TYPE
("B" CIRCUIT)
GENERATOR REGULATOR

After making all connections but **BEFORE** starting engine:

1. Disconnect "Fld" wire from regulator terminal.
2. **Momentarily touch** this "Fld" wire to "Bat" terminal of regulator. (The occurrence of a spark is normal.)
3. Reconnect "Fld" wire to "Fld" terminal on regulator.

CAUTION: Never touch battery lead to "Fld" terminal of the regulator as this will damage the regulator.

bring it up to a full charge. At this point, resistances automatically cut back into the circuit to reduce generator power so it will just maintain the battery charge and keep its voltage within safe limits.

If trouble is indicated in your regulator, make the ground test first. Connect the jumper from regulator base to a good ground on the car body. If your regulator has a separate ground terminal, see that connections here and at generator ground terminal are clean and tight. After starting up and running engine at a fast idle, your idiot light should go out or ammeter show positive. If not, your regulator grounding is defective.

For further tests of a dual contact regulator in a Delco-Remy system, refer back to the generator test procedure.

If you have an externally grounded generator, connect jumper between field terminal on regulator and a good ground. If the regulator has a ground terminal, connect jumper between it and the regulator body. If you get a charge signal during a fast idle, the regulator is at fault.

On internal ground systems, make this test by connecting jumper between armature and field terminals of the regulator. This hookup can be used in an emergency to drive the car short distances at low speeds until you can get the regulator fixed or replaced.

Too Much Charge. If your battery is fully charged and a high charge rate is still indicated, run engine at a fast idle and remove wire from the regulator field terminal. If charge rate continues, you probably have a grounded or shorted wire somewhere in the wiring harness of the car. If the rate drops to zero, the trouble is in the regulator. Continued high charging may seriously damage generator armature, contact points and coil as well as burn out your car lights prematurely.

Too Little Charge. If battery and charge rate are both low, check for the most common causes—loose battery cable connections and corroded battery terminals. If they are cleaned and tight, run engine at a fast idle and cut the regulator out of the charging circuit. To do this on externally grounded systems, place a jumper between field and ground terminals of the regulator; on internally grounded systems, make the hookup between field and armature terminals of the regulator. If trouble is in the regulator, the charge rate should increase noticeably.

Since few faulty regulators are repairable, it's a good idea to buy a new one (around $10 to $15) when you find yours at fault.

Repolarization. After testing or repairing a generator, make sure its polarity is the same as that of its regulator and the battery it will charge. Before starting, if you have a dual-contact regulator, slip cardboard strips between brushes and commutator for insulation.

On externally grounded generators, make a "flash" jumper wire connection between "B" (battery) and "A" (generator armature) leads at the regulator. Polarizing action occurs instantly. On internally grounded units, remove field lead from regulator and contact it momentarily with the "B" regulator terminal.

This is the ultimate in charging systems—an alternator with built-in voltage regulation.

41

Maintaining Alternator Output

VIRTUALLY ALL CARS built in recent years (Volkswagen a notable exception) have AC generators, commonly called alternators.

The alternator electrical system represents a high achievement in obtaining the most electrical power from a minimum draw on engine output. It has been termed the ultimate electrical power source for automotive use.

The alternator offers the potential for longer battery life in addition to its primary advantage—higher output. The higher output is obtained due to the comparatively low weight of the rotor and coil assembly allowing greater pulley ratios for higher r.p.m. The result, of course, is higher output—even at engine idle. Maintaining the advantage an alternator gives your

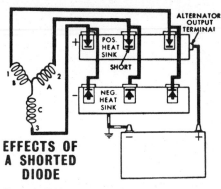

EFFECTS OF A SHORTED DIODE

Shorted diode will allow current to flow in both directions. It will flow back to the A winding instead of to the battery.

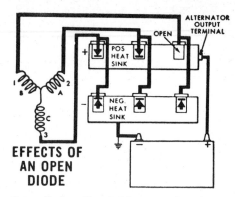

EFFECTS OF AN OPEN DIODE

Open diode will not let current flow in either direction. The circuit is not complete through the B winding to battery.

The diode, also called rectifier, converts the AC output of the alternator into DC by permitting current to flow only one way.

electrical system is just a matter of knowing the alternator and keeping it in top tune.

Construction. All alternators consist of a stator, which corresponds to the generator's field circuit, and a rotor, which corresponds to the generator's armature. The only essential difference between the two is the method used to convert alternating current to direct current. Alternator construction can be seen in the accompanying illustrations.

In generators, as you've seen, brushes are used to pick the alternating current off a commutator, converting that current to direct. Alternators, however, employ silicon rectifiers or, for short, diodes. Don't be confused by the fact that alternators also contain brushes because they are used for a different purpose than in a generator. Alternator brushes supply field current to the rotor by connecting two slip rings mounted concentrically on the rotor shaft.

The rectifier in the alternator is a chemical disc that changes alternating current to direct current since it permits current to flow in one direction only. In other words, the rectifiers used in alternators have a low resistance to the flow of electrical current in one direction and a high resistance to the flow of electrical current in the other direction.

This low resistance allows current to flow from the alternator to the battery, but the rectifier's high resistance prevents a return flow from the battery to the alternator when battery current exceeds alternator output, as it does when the engine idles.

Both alternator and generator have regulator units, but the makeup of each is different. One difference is the absence of a circuit breaker (the cut-out rely) in the alternator regulator.

In the generator's regulator, as you've seen, the circuit breaker connects and disconnects the battery and generator at the proper time. Since the

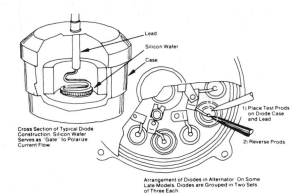

Lead
Silicon Wafer
Case

Cross Section of Typical Diode
Construction. Silicon Wafer
Serves as "Gate" to Polarize
Current Flow.

1) Place Test Prods
on Diode Case
and Lead

2) Reverse Prods

Arrangement of Diodes in Alternator. On Some
Late Models, Diodes are Grouped in Two Sets
of Three Each.

Left: Testing diode requires a 12-volt test lamp with battery built in or a third connector for car's battery. Test prods should be touched at points shown in illustration, then reversed. Test lamp bulb should light in only one direction. If it fails to light in either connection, or lights in both connections, at least one diode in a group is defective. Left: Defective diode replacement is not for the weekend mechanic, as special tools to press out and install are necessary. Below left: Alternator rotor should be checked for internal ground—a defect—with diode test lamp, as shown. If lamp lights, stator is internally grounded and should be replaced. Below: Alternator output test requires an ammeter and voltmeter, connected as shown, and a fully-charged battery. Carbon pile is a load-adjusting rheostat, but you can also load battery by turning on accessories and lights. For this test, disconnect battery cables and alternator connections. On some GM Delcotron alternators, field terminal has "2" below it; on all others, the letter "F" is used. When fully loaded, alternator should put out within three amps of specifications. If five amps or more below specifications, bad diode is indicated.

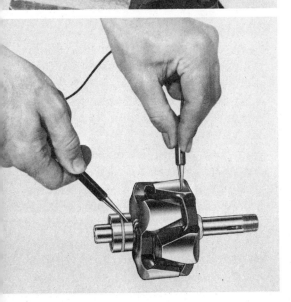

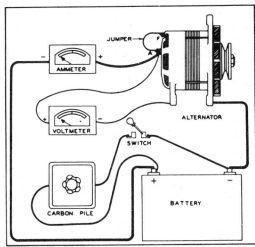

JUMPER F

AMMETER

VOLTMETER

SWITCH

ALTERNATOR

CARBON PILE

BATTERY

+   —

281

alternator is self-rectifying, though, allowing current to flow only in one direction—toward the battery—there is no need for a circuit breaker. The constant, steady flow of current from the alternator to the battery allows the battery to maintain a full state of charge.

Another difference is the absence of a current regulator. The alternator cannot overcharge so long as the voltage regulation is correct, so there is no need for other than a voltage regulator.

The simple requirements of the alternator for regulation hastened the development of the fully-electronic voltage regulator.

Now used on virtually all cars with alternators, the fully-electronic regulator has no vibrating contacts and is not adjustable. Either it works or it doesn't, and it usually does.

On most cars, the fully-electronic regulator is either a plug-in to the alternator or built into it.

The service information in this chapter on voltage regulators, therefore, refers to the vibrating contact type used through the 1960's.

Maintenance. The alternator is no harder to tune than the generator. If trouble is apparent, you don't usually have to replace the entire unit. The unit breaks into two parts—the stator and rotor—allowing you to replace the one that is giving the trouble.

In many cases, you don't even have to replace one of those major components. A common problem, low output, is normally traced to either of two things: a slipping fan belt or defective diodes (rectifiers).

Fan belt tension is critical with the alternator. Always make sure the belt is in good condition and adjusted to specification.

The one precaution you must keep in mind when working with the alternator is guarding against reverse polarity. Reverse the polarity of the alternator or the battery for even an instant and you stand a chance of burning out the rectifiers. To prevent accidental grounding, furthermore, you should always use insulated tools when working in the area of the alternator.

Following adjustment of the fan belt, turn your attention to the regulator. Make sure all connections at this unit are tight. Follow this by checking the condition of the regulator points. If you find they're burned or pitted, you'll have to replace the regulator. Now, check and tighten all connections including those to the ignition switch, the ballast resistor, the regulator and the conducting surfaces of the fuse and holder.

Unscrew the brushes from the alternator and inspect them for wear. If worn, replace them.

In some cars, the brushes can be removed from the alternator with the unit in the car. This is done by unscrewing the external cap screws to which the brushes are attached. In other cars, the unit must be removed from the car to reach the brushes, which can then be unscrewed.

If it becomes necessary to take the unit apart, remove it from the car and split it open, separating the stator from the rotor. Test the rectifiers first. This can be done with a commercial diode tester, although you can also use any continuity tester, such as an ohmmeter or a test lamp that plugs into household current. The test connections are illustrated.

If a diode is defective, it must be replaced. This requires special tools and should be left to a professional shop.

Next inspect the stator winding carefully for breaks. To be absolutely sure there are none, you should test from the stator leads to the stator core with a 110-volt test lamp or other suitable tester. If the lamp lights, the stator is grounded and should be replaced.

Finally, test the field windings in the rotor part of the alternator. This is done with an ammeter hooked to the alternator battery output terminal while turning the rotor shaft by hand. The correct field current draw should be recorded on the meter. This reading differs from car to car, so check your service manual.

The above description tells you what to do if you are not getting output from the alternator. However, there are things a faultily adjusted or malfunctioning alternator can cause—most can be checked on the car.

Low Charging Rate. A low charging rate is indicated when the ammeter or trouble-light in your car begins to show discharge at low engine speed and idle. It is also indicated if a battery gets run-down.

Look at the fan belt first and make sure it's properly adjusted. Then check the battery terminals where high resistance could be causing the trouble. Remove the cables and clean the terminals and posts. Make sure the ground cable is clean and tight.

Finally check at the alternator for loose connections. If the trouble still persists, replace the brushes in the alternator since poor contact between brushes and slip rings is a major factor for a low charging rate. As a final tuneup procedure, remove the alternator from the car and check the stator. Open windings cause an unsteady low charging rate.

If the ammeter troublelight flicks on and off at all speeds and you get a rundown battery, which indicates low voltage output, check the regulator first. To do this, hook the negative lead of a voltmeter to the battery's negative post and the positive to the positive post. Connect a jumper wire from the ignition terminal to the field terminal on the regulator and then start the engine. The voltmeter should read about 14 to 15 volts for a 12-volt charging system. If not, the regulator is faulty. Try adjusting the regulator points; if that does not increase the voltage output, get a new regulator.

But if the regulator does check out, go to the alternator and tighten all connections. The trouble could also be a shorted rectifier or grounded stator, so check them as well.

High Charging Rate. It is possible for the alternator to throw out too much charge. An over-charge condition will show up by acid salts on the battery and the battery beginning to use too much water. Check the regulator first; if it's set too high, adjust the points. If this doesn't help, don't scrap the regulator yet.

First remove the unit and clean its mounting surface. A poorly grounded regulator could be causing the problem. If not, the problem is either that the regulator points are stuck or that there are open windings in the unit. If so, replace the regulator.

If the battery is using too much water or a lot of acid salts begin to form, it could also mean that the regulator points are oxidizing. The cause could be a loose or dirty ground connection, so clean the mounting surface and tighten all attaching bolts. Now, test the regulator. If the meter shows a high voltage, set the points.

Finally, check and adjust the regulator air gap to specification as given in your car's manual. To do this, connect a test lamp between the regulator ignition and field terminals. Insert the proper wire gauge (one of 0.48 in.). Press the armature plate down. The contacts should open and the test lamp should dim.

Now, insert a larger wire gauge in the same position (usually one of .052 in.). Depress the armature plate. The uper contact should be closed and the test lamp should remain lighted. If the air gap doesn't check out, adjust it by bending the upper contact support until you get the right openings and test readings.

Another reason for oxidized points could be shorted field windings in the rotor pole. In this case, the rotor has to be replaced.

Again, excessive use of water by the battery and acid salts on the battery are indications of another condition—burned regulator points. The trouble is probably a regulator set too high or shorted field windings in the rotor pole. In the former case, adjust the points—in the latter, replace the rotor.

Mechanical Problems. An alternator that is noisy is one that is either loose on its mountings or one that has internal problems. First check the mounting bolts and make sure the alternator is tightly connected. The drive pulley could also be causing the noise, so ensure that it is tight.

If this fails to stop the noise, remove the alternator from the car and break it open. Inspect the rotor fan blades. If bent, replace the rotor. Now test each rectifier for a short. If this doesn't stop the trouble, the problem is a sprung rotor shaft, worn shaft bearings or open or shorted windings in the stator and a rubbing rotor pole.

In the event of a sprung rotor shaft, replace the rotor. If the problem boils down to worn shaft bearings, you can have them replaced too. If, though, the stator windings are shorted and the rotor poles are rubbing, you'll have to replace the entire alternator.

If the battery keeps running down for no rhyme or reason, it indicates that the regulator points are stuck closed. This was probably caused by a poor ground connection between the alternator and regulator. The only course is to replace the regulator and make sure the new unit is properly grounded so the trouble doesn't recur.

Batteries come in many shapes, sizes, capacities, and construction features. This one has a prismatic cell cap for a visual indication of whether or not water is needed.

42

Guard Your Battery

PITY THE POOR car battery. At best it is ignored by its owner; at worst it is abused brutally. And yet it takes its punishment stoically, with hardly a complaint.

Toward the very end of its life, the battery tries to warn its owner in a tactful way—perhaps by sulfating its posts or by faltering momentarily when cranking the engine. At last, after perhaps two years of thankless toil, it abruptly expires. Has its owner learned his lesson? Hardly. He simply buys a new battery to abuse.

Fortunately, the battery manufacturers have given up on the average motorist and are busily developing permanently sealed batteries that will hold up. In fact, your car may have a sealed battery, but more likely it does not.

If it doesn't, you should give the battery some service. It requires very little—just keep it reasonably clean, satisfy its modest thirst, check its strength occasionally and extend a few other common sense courtesies.

To better understand a battery's needs, you first must understand what it is and how it works. To begin with, a battery doesn't manufacture electrical energy; it simply stores it, and then delivers it on demand. Energy is fed into a battery in the form of direct-current electricity, stored in the form of chemical energy, and released again as direct-current electricity. When a battery is accepting current, it is "charging"; delivering current, it is "discharging."

A battery consists of several cells, each containing two groups of plates made of unlike metals. These plates are immersed in electrolyte, a chemical solution that reacts with them chemically. In the lead-acid automotive battery, the positive plate is made up of lead peroxide; the negative plate is made up of a different form of lead oxide called sponge lead. Though both of these materials basically are lead, they react like unlike metals. When they are submerged in the electrolyte —a solution of sulfuric acid and water —a voltage is set up and electrical current flows when the circuit is completed. During discharge, the sulfuric acid combines with the active materials in the positive and negative plates and gradually changes both to lead sulfate. If this change is allowed to go on to completion, the battery no longer has two dissimilar metals, and electrical current no longer flows. The battery is then completely discharged.

A discharged battery must be recharged before it can deliver electricity again. This is done by applying direct current from an external source (the car generator or alternator, or a plug-in battery charger) to the battery terminals. From the terminals the current passes through the battery, in the opposite direction to the current flow when the battery is discharging. This restores the sulfated plates to their original forms—the positive plates to lead peroxide, the negative plates to sponge lead—while the sulfuric acid returns to the electrolyte. With two unlike metals in an acid solution, the battery is ready to deliver electricity again.

This cycle can't repeat itself indefinitely. Sometimes, as the plates turn to lead sulfate, large, hard crystals form that can't be broken down by recharging. Also, some of the plate material occasionally flakes off the plates and sinks to the bottom of the battery. If enough of this material accumulates, it can short-circuit a cell. Also, a battery can suffer internal damage from excessively high temperatures, rough treatment, and other causes.

Measuring a battery's strength. Acid is heavier than water. Thus, when all the acid returns to the electrolyte during recharging, the electrolyte becomes heavier. This change can be measured in terms of specific gravity—the weight of the electrolyte as compared with an equal volume of water. From this it follows that the specific gravity of the electrolyte is an excellent indication of the state of charge of a battery.

Here is where the hydrometer comes in. A simple, inexpensive instrument, it is a wise investment for any motorist. It consists of a calibrated float in a syringe-like glass or transparent plastic tube, into which a sample of the electrolyte in each battery cell can be drawn with a rubber suction ball. When specific gravity is high, the float rises higher in the electrolyte than when specific gravity is low.

At 80° F. the specific gravity of the electrolyte in a fully-charged battery

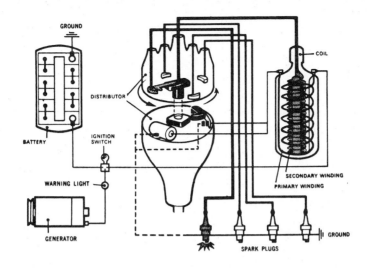

GROUND

DISTRIBUTOR

COIL

BATTERY

IGNITION SWITCH

WARNING LIGHT

SECONDARY WINDING

PRIMARY WINDING

GENERATOR

SPARK PLUGS

GROUND

BATTERY

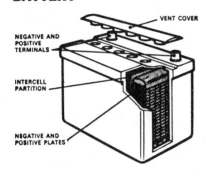

VENT COVER

NEGATIVE AND POSITIVE TERMINALS

INTERCELL PARTITION

NEGATIVE AND POSITIVE PLATES

Above: Heart of the ignition system is the battery, which supplies the spark that ignites the fuel mixture in the cylinders. While the engine is running, the generator or alternator generates electrical power.

Left: Basic battery components are shown here. Multiply the number of cells by two to determine voltage. The capacity depends on the size and number of the plates.

should be 1.260 or higher; discharged, 1.160 or lower. (Deduct .004 from these figures for each 10° that the battery exceeds 80°; add .004 for each 10° below 80°.) All cells should test within .050 of each other. A greater variation indicates the battery must be replaced.

A discharged battery will freeze more easily in winter. For example, a battery with a hydrometer reading of 1.140 will freeze at 8° F., while a battery with a 1.280 reading will freeze at *minus* 92°. A hydrometer check every few weeks can help extend battery life and prevent annoying failures.

A small charger is helpful, especially in winter or whenever heavy demands are made on the battery.

Such home chargers, however, are not too effective for recharging a badly run-down battery. Here a larger commercial charger, as found in service stations, is needed. If possible, have the battery slow-charged; this may take from 12 to 24 hours. In cases of urgency, a fast charge (30 to 90 minutes) may be applied to get the battery up to about 70 or 80 percent of capacity. There is no risk of damage provided the battery is healthy and the current is reduced progressively. Careful supervision is necessary to make sure the battery temperature doesn't exceed 125° F. Excessive temperatures can buckle and ruin the plates.

Before placing the battery back in service, check the voltage regulator and generator or alternator output against the manufacturer's specs: too low an output causes discharging, while too high an output raises the battery temperature and increases chemical activity; either way the battery can suffer permanent damage.

Buying a battery. If your battery is defective and must be replaced, what should you look for in a new one? The first consideration, obviously, is outside dimensions. The new battery must fit the holder; a loose, improperly-mounted battery will quickly bounce itself to death.

Secondly, the voltage must be right. Each cell in a car battery puts out about two volts; thus a six-volt battery has three cells, a 12-volt battery has six cells. All modern domestic cars and practically all imports have 12-volt electrical systems.

For many years, batteries have been rated according to their ability, when fully charged, to deliver a specified quantity of electricity over a definite period of time (usually 20 hours).

Basically, capacity is determined by the number and size of the plates and by the amount of sulfuric acid in the electrolyte. It is expressed in ampere-hours, a unit of measure obtained by multiplying the current flow in amperes by the time in hours during which the current flows. For example, a battery delivering five amperes for 20 hours has a 100-ampere-hour capacity.

Battery capacity also is rated in watts. The "Peak Watts Rating" is a measurement of starting power, with 3,000 the normally required Peak Watts Rating for the battery needed by the average car.

In fact, the Peak Watts Rating was the first successful attempt to supplant the amp-hour rating. After all, what you want is a measurement of starting power, not the ability of the battery to deliver a small amount of current over a 20-hour period. The amp-hour rating might be a convenient way of telling if your battery will have any juice left if you leave the parking lights on overnight, but that is about all.

There actually is a rating that gives you an indication of starting power. Called the "Five-Second Voltage," it indicates the number of volts the battery can maintain at zero degrees after a starting drain of 150 amps.

A good battery would have a rating of 9.4 to 10.2 volts. Of course, starting amperage draw is greater than 150 (more like 350-500 amps), but at least this rating tells you something.

Under a newer system, the battery is rated in amperes discharged in 30 seconds without voltage dropping to less than 1.2 per cell (7.2 for the battery)—high enough to start the car

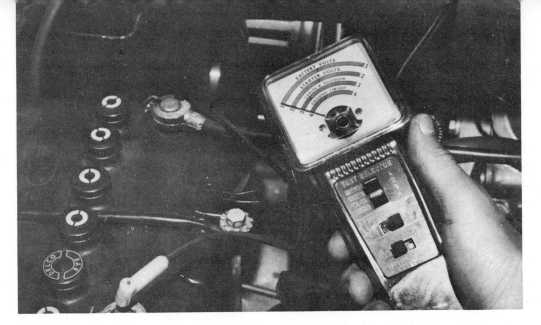

If a battery is questionable, it should be checked with a battery-starter tester. Type shown is an inexpensive type that a weekend mechanic might consider.

until perhaps the last second. With this system, a good battery will have a rating in excess of 375, a premium battery in excess of 450. To calculate reserve capacity, another newer rating counts the number of minutes a fully-charged battery at 80° F. will deliver 25 amps—indicating how long you can drive a car with a defective generator and still use important accessories, such as windshield wipers, lights, etc.

A replacement battery should have at least as great a capacity as the original one. If your engine isn't in the best mechanical condition and requires lots of cranking, or if you've added electrical accessories since buying the car, splurge for a greater capacity (heavy-duty) battery. An underpowered, bargain-basement battery is no bargain; it will give poor service right from the start, and will fail sooner.

Mounting the battery. Secure the battery hold-down straps snugly, but not so tightly as to crack the battery case. Examine the battery cables, and replace them if they are suspect. Remove corrosion from terminals by dipping them in a solution of sodium bicarbonate and water and then flushing with clean water. If necessary, wire brush the terminals and battery posts lightly for good electrical contact. If the terminals fit the posts too loosely, wind copper wire tightly around the posts. Attach the ground cable last to avoid short circuits. (When removing the battery, reverse this procedure and loosen the ground cable first.)

Once the terminals are on clean and tight, lightly coat them and the top of the battery post with petroleum jelly. Do not apply this coating to the sides of the battery posts before the terminals are attached, or you will impede current flow.

On General Motors cars with the sealed side terminals, the only service necessary is to occasionally check the cable terminal for corrosion and wire brush if necessary, making certain the terminal is tight. Don't grease anything.

Once the battery is installed, make sure connections are made properly. Turning on the headlights should show a discharge reading on your ammeter (if you're lucky enough to have one in your car) or, with ignition key on and the engine not running, should cause your generator warning light to glow. If the ammeter shows charge or the warning light doesn't glow, turn the battery around and switch the connections. Finally, smear the terminals and posts with petroleum jelly to reduce corrosion.

Keeping your battery healthy. Check the electrolyte level in each cell at least twice a month (more often during hot weather or fast, long-distance driving). As electricity passes through the cells, some of the water in the electrolyte is converted into hydrogen and oxygen gases and escapes through the vent holes in the battery caps. Normally a battery uses only a slight amount of water every few weeks. An excessive thirst indicates overcharging; check the electrical system.

Experts disagree on whether ordinary tap water may be added to a battery. Some say naturally soft, clear tap water is acceptable, but most recommend using distilled water (sold in auto accessory stores), rain water gathered in non-metallic containers, or clean melted snow. Rather than letting a service station attendant fill your battery, you'd be wise to carry your own plastic bottle of distilled water in the trunk. Never add acid to a battery; this subjects the plates to higher current densities, causing faster deterioration.

Check electrolyte level with a flashlight if necessary, but never with a match or other open flame; gases produced by batteries are highly explosive. Most batteries have markers to show proper electrolyte level. If yours doesn't, fill each cell no more than $\frac{3}{8}$ inch above the plates. When the electrolyte level drops below the tops of the plates, the concentration of acid increases dangerously. Overfilling also is harmful. As battery temperatures rise, the electrolyte expands until it overflows through the vents. It then can form a bridge on top of the battery across which current can flow, draining the battery. Or it may damage the battery holder, body panels, and engine.

Special battery fillers are available that stop water flow automatically when proper electrolyte level has been reached. In a pinch, use your hydrometer to fill the battery. Pouring in water from a cup or bottle is unwise; the flow is hard to control.

In cold weather, add water only if you plan to run the car immediately afterward. Otherwise the water may freeze and crack the battery case. Also, do not take hydrometer reading immediately after adding water.

Those "miraculous" additives. Notwithstanding the fantastic claims made by manufacturers of various battery additives, none of these products has been proved effective in rejuvenating

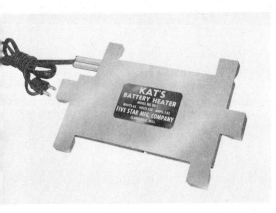

If you live in a very cold area, a battery heater can make winter starting easier. The battery heater is placed in the bottom of the battery case, the battery sits on it, and the heater is plugged into a household outlet.

or extending the life of a healthy battery; more likely, additives will ruin your battery and void the warranty.

If the electrolyte level in one cell drops faster than in the others, suspect a leak. Small cracks in the battery case can be sealed with pitch or commercial sealer applied with a soldering gun. A large crack will necessitate replacement of the battery. Only when refilling a repaired cell should you use an acid solution. Check with a hydrometer to make sure you get the right concentration.

Besides checking electrolyte level, and state of charge and cleaning away corrosion, what else can you do to add years to the life of your battery? For one thing, you can keep your engine well-tuned and your starter motor in top condition to reduce current drain during starting. Also, remember the following driving hints:

- *Before starting the engine,* shut off headlights and other electrical equipment. If you have a manual transmission, shift into neutral and hold the clutch disengaged. Cold, viscous transmission oil puts a considerable drag on transmission gears; but with the clutch (and transmission) disengaged, the starter motor has to crank just the engine.

- *On cold days,* keep the battery warm, if possible. A fully charged battery at 0° F. loses 60 percent of the cranking power it has at 80°; and an engine at 0° requires two and a half times as much starting power as at 80°. That's why a weak battery may get you through the summer, but will fail during the first cold snap. Inexpensive battery warmers that plug into a household outlet are available.

- *In slow-moving,* stop-and-go traffic, especially at night, when headlights are in use, avoid using other electrical accessories if possible. When traffic comes to a stop for a few minutes, switch down from headlights to parking lights (but don't forget to switch back when you start moving).

- *Jumper cables are good* to have in your trunk—just in case. If you should have to use them, be sure you wire the posts of the two batteries from positive to positive and negative to negative; otherwise the wiring and other components may be damaged. The posts of most batteries are marked.

According to battery manufacturers, the average life of a car battery is 26 months. And yet some savvy motorists have squeezed five years' service from their batteries—evidence that a little tender loving care pays big benefits.

43

Checking Dashboard Gauges

THE MAN WHO likes to take care of his car is also the type of person who will order his new car with every optional dashboard gauge available, so he can spot problems before they get serious.

Problems also can occur with gauges. Not too long ago, pulling an instrument gauge cluster and putting it back was a time-consuming horror.

Today, many cars have quick-pull instrument clusters, such as American Motors cars, Maverick and Pinto, Pontiac and Chevy Vega. General dashboard gauge accessibility on almost all cars is markedly improved.

In many cases, too, problems can be cured without removing a gauge or cluster.

Electric Circuit. An electric gauge circuit usually is quite simple. One wire (or printed circuit) goes from each gauge into a master connector, and one wire from that connector goes through a fuse to a terminal on the ignition switch. Another wire goes from the gauge to a sensor (also called a sending unit), on the engine for water temperature or oil pressure, in the gas tank for fuel level.

General Motors cars all use a conventional 12-volt circuit. Ford and

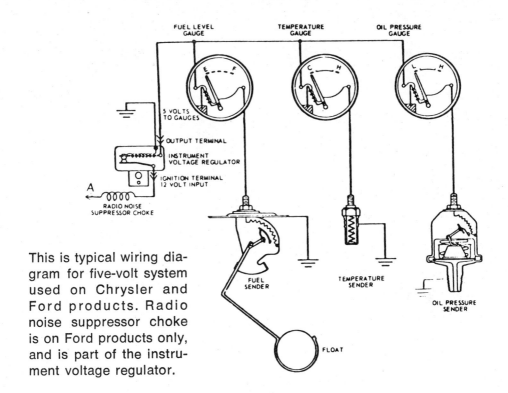

FUEL LEVEL GAUGE   TEMPERATURE GAUGE   OIL PRESSURE GAUGE

5 VOLTS TO GAUGES

OUTPUT TERMINAL

INSTRUMENT VOLTAGE REGULATOR

IGNITION TERMINAL 12 VOLT INPUT

A

RADIO NOISE SUPPRESSOR CHOKE

FUEL SENDER   TEMPERATURE SENDER   OIL PRESSURE SENDER

FLOAT

This is typical wiring diagram for five-volt system used on Chrysler and Ford products. Radio noise suppressor choke is on Ford products only, and is part of the instrument voltage regulator.

Chrysler products have gauges designed to operate on five volts, and the wire from the ignition switch to the gauges is split and a special voltage regulator is inserted in the circuit. This special regulator keeps voltage to the gauges at the specified five.

This special regulator is mounted under the dashboard, on the back or top of the cluster on Ford products and some Chrysler cars. It also is built into the fuel gauge on other Chrysler products. (If you check with a parts house, you'll find out if the special instrument regulator is a detail or only available with a fuel gauge.)

Gauge Operation. The electric gauge

operation, regardless of function, is basically the same. In the fuel gauge, for example, the fuel in the tank controls the position of a float, which is attached to a variable resistor with a movable contact.

When the fuel level is low, the contact is moved by the float to a high resistance portion of the resistor, limiting current that can flow from the ignition switch to the gauge.

When the fuel level is high, the float moves the contact to a low resistance portion of the resistor, allowing more current to go to the gauge.

The gauge itself has a pointer controlled by a bimetal strip, which is

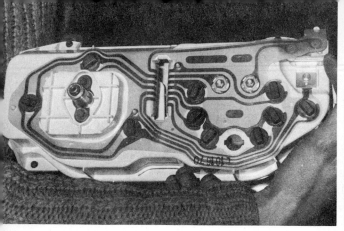
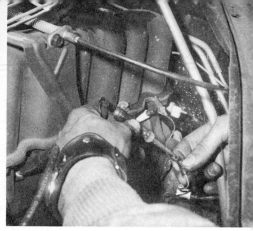

At left is the back of a Maverick instrument cluster. Plastic sheet with printed circuit is used instead of wiring. Finger points to location of instrument voltage regulator at upper right. Photo right: Instrument regulator can be checked out by disconnecting a sending unit on engine (oil pressure sender is one disconnected in photo) and connecting a test lamp (alligator clip to ground, probe to wire from sender). Turn on ignition and if regulator is good, test lamp bulb should flicker.

heated by the current flow from the ignition switch. When the current flow is low, there is little heat and the pointer moves only a bit. When the current flow is high, the bimetal strip is heated more, and deflects the pointer further along the gauge.

The temperature gauge system is different only in that a temperature-sensitive resistor is used as a sending unit. When engine temperature is low, the temperature-sensitive resistor produces high resistance for minimum deflection of the gauge pointer. When engine temperature rises, the temperature-sensitive resistor's contact is moved to a low-resistance position, permitting greater deflection of the gauge pointer.

The oil pressure gauge sending unit uses a pressure-sensitive flexible diaphragm to control the movable contact in a variable resistor.

Common Problems. The most common gauge problems are:

1. No gauges work at all.

2. All gauges are pegged, that is, all the way to the high end of the scale.

3. A single gauge of the group fails to function.

Failure of any gauge to work is most common, and usually is nothing more than a blown or defective fuse. Fuses are cheap, so even if a fuse looks good, try replacing it before attempting anything more complex. (You can "borrow" a fuse from another circuit. Just make sure it is of the same amperage rating.) Some fuses that look good have suffered a separation at one of the metal cap ends.

Another possibility is a break in the circuit from the ignition switch to the master connector to the gauges. On GM and American Motors cars, check for a loose connection at the ignition switch.

On Ford and Chrysler products, the loose connection is possible, but more likely is a defective instrument voltage regulator.

Test Regulator. To check the regulator, disconnect the wire from the engine temperature or oil pressure sending unit in the engine, whichever is more accessible.

Connect a test lamp in series—one wire of the test lamp to a good ground, the other test lamp wire to the terminal of the wire you took off the sending unit.

Turn on the ignition. The test lamp should flicker if the instrument regulator is good.

(Note: if you have a voltmeter, make the same connections and if the regulator is good, the voltmeter needle should flicker.)

If the regulator is defective, it must be replaced. It is a sealed unit and cannot be serviced. See the illustrations which show the unit and its mounting.

If the regulator tests out well, and the gauges still don't work, the problem must be in the master connector to the gauges or in the printed circuitry on cars so equipped. If you can't find an obvious bad connection, leave the job to an electrical specialist. Fortunately 98 percent of the time, the problem will be in the areas you can handle.

(Note: some Ford instrument regulators incorporate a radio suppression device called a "choke," and if this is defective, it can cause all gauges to stop functioning. To check the choke, see the illustration.)

Pegged Gauges. (This applies only to Ford and Chrysler five-volt systems). If the gauges all are pegged, there are two possible causes:

1. The instrument voltage regulator is defective (you now know how to check that out).

Left: Unsnap two buttons to expose instrument regulator and unbolt as shown to remove. Right: On models without printed circuitry, instrument voltage regulator may be a plug-in unit as shown.

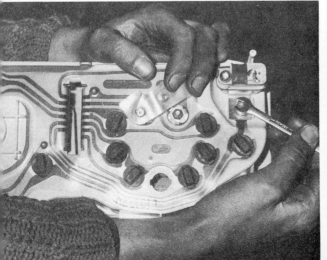
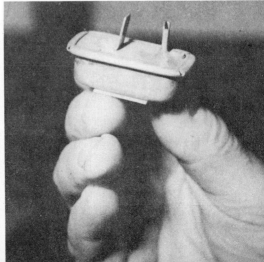

2. Whatever is used to ground the regulator and gauges is not providing a satisfactory ground connection.

The regulator and gauges usually are grounded by the mounting screws, and if they are loose, the ground circuit is poor. A poor ground circuit provides a false signal to the instrument regulator and causes it to pass higher voltage.

Jumper wires from the instrument regulator body and the instrument cluster to a good ground can be used to pinpoint the problem. If the use of jumper wires causes the gauges to operate properly, tighten the mounting screws.

If the problem was cured with jumper wires but won't go away when you tighten the screws, run separate jumper wires.

Individual Gauges. If an individual gauge does not indicate, the problem is either in the sending unit, the wiring or the gauge itself. The common problems in the wiring are poor or loose connections, which can be checked for visually.

To check out a gauge, disconnect the wire at the sending unit, and connect it to ground by means of a jumper wire with a 10-ohm resistor in it. You can make such a jumper wire with a 10-ohm resistor purchased from a radio supply store, a couple of pieces of wire and a couple of alligator clips. Attach one end of each wire to a terminal on the resistor, and the alligator clips to the other ends of the wires.

With the sending unit wire attached to the special jumper wire and the wire connected to ground, the gauge pointer should swing all the way to the high side. If it doesn't, the gauge is defective and should be replaced.

If the gauge is good, check the sending unit for a good ground by connecting a jumper wire (without the resistor) from the sending unit body to the engine. If the gauge now operates normally, take out the sending unit, clean its threads and the sending unit bore with a brush and reinstall.

If a bad ground isn't the problem, and the gauge is good, the odds are that the problem is a defective sending unit. The only practical way to test one is by substitution with a new unit. With a fuel sending unit, this requires dropping the gas tank, a somewhat time-consuming procedure. But your time is a lot cheaper than a professional mechanic's, and sending units, fortunately, are inexpensive.

Special Problems. Other possible gauge problems and their solutions are:

1. Flickering gauges. This is almost invariably limited to cars with five-volt systems and is caused in such cases by bad contact points in the instrument regulator. Replace it.

2. Individual gauge is pegged. This is caused by a shorted wire in the harness or shorted sending unit. The more common situation is a shorted sending unit, which should be checked by substitution. If the sending unit is good, the only practical cure is to disconnect the wire from the sending unit to the master connector, tape it at both ends and run a new wire outside the wiring harness. Although the wiring problem could be checked with a jumper wire, eliminating the possibility of unnecessarily buying a sending unit, it is somewhat remote and may be very

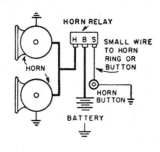

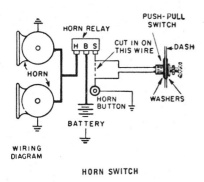

WIRING
DIAGRAM

HORN SWITCH

First, drill a hole large enough to accommodate the switch at a convenient spot on the dash. Lift the hood and locate the horn relay. If you're unsure about which metal box is the horn relay, trace the wires from the horn. Take two lengths of #14 insulated wire and thread through the firewall; if possible, using a hole in the firewall through which other wires pass. If you drill a new hole, install a rubber grommet so that the insulation on the wires won't scrape against metal.

Loosen the screw on the horn relay terminal marked "S" (switch or horn button) and remove the wire from the horn relay. If there is no "S," the smallest wire leading to the relay is the horn-ring, or button, wire.

Attach one of the new wires to the "S" terminal on the relay; lead the other end of the wire through the firewall and attach to either switch terminal. Solder and tape one end of the second piece of new wire to the end of the wire removed from the "S" terminal on the horn relay. Lead the free end of this wire through the hole in the firewall and attach to the other switch terminal. Install the switch, using washers.

Now to test your job. With the switch pushed *in,* a tap on the horn-ring or button should make the horns blow. With the switch pulled to *off* position, the horns should not blow. If it's the other way around, reverse the two switch wires.

When you leave your car, get in the habit of pulling the switch to the *off* position. This cuts the horns out completely.

time-consuming on older cars. If you have a car with a quick-pull instrument cluster, the job can be done easily, provided you have a wiring diagram and can identify the one in the master connector that provides juice for the offending gauge. Clearly, this job can present problems and you may wish to leave it to a professional mechanic.

3. All gauges read low on Chrysler or Ford five-volt system. The problem is normally a defective instrument voltage regulator.

Be Sure Your Horn Won't Blow at Midnight. By installing a simple push-pull switch on your dash, and cutting into one wire, you can be certain that *your* car horns will never blow at midnight.

297

Noise from misaligned hood can be corrected by repositioning. Loosen bolts in elongated holes in mounting brackets.

44

How to Spot That Noise— and Cure It

WOULDN'T YOU LIKE to choke that little "canary" somewhere in the front end of your car that's been pestering you? Or, maybe you've got one of those thumpy clunks that only shows up now and then at certain speeds. Suppose your car runs like the proverbial jackrabbit but when you hit around 45 or so, some sort of a howl or wheeze comes in that makes your passenger ask "What makes it do that?"

Noises often come from a source least expected as knocks, growls, groans, squeaks, whistles and so on have a way of seeming to be where they ain't. Even the best shops are often stumped by odd sounds, especially when everything seems to be tip-top. There is always that "mysterious" knocking or rattle, hard to pin down. But even the most evasive squeak can be located by following these methods.

Unwanted noises plague new and old cars, big and little cars. Those little tingling noises that are often heard only when the car is in motion can keep you guessing. And for the life of you, you can't reproduce them by bouncing or shaking your car. Weather has a lot to do with car noise too.

Some squeaks and rattles ride with you on hot, dry days but fade away during rainy weather. Sometimes all you can do is localize foreign noise, and you would have to tear down the unit to find the cause, like a transmission, for example. You may have traced a low speed "howl" to a manual transmission. Tearing down the transmission might show a defective clutch pilot bearing, binding clutch hub or misalignment of the clutch in the flywheel as the direct cause of the growl.

While a complete chassis lubrication, including under hood engine units, stops many noises, don't depend too much on a chassis lube job to take care of the squeaks and groans permanently. There may be a worn spring shackle that quiets down with a lube job, but lubricant won't take the place of worn rubber or metal. Once you've traced such a noise, better get some new bushings in the shackle. Higher car speeds and more powerful engines tend to amplify small noises you never have heard before at lower speeds.

When trying to locate noises under the hood and coming principally from the engine, a sounding rod helps to localize the source. The rod can be 5/16 or ⅜-inch diameter steel, and about 3 feet long, or use a broom stick of about the same length. To "sound" a noise, place one end of it on the spot to be tested and bring the other end close so your ear rests on your closed hand. To organize your attack, split up the engine section into zones.

While using the sounding rod, "short out" the spark plug of the cylinder being tested. If the engine knock becomes less audible, louder or changes in any way with a spark plug dead, you are pretty sure to have located the troublesome cylinder. Of course, if all connecting rod bearings are worn and loose, you will hear a clatter no matter where you put the end of the sounding rod on the crankcase. Speeding up the engine makes such clatter louder.

Actually the foreign noises we are interested in are those "funny sounds" —klunks, whistles and squeaks that might come from any part of your car.

Since many car owners recognize run-of-mine knocks, spark rap, valve tappet clatter, hydraulic valve lifter click, carbon knock and such, we'll skip those and talk about the ones that are harder to track down.

Table A lists the more common noises, parts affected, probable trouble, how to check for it and how to fix it. You can't always apply the same information to every make of car. Take #9, if the car has an automatic transmission, you can't check for end play as prescribed because there is no pedal to push. In this case check for excessive end play with the oil pan off using a heavy screwdriver or pinch bar between the main bearing cap and crank cheek. Or, in #13, piston slap may occur in even a new or rebuilt engine with some types of aluminum pistons when the engine is cold, but the pistons will quiet down as the engine reaches correct operating temperature.

Whether you call it a knock, squeak, hiss, rattle, or pound (see Table B for definitions), a noise can be caused by one or more of the conditions illustrated. Friction will set up a squeak, for example, when a bolt becomes loose enough to allow adjacent parts to rub together. Squirting a little oil around the parts usually quiets it, but for a permanent remedy, tighten the bolt. Friction, too, produces the squeak from a glazed fan belt. A little wax or aerosol belt dressing on the belt quiets it for a time, but you really need a new belt.

Out-of-round parts that wobble or hop can produce a wump-wump-wump noise like an out-of-balance wheel or engine flywheel. One grumble, accompanied by noticeable car vibration, is often traced to an unbalanced propeller shaft with undercoating on one side. Undercoating is fine for fenders or gas tank, but if a blob gets smeared on the propeller shaft (actually a tube), it can set up a mighty unpleasant vibration at high speeds. Since the undercoating is not evenly spread around shaft, it runs lop-sided—the higher the speed the worse it gets. It takes only a few ounces on the shaft to cause a noise.

An out-of-round or worn ignition distributor shaft can cause your car's engine to run "rough," particularly at low speed, along with a sort of "loping" exhaust. Wear can turn the bushing oval allowing the distributor shaft to be pushed back and forth in the oval opening by pressure from the bent shaft. In a six-cylinder engine distributor, for example, only two of the cylinders have the correct "dwell" or closure time for the contact points. Other cylinders are firing "early" or "late," causing an unbalanced or "rough" running engine.

Misaligned parts, such as two shaft ends which do not slide concentrically into a coupling, cause severe strains on the supporting bearings and wear the bearings excessively to produce noise. Clutches, transmissions, propeller shafts and rear axles are subject to these misalignments, particularly on older cars or those recently repaired. Transmission noises are difficult to track down because some noises, which seem to be coming from the transmission, actually are being "telegraphed" from their origin in the rear axle.

Adjustments for correcting misaligned parts are provided, for example, at the hood hinges, hood lock dowel and guide. Usually elongated holes at hood hinges permit fore and aft movement of the hood hinge brackets. To align hood, loosen hinge adjusting screws, grasp front of hood and shift it around until it is centered. Then carefully raise the hood and tighten the hinge screws.

Minor adjustments can be made on the trunk lid at the hinges. To find out if an adjustment is necessary, chalk the edge of the body flange with white chalk and close the lid. If chalk marks on the weatherstrip are not visible all around (spotty), adjustment is necessary. Loosen hinge support bolts and shift the deck lid in elongated holes at the body hinge support brackets. After alignment, tighten the bolts.

Shock absorbers are often blamed for noise when actually the fault may be elsewhere. There may be loose parts in the car's trunk, or spring shackles and clips may be loose. Fenders or bumpers may require tightening. Most shock absorber noise results from units that are empty or low in fluid, have worn links and bushings or loose mountings. Simplest way to correct shock absorber noise is to replace units.

TABLE A

ENGINE AND UNDERHOOD NOISE

CHARACTERISTIC SOUND OR BEHAVIOR	PART OR PARTS AFFECTED	PROBABLE NATURE OF TROUBLE	CHECKING	REMEDY
1. Hissing	Spark plug	Broken or loose	Squirt oil around plug base; bubbles indicate leak	Tighten or replace plug
2. Click or rattle	Fan	Bent blade, loose pulley	Look for shiny spot on blade. Inspect pulley	Replace fan—do not sraighten. If problem is caused by weak engine mounts, replace them, too
3. Loud report in muffler	Muffler	Exhaust valve not seating. Ignition out of time. Rich or too lean mixture	Accelerate engine for smoke from exhaust pipe	Reface & regrind valve. Retime ignition to engine. Clean carburetor jets or adjust fuel level
4. Sharp snap Engine pulling	High-tension Ignition System	Cracked distributor head. Cracked plug insulator. Damaged wire insulation. Loose distributor wire	Wipe distributor head and plugs. Examine wire insulation. Test wires in distributor sockets	Wipe parts clean or replace with new. Tape wires or replace. Push wires firmly into sockets
5. Dull thump or Pound upon acceleration	Engine mount or mounts	Loose or deteriorated rubber in mount	Visual inspection	Tighten bolts of mount or replace rubber blocks
6. Metallic rattle upon acceleration	Muffler or tail pipe	Muffler baffles loose. Tail pipe strikes frame	Use sounding rod on muffler (rear end on jacks) shake tail pipe	Install new muffler. Bend tail pipe and tighten clamps
7. Squeal (generally at idling speed)	Generator Fan bearing Water pump	Generator brushes too hard. Fan bearing dry. Dry water pump seal	Use sounding rod on suspected units	Install new generator brushes—or sand commutator. Lubricate fan bearing. Use soluble oil in cooling system
8. Knock (upon accelerating or pulling)	Ignition Distributor	Automatic advance stuck. Spark timed too early. Vacuum control not functioning	Test governor weights for free action. Check timing with a timing light. Check vacuum control	Clean and lubricate governor advance. Retime ignition to engine with timing light. Install new diaphragm
9. Intermittent rap (engine idling)	Crankshaft	Excessive end play in crankshaft	Noise affected by applying or releasing clutch	Install new end-thrust bearing or bronze washer
10. Loud knock or "bump" (engine pulling hard at low speed)	Crankshaft main bearing	Loose or worn main bearing	Short out spark plugs with screwdriver on block or head	Replace worn bearing or bearings with new or adjust with shims
11. Well defined knock or "tap" on accelerating more pronounced when releasing pedal	Connecting rod	Worn bearing	Allow engine to "pull" at approximately 35 mph. then release accelerator pedal pressure	Install rod or rods with new bearings

Continued

301

TABLE A (Continued)

	CHARACTERISTIC SOUND OR BEHAVIOR	PART OR PARTS AFFECTED	PROBABLE NATURE OF TROUBLE	CHECKING	REMEDY
			ENGINE AND UNDERHOOD NOISE		
12.	Light metallic knock or tap (engine idling)	Piston pin	Worn pin	Hold sounding rod on block from cylinder to cylinder. Short out plugs one by one	Install new pin or pins
13.	Decided "slap" or knock with cold engine	Pistons	Pistons loose in cylinder. Connecting rod misaligned. Excessively worn cylinders	See whether noise disappears as engine warms up	Recondition cylinders. Install new pistons, rings, pins and align connecting rods
14.	"Spark" knocks (when open throttle)	Ignition Distributor	Sticking distributor breaker plate. Governor advance springs weak	Visual inspection of plate. Test distributor, after removal in test machine	Clean and "free-up" breaker plate. Install new governor springs.
15.	"Whistle" (partly open throttle)	Heat riser tube	Loose tube	Idle engine. Remove air cleaner. Hold bundle of rags over exhaust tail pipe. Stop engine. Check for smoke from carburetor air intake	Install new riser tube to replace burned out tube
16.	Hissing sound (in crankcase)	Pistons and Rings	Loose pistons or stuck rings causing "blow-by"	Look for smoke coming from breather pipe or crankcase. Insert rubber hose in breather. Crank engine and place ear on other end of hose	Recondition cylinders, new pistons and rings, or free-up rings with solvent
			DRIVE LINE NOISE—CLUTCH, TRANSMISSION AND PROPELLER SHAFT		
17.	Chatter	Clutch	Facings worn or glazed	Accelerate car slowly. (also check for excessive end play in rear spring front shackles)	Install new clutch facings. New pressure plate may also be required
18.	Grinding noise	Clutch	Worn release bearing. Bearing requires lubrication	Press clutch pedal intermittently	Install new release bearing
19.	Squeaks	Clutch	Insufficient pedal-to-floor board clearance	Test for pedal striking floor board	Adjust screw or pedal shaft clearance, to correct specification
20.	Whining noise	Fluid flywheel	Fluid level low	Constantly audible	Add fluid to correct level
21.	Whistle—long, low	Driver or passenger	Curvaceous blonde on street	Glance quickly around area	Turn sharply at next corner
22.	Gears noisy when shifting	Transmission and Clutch	Wrong clutch pedal adjustment	Noise evident when shifting into any speed while pressing clutch pedal	Adjust for correct "lash" and floor board clearance

302

No.	Noise	Location	Probable cause	Test	Remedy
23.	Grinding noise from transmission at high speed	Transmission and Propeller shaft assembly	Worn transmission rear bearings. Worn universal joints	"Whip" of propeller shaft usually can be felt at high speed	New transmission bearings (other parts may be needed too). Renew worn universal
24.	Howl (shift lever in "low")	Transmission (manual)	Worn clutch pilot bearing in flywheel recess	Noise usually disappears in 2nd and high	Remove clutch & transmission assembly & install new pilot bearing
25.	Growl or hum (in "neutral")	Transmission (manual)	Pinion shaft bearing and gear probably excessively worn	Depressing clutch pedal usually stops noise	Overhaul transmission (other gears and bearings usually are worn, too)
26.	Whirring noise (under car, with considerable vibrating)	Propeller shaft	Worn universal joints and unbalanced propeller shaft	Drive at fairly high speed. Shift to neutral. Let engine idle. If vibration persists, suspect propeller shaft	New universal joint parts (also perhaps, transmission rear bearing)

CHASSIS, SPRINGS, SHACKLES, AND SHOCK ABSORBER NOISE

No.	Noise	Location	Probable cause	Test	Remedy
27.	Rattle	Under hood chassis parts (front)	Loose radiator shell. Independent coil spring pads missing. Car heater bracket loose	Visual inspection of parts; test for looseness with heavy screwdriver	Replace missing parts, screws or bolts and tighten securely
28.	Rattle	Muffler or Tail pipe	Muffler and tail-pipe bracket loose	Grasp and shake end of tailpipe. Visual inspection underneath car	Replace missing parts screws or bolts and tighten securely
29.	Drumming noise	Under hood parts	Loose engine mountings	With carburetor throttle rod accelerate engine in short "jerks" and observe engine mountings for movement	Tighten engine hold-down bolts (or replace rubber mounts on newer engines)
30.	Heavy bumping noise	Under hood	Battery loose in its cradle	Visual inspection	Tighten battery hold-bolts (also see if cable has been chafing)
31.	Dull thud	Spring shackle or bolt	Worn or loose rubber or metal bushings	Place pry bar between frame and leaf spring and apply pressure to test looseness	Install new rubber bushings (some equipped with metal bushings)
32.	Squeaky noise (slowing down or stopping)	Shock absorber	Linkage joints	Examine for lack of lubrication	Lubricate linkage
33.	Rattle (from vicinity of wheels)	Shock absorbers	Loose on frame—Arm striking frame or other parts. Bushings or attaching eyes (telescoping type) worn or loose	Visual examination of parts. (Also check spring shackles, sway bar mounting and spring U-bolts for looseness)	Tighten bolts, align parts or rebush attaching parts. (Noise seldom within shock absorber itself)

REAR AXLE NOISE

No.	Noise	Location	Probable cause	Test	Remedy
34.	Humming noise (continuous)	Rear axle pinion and drive gear	Pinion bearing incorrectly adjusted giving high tooth contact	Best done by driving on asphalt road. (Have correct seasonal lubricant in axle). Often can be tire noise	Move pinion towards drive gear (drive gear may require shifting also). Axle must be "taken down" for work
35.	Gear noise (decelerating)	Rear axle Differential	End play in differential bearings excessive	Audible when releasing accelerator and car slows down	Rear axle must be opened. Loosen bearing saddle clamps and adjust bearings. Lock assembly

Continued

	CHARACTERISTIC SOUND OR BEHAVIOR	PART OR PARTS AFFECTED	PROBABLE NATURE OF TROUBLE	CHECKING	REMEDY
	REAR AXLE NOISE				
36.	Hum while coasting	Axle wheel bearings	Excessive end play in axle shafts (or both shafts)	Audible when coasting. Jack up rear wheels and pull and push on wheels in line with axle shaft	Remove wheel, brake drum and adjust end play with shims inside backing plate
37.	Noise or Growl on turns	Rear axle side gear thrust washers or inner axle oil seal	Thrust washers worn, seal burned out	Most audible when making left turn	Remove, disassemble differential and install new thrust washers (perhaps gears also). Install new axle oil seal
38.	Chatter (limited Slip Differential only)	Differential clutches	Improper lubricant	Most audible in turns	Draw all old oil out with siphon. Refill with limited slip oil.
	BRAKE, TIRES AND WHEEL NOISE				
39.	Chatter (applying brakes)	Brakes (one or more wheels)	Loose wheel bearing. Loose spring U-bolts. Loose spring shackle	Jack up wheel, grasp it top and bottom and test for "play." Inspect U-bolts for tightness. Test shackles	Adjust wheel bearing. Tighten U-bolts, Re-bush spring shackles
40.	Loud squeal—when applying brakes	Brakes	Non-concentric shoes produce local high pressure areas. Drums distort under braking pressure	Remove wheels and brake drum. Check lining for uneven wear spots. Have mechanic check drums with gauges	Have shop true-up brake shoe linings with lining grinder. Install new brake drums
41.	Squeal or whistle (on curves)	Tires	Lateral slippage caused by front wheel misalignment	Check tires for uneven tread wear, scuffing and cupped condition; check for bent frame	Front end alignment for toe-in camber, caster and king pin inclination. Straighten frame
42.	Thumping noise	Tires	One or more tires "egg-shaped"	Jack up wheel; place carton or box on ground close to center of tread. Rotate tire slowly; note variation in distance between tire and box	Tire should be retrued (new tires should be driven 1500 miles or so for breakin before truing)
43.	Rattle (front wheel)	Bearings	Broken ball or roller	Remove bearings and make visual inspection	Install new bearing assembly and adjust bearing
	BODY NOISE				
44.	Rumble or Rattle (front end)	Hood	Hood fastener has insufficient spring tension Anti-rattlers missing	Testing for trouble is also the cure. Loosen lock nut and turn dowel inward with screwdriver for correct fit and tighten nut. Check for missing rubber or fabric anti-rattlers	Correct tension removes "play" Install new anti-rattlers

No.	Symptom	Part	Condition/Cause	Check	Remedy
45.	Squeak	Door panel	Panel scrapes against hinge pillar	Look for "rusty" or shiny edge on door panel and hinge pillar	Open door, insert screwdriver in crack and press on door so as to close against it. Metal will spring back at flange
46.	Front fender "squeak"	Fender and door	Too little clearance between fender and door	Visual inspection	Loosen bolts (engine compartment) holding fender rear edge to cowl. Shift fender forward or rearward with pinch bar for clearance, tighten bolts
47.	Rattle (cowl)	Ventilator	Gasket rotted out or deteriorated	Visual inspection of gasket	Remove old pieces of gasket, clean channel, fit new gasket
48.	Squeal or whistle (40-50 mph)	Body louvers on side of car	Air stream passing through louvers	Fasten a cloth over louvers and see if noise ceases	Break up air stream with wire fastened lengthwise in louvers
49.	Rumbling sound	Doors and body panel	Vibration due to insufficient sound deadening	Difficult to check	Undercoating possibly best answer
50.	Bumping noise (rear end of car)	Spare wheel and tire	Loose in its mounting. Loose body bolts	Visual inspection	Tighten clamp screw or nut. Tighten body bolts
51.	"Buzzing" sound	Speedometer	Cable tip not correctly seated in speedometer head drive gear. Cable too long	Unscrew sleeve on rear of speedometer and examine parts	Seat tip into drive gear and tighten sleeve. Install cable of correct length.

TABLE B

The dictionary says this about different kinds of noises:

GROWL To utter a deep guttural sound

HUM A low monotonous noise...of a swiftly revolving top or a whirling wheel.

KNOCK ...a knocking noise as from loose parts knocking against each other.

SQUEAK A sharp, shrill, piercing noise as of wheels turning on dry axles.

THUMP A blow or knock as with something thick or heavy ... to cause a dull sound.

RATTLE To make, cause or emit a rapid succession of short, sharp noises as through shaking or recurrent collisions of hard bodies.

Lubricating hood hinge pivots.

45

Lubrication for Noise Prevention

IN ADDITION TO curing rattles and noises, there are some things you can do to keep some parts of your car from developing unwanted chirps as they age.

These include windshield wiper arm pivots, door hinges, hood hinges and door push buttons (not the locks), which should be given a squirt of engine oil.

Other alternatives are door strikers (a stick lubricant), window channels (aerosol silicone lube), door lock and speedometer cable (graphite lubricant), hood latch (grease), spring shackles and shock absorber bushings (brake fluid), fender skirts (silicone lube) and pedal linkages (aerosol silicone lube).

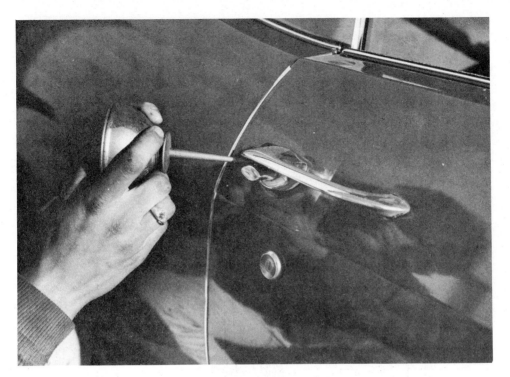

Lubricating door push button.

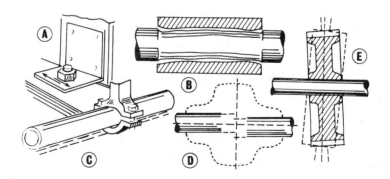

A few causes of knocks, squeaks, and rattles. **(A)** friction of loose, dry parts rubbing together; **(B)** excessive wear in a shaft and its bearing or bushing; **(C)** loose part, like muffler tail pipe; **(D)** misaligned shafts, causing excessive wear and "pound" **(E)** gears, pulleys, etc., that run out-of-true.

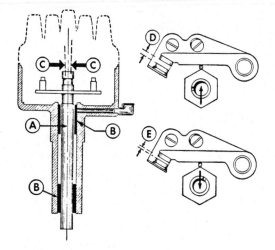

Engine's "wump, wump, wump" at idle may be caused by a worn or bent ignition distributor shaft. Note how shaft **(A)** in top bushing **(B)** wobbles so its center line oscillates from **C** to **C.** As the distributor cam is pushed toward or away from the contact point breaker arm, the point opening is either too great **(D)** or too little **(E).**

Typical forward engine mounting. **(A)** frame bracket; **(B)** engine; **(C)** rubber shock dampening insulator. If rubber deteriorates, a knock or thump may result as the engine rocks during accelerating.

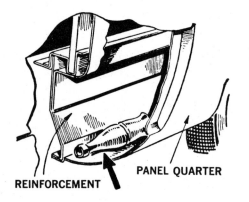

REINFORCEMENT   PANEL QUARTER

A "mysterious" rattle like this soda bottle which some factory employee unthinkingly welded in the panel quarter is usually found only by sheer accident.

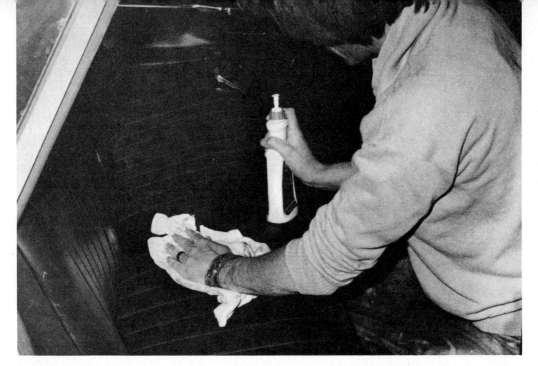

Modern vinyl upholstery is normally cleaned with household spray cleaners.

46

Servicing Upholstery

THE BEAUTIFUL OUTSIDE appearance of a carefully washed and waxed automobile is meaningless if the interior does not match.

Fortunately, today's vinyl upholstery is extremely easy to keep clean and, with special products available, also easy to repair and recolor.

Most mild household spray cleaners will do a very nice job on car vinyl upholstery, removing dirt easily, and doing a reasonable job on stains.

If your car's upholstery is beyond quick cleanup, a recoloring is the answer.

The leading product in the field is Vyna-Chem "Wipe-On Liquid Color," and it works on vinyl, leather and Naugahyde. It is available in a variety of colors, and can be mixed or matched to just about any color you want.

The color coats in such a way as to resist cracking.

The same company produces a highly-effective vinyl upholstery and top repair kit, "Vyna-Weld."

You just trim the ripped area. Apply the repair material, a sort of vinyl putty, with a spatula. The material is available in colors to match original equipment upholstery.

Smooth over the damaged area with the spatula.

Select the proper graining paper. (The kit comes with paper that is grained to match different car upholstery.) Place the graining paper on the damaged area and heat with an iron. Remove the graining paper and you actually will not be able to find the "patch" a week later.

If your car is an older one or an economy model, with broadcloth or flatcloth upholstery, keeping it clean presents some problems.

Broadcloth and Flatcloth. Avoid using any solutions containing water on broadcloth no matter how efficiently they remove signs of soiling or stains. Broadcloth finishes are produced by a process employing multiple pressings and other operations which result in the fine finish of this fabric. Water causes the nap to curl and become rough. The result is an unsightly appearance and restoration of the original finish is impossible.

The use of a volatile cleaner is recommended on both flatcloth and broadcloth upholstery. Naphtha or gasoline may be used, but make sure that no coloring or tetraethyl lead is contained in the solvent. Since naphtha and gasoline are dangerous as a fire hazard, they should only be used as a last resort when a safer type of cleaner such as carbon tetrachloride is not available. Make sure there is plenty of ventilation when using any type of volatile cleaner since the fumes are toxic in large amounts. Also, remember to wear rubber gloves to protect the skin if it is sensitive to irritation.

After all dust and dirt have been removed from the material, wet a cloth with the volatile cleaner. Spread the cloth open and permit the cleaner to evaporate so that the cloth is just damp. Apply the cloth to the upholstery with a very light pressure and rub over a small area at a time. Change to a clean portion of the cloth every few strokes.

If the material is to be gone over again, give it time to dry thoroughly. This will prevent the solvent from penetrating to the padding underneath. Avoid soaking or heavily wetting the upholstery with any volatile cleaner.

Upholstery on doors is treated in the same way. Remove all seats that can be easily taken out of the car for cleaning or clean them inside the car using the same procedure. For best results, all the upholstery should be dry before using.

Leather, genuine or imitation (such as Volkswagen's), requires the use of neutral soap which is obtainable at almost any drugstore. Never use volatile cleaners, household detergents or soaps, furniture polishes, oils or bleaches. These may mar the finish of the leather permanently.

There is a natural tendency for leather to show signs of wrinkling; it may also bear the marks from the animal's encounters with barbed wire and other scars. Such marks do not impair its durability or quality. However, wrinkles and scars are natural collec-

Vinyl patch kit can make this tear disappear. Start by cutting around tear to eliminate tear flap.

Apply paste vinyl to hole and smooth down.

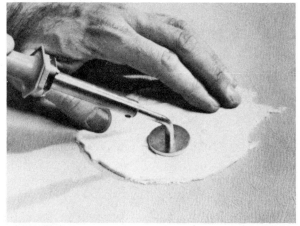

Place texturing paper over paste and heat with iron to cure paste.

Remove texturing paper and the repair is perfect. Texturing paper has matched repaired area to rest of upholstery. Kit has papers with different textures to match all cars.

tors of dirt and dust, and if this condition continues, the dirt becomes a hard and abrasive grit. Under pressure, this grit will cut into the finish and will be the cause of color bleeding and cracking in pressure areas.

To restore the original bright color, use lukewarm water and a neutral soap. Work up a heavy suds and apply *only* the suds to the leather. Next, go over the leather again, but this time use only a damp, clean cloth. Then wipe the leather with a soft, dry cloth. This same treatment can be used in the treatment of imitation leathers.

Ceilings and Floors. Ceilings should be cleaned in the same way as the rest of the upholstery. Use the cleaning agent recommended to the type of material.

Floor carpets are best maintained by frequent and thorough brushing and the use of a vacuum cleaner. If this does not remove the dirt, use a foam-type cleaner to do the job. Do not apply the foam cleaner to more than one square foot of carpet at a time. Use a vacuum cleaner to remove the foam from each processed section. After cleaning, the carpet may be fluffed by working a soft bristle brush gently over the nap. Make sure the carpet is completely dry before using and open the windows to prevent mildewing.

If a carpet has been badly stained and must be removed for cleaning, care must be taken to prevent damage. Carpets are cemented or held in place with metal molding, or both. First, remove screws and molding; then turn back a corner of the carpet. Use a wide-blade putty knife to separate the carpet from the cement. Do not pull or jerk the carpet. Avoid getting any of the cement on the face of the carpet. Once removed, use a volatile cleaner to remove oil or grease spots; then clean with foam as outlined earlier.

STAIN REMOVAL

Different kinds of stains require different treatments and the use of the wrong treatment may cause even worse damage than the stain itself. However, the removal of the most common stains is well within the ability of the average person. It should be remembered that the sooner after occurrence the stain is treated, the better will be the results.

Battery Acid. Saturate affected area with common household ammonia. Allow it to remain on the stain about one minute to neutralize the acid. Rub the spot with a clean cloth wet with cold water. Blot with dry cloth and repeat wet rag application. Action must be immediate to limit destructive action of the acid on the fabric.

Blood. Never try to remove blood with hot water or with soap and water. The action may set the stain and make removal almost impossible. With a clean cloth wet with *cold* water, rub the blood stain to remove as much of it as possible. As the wet cloth absorbs the stain, fold it to present a clean portion to the stain. Failure to do so will work the stain in a diluted form back into the material. If done soon after the stain's occurrence, this procedure should remove all of it. Should the stain be obstinate after this treatment, apply a bit of household ammonia. Let stand a minute or two, then rub the stain with a clean cloth saturated with cold water. Should the water and ammonia treatment fail to have the desired effect, another remedy must be used. Make a thick paste of corn starch and cold water and apply it to the stain. After the paste has dried, remove it to determine if the paste has absorbed the stain. If not, several applications may be necessary.

Candy. Non-chocolate candy stains are best removed by applying a cloth soaked in very hot water to the stain. Rub gently and allow to dry. Should some sign of stain remain, remove by applying a cloth wet with volatile cleaner. For chocolate candy, the same treatment is recommended except that lukewarm water instead of very hot water should be used.

Chewing Gum. Apply an ice cube to the gum to harden it. Scrape off hardened particles with a dull knife or edge of a spoon. If all the gum cannot be removed, moisten it with a volatile cleaner. While the gum is moist, remove it by separating it from the material with a dull knife or spoon.

Fruit, Liquor or Wine. Apply very hot water with a clean rag, and wet thoroughly. Rub briskly with hot water soaked cloth. If the stain persists, scrape with a dull knife or spoon while wet, and allow to dry. If signs of the stain remain, then rub lightly with a cloth dampened with a volatile cleaner. Never use soap and water since such treatment may permanently set the stain. Also, never use heat to dry the treated area.

Enamel, Lacquer or Paint. Wet a clean cloth in turpentine. Rub over the stain to remove as much as possible. If the stain is stubborn, saturate with a mixture of one part denatured alcohol and one part benzine. Apply dull knife or spoon to stain and scrape away as much as possible. Repeat if necessary. Apply a final saturation of the mixture and follow immediately with a vigorous rubbing with a cloth soaked with lukewarm soapsuds. Rinse by sponging with cold water.

Tar. Moisten the tar slightly with a volatile cleaner. Use a dull knife to scrape away as much as you can. Rub the spot gently with a cloth dampened with a volatile cleaner until it disappears.

Grease or Oil. Remove as much of the grease or oil as is possible with a dull knife blade or kitchen spatula. Rub lightly with a cloth wet with a volatile cleaner over the affected area. Rub from the outer edges of the stain toward the center to reduce the possibility of spreading the stain. Keep applying cleaner on fresh cloths as needed. Confine oil or grease to as small an area as possible by pouring a small quantity of the cleaner directly on the stain. Keep doing this until no more grease or oil can be blotted up. This method also aids in the preventing of a ring formation. If repeated treatments with the solvent still leave a dirty stain, rub the area with lukewarm soapsuds. Rinse with cold water applied with a clean cloth. Always rub from the outside to the center of the stain.

Ice Cream. Wet the stain with very hot water applied with a clean cloth. Scrape wet area to remove as much of the stain as possible. Rub vigorously with very hot water again. If the stain is stubborn, rub it with a cloth wet with warm neutral soap suds. Rinse by rubbing with a cloth wet with cold water, and allow to dry. If faint signs still remain, rub with a cloth dampened with a volatile cleaner.

Mildew. Rub mildew vigorously with warm soap suds and rinse by rubbing with a cloth dipped in cold water. Old mildew stains are harder to remove. The only treatment recommended for treating discolorations caused by old mildew growths is the use of oxalic acid. Wet the mildew with a 10% oxalic acid solution. Let it soak a minute or so. Next use a blotter or absorbent cloth to blot up acid. Rinse with either hot or cold water. Repeat this sequence as often as is necessary.

Shoe Polish. White shoe polish should be allowed to dry completely. With a brush, go over the dry stain briskly until it disappears. Should it persist, moisten it with cold water. Allow to dry, then brush vigorously until it vanishes. Wax or paste type shoe polishes need to be rubbed gently with a cloth dampened with a volatile cleaner. Rub from the outside of the stain to the center, changing to a clean portion of the cloth frequently.

Lipstick. Different brands of lipstick are made of varying components which make stains difficult to remove. Use a spoon or dull knife to scrape away as much as possible. Rub lightly with a cloth dampened with a volatile cleaner. Repeat several times. Should some stain remain after repeated treatments, it is recommended that no more be done to it. Other measures might do more harm than good.

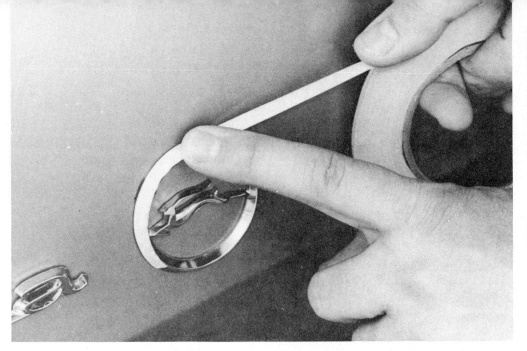

Careful masking with tape of all chrome parts not to be removed is essential.

47

Paint Your Car Like a Pro

IF YOU CAN afford to buy a brand-new car every year or two, this article is not for you. But if, like most people, you have to squeeze three, four, or more years out of every car you own, there is one quick way to at least make your car look new: repaint it.

Don't get us wrong; the job is not a snap. Figure on at least four or five full days. On the other hand, you don't need any special skills or experience.

With today's modern paints and sealers, even an amateur can do a professional job.

You don't even need to buy expensive tools. Nearly every town has a shop that will rent you an air compressor, spray gun, and (if you don't already have one) an electric drill. Add a few basic hand tools that you probably already own, plus $40 or $50 worth of materials, and you're ready to start.

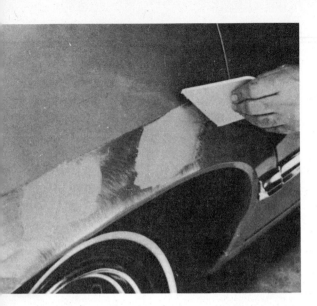

Application of putty to fill in dents can be done using kit available in auto accessory stores.

You say you can get a professional paint job for the same money? Don't you believe it. High-quality car refinishing can cost $250 or more. The fast-buck operators who offer "cheapie" deals have to cut corners to make a profit. Most do very little sanding of your old finish—a vital step if the new paint is to stick. Instead of removing trim, they usually mask it off; this gives a sloppier job, and may promote corrosion. They won't do any body repairs unless you pay extra. They apply few coats of paint, and the materials they use often are inferior. With a little care and patience you can do much better.

One important point: a fully enclosed garage (with heat, if the weather is cold) is a must. Never, never try to paint a car outdoors.

You'll need plenty of newspapers for masking, plus clean, lint-free rags for wiping body surfaces. Start saving these a couple of weeks before you start working. Buy your materials from a body-supply store, not an ordinary hardware store; that's the only way to be sure you're getting materials designed for auto bodies rather than furniture or the back-yard fence.

Your first job is to remove the bumpers, grille, outside mirrors, door and trunk handles, bright-metal headlight rims, side trim, emblems, and all other brightwork. Some trim, especially on older cars, may be hard to remove because of corroded nuts and bolts. Apply penetrating oil to problem areas. As a last resort, use a hammer and chisel and then replace the nuts and bolts. As you remove small hardware, drop it in labeled envelopes for easier identification during reassembly.

Now check the stripped body for dents, gouges, holes, and rust, and make all necessary repairs; blemishes will show up prominently under shiny new paint. In case of major damage, let a body shop make the repairs. Tell the proprietor you want the area primed but not painted; that should cut the price.

You can fix small dents and holes easily with the inexpensive do-it-yourself patch kits sold in auto accessory stores. (These kits come with instructions.) Caution: Be sure you buy an epoxy resin kit intended for cars; some patch kits intended for fiberglass boats give poor results on metal.

Grind away rust spots with a rotary grinder or electric drill equipped with a sanding disk until you're down to shiny bright metal. If the rust goes all

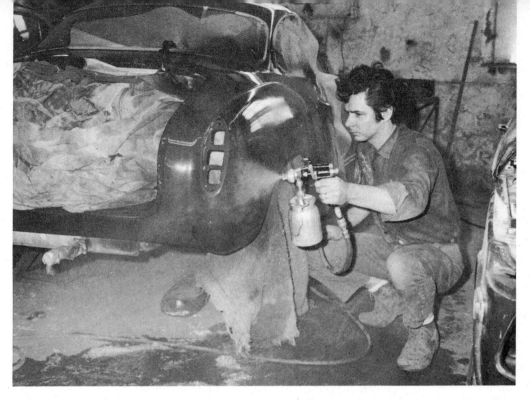

Spray paint in as dust-free an area as possible.

the way through, cut away the cancerous area and patch with fiberglass. For larger holes, have new metal welded in. Incidentally, don't go overboard with the grinder; those rotary grinding scratches are hard to sand smooth.

Now for an important decision: is your old finish sound enough to form a base for the new paint? In most cases it is. But if your old paint is chipping and peeling, don't expect new paint to adhere any better. Your only sensible solution then is to remove all the old paint, right down to bare metal.

This isn't as hard as it sounds. You can buy a chemical paint remover that will quickly loosen the old paint. Operating procedures vary from brand to brand, so follow the instructions on the container. After the paint is removed, flush thoroughly with water and wipe

dry. To prevent surface rust, which forms very quickly, apply etching solution panel by panel.

If the old paint is satisfactory, clean it thoroughly with degreaser-solvent, rubbing in the liquid with clean rags to remove old wax and grime. From that point on, don't touch the metal with your bare hands; the oil in your skin could impair adhesion of the new paint. If you should accidentally touch the metal at any time right up to the final spraying degrease the area immediately.

Now sand the entire car to remove the oxidized top surface and to give the new finish a good grip. The way you sand the body will make the difference between a smooth, long-lasting job and one that starts peeling in days or weeks.

317

A rigid sanding block has too small a contact area on curved body panels, and hand-held sandpaper gives high and low spots because of uneven finger pressure. Instead, use a rubber sanding block; it will conform to the surface while distributing pressure evenly.

Use waterproof auto body sandpaper, and dip it in a pail of clean water frequently. The water clears residue from the sandpaper and acts as a lubricant. Start with the coarsest (220-grit) sandpaper, taking special care to remove all traces of rotary grinding and to featheredge chips and scratches. Sand back and forth in a front-to-rear direction. Never cross-sand.

After sanding every inch of the body, repeat the wet-sanding operation with the next-finer #320, and then with #400 sandpaper. Then wash away all sanding dust with plain water and a clean rag, dry the surface, and let the car stand for several hours, preferably overnight. Leave the garage doors or windows cracked open for ventilation.

Before resuming work, pull the car out of the garage. wet down the garage floor with a hose, and sweep out the dirt. Then drive the car back inside and mask off any areas not to be painted—windows, wheels, headlights, etc. The easy way to do this is to apply masking tape to the edge of the paper first, and then to the car. Go over the entire car with a tack cloth—a special, slightly sticky rag—to remove dust. Now you're ready to spray on the primer-surfacer, or undercoat.

When you select the spray gun and compressor (large paint stores as well as body supply shops rent them), be sure you get the right ones. Two main types are available: the preferred siphon-feed type, in which air pressure passes over the opening in the fluid nozzle and creates a suction that draws the material from the cup, and the pressure type, in which the material is pushed out of the cup by air pressure. (This kind clogs easier.) A third type of gun, known as the airless spray type, subjects the paint to tremendously high pressure by means of a self-contained pump. This type of gun makes it difficult to control film thickness, and causes runs and sags on contoured surfaces. Stay away from it.

The compressor should put out at least 40 pounds per square inch. And don't forget an inexpensive, disposable face mask to protect your lungs from the paint fumes.

Mix one part primer-sealer with one and a half parts thinner (or follow the manufacturer's instructions, if they differ), making sure the materials are compatible with the type of paint you will be using. (Lacquers are easier to use because they dry quickly.) Set the spray gun to form a fan-shaped pattern about nine inches wide, two or three inches high, and practice on some scrap cardboard.

Hold the gun from six to ten inches away and always keep it perpendicular and equidistant to the work. Never spray with the gun stationary; start the sideward motion before squeezing the trigger, and release the trigger just before finishing the stroke. The material should be wet when it hits the surface, but not so wet that it sags and runs.

CAUSES OF IMPROPER SPRAY GUN OPERATION

SPITTING

A. Vent hole in cover may be clogged.

B. Fluid nozzle worn or cracked. Dirt between fluid nozzle seat and body.

C. Loose or defective swivel nut on siphon cup or material hose.

D. Loose fluid tube.

E. Worn or imperfect needle.

CURVED SPRAY PATTERN

A. One air nozzle hole clogged.

B. Air nozzle worn.

OUT OF BALANCE SPRAY

A. Dried material in or on fluid nozzle.

B. Jets in air nozzle may be partially plugged.

C. Worn or imperfect nozzle or needle.

SPLIT SPRAY

A. (Split spray refers to a fan pattern that is heavy on each end and weak in the center.) Air pressure too great.

B. Material too thin for wide spray pattern.

EXCESS OVERSPRAY

A. Excessive air pressure in proportion to weight of material.

B. Material too thin.

C. Gun not close enough to the surface being refinished.

DRY DULL FINISH

A. Insufficient compressor capacity.

B. Pressure drop due to line friction obstruction or leaks caused by badly worn hose.

C. Vent hole in cover clogged.

D. Air control valve partially closed.

Once you learn the proper motion, start spraying the car in long, horizontal strokes, overlapping considerably to avoid blotches and streaks. Then relax for 30 or 40 minutes while the primer-sealer dries.

Next examine the body for low spots, scratches, or other imperfections. You have to look closely to spot these when they're covered with dull primer; but if you miss any, they will be very obvious under the paint. Some pros prefer to spray a very thin, different-colored coat of primer over the first, and then wet-sand the body with #320 sandpaper. As they sand through the high spots, the low spots immediately show up.

Fill low spots or scratches with body glaze, applied with a rubber squeegee. If you must fill a deep area, use two or more thin coats of glaze rather than one thick one. Even better, hammer out the indentation first.

Allow several hours for the glaze to harden all the way through. (Hardening time varies with temperature and the thickness of the filler coat.) Then, using a *wood* sanding block long enough to bridge the patched area, dry-sand the glaze until it is perfectly flush with the primed surface. Start with coarse #180 sandpaper and work your way down to a #400 sheet. Wipe the area with a clean cloth, then a tack cloth, and reprime. Most primer-sealers do not require sanding however, with some a light spot scuff is permitted to remove dirt nibs. Follow the manufacturer's instructions.

Clean the spray gun thoroughly with thinner before switching to the paint. Refer to the paint label for the proper proportion of paint thinner to be added, making sure the right kind of thinner is used. Stir the thinned paint thoroughly, working the pigment from the bottom up. A coathanger wire bent into a hook and chucked in an electric drill makes stirring fast and easy. Then pour the paint through a special strainer to filter out lumps that might clog the gun.

Wipe the entire car lightly with a tack cloth and start spraying on the color coats. Keep working around the car in a set pattern without stopping between coats. By the time you're ready to start the next coat, the previous one will have dried. After applying five coats, wet-sand lightly with #600 sandpaper and dry with clean rags. Let the paint dry overnight, go over the car with a tack cloth, and spray on four or five mist coats, using 50 percent more thinner than before. This gives a deep, shiny finish.

Wait another day before compounding the finish and remounting the chrome trim. A wax job should be postponed for at least two months; this will give the solvents in the paint a chance to evaporate, giving you a hard, durable finish that looks like a professional job, yet costs much less.